Postwar British Politics

Postwar British Politics challenges established interpretations of postwar British politics and offers in place of these a novel evolutionary account of public policy and the state of Britain since 1945.

Peter Kerr provides a highly critical analysis of the dominant view amongst political scientists and contemporary historians that postwar British politics before the election of the Blair government was dominated by a period of consensus, followed by a radical restructuring of the state by the Thatcher governments. The book argues persuasively why we should reject the idea of a postwar consensus, and, with it, the notion that the Thatcher governments fundamentally altered the direction of British public policy. Instead Peter Kerr shows that postwar British politics can be largely characterised in terms of a significant degree of continuity, and a gradual evolution from a period of conflict over the primary aims of government strategy to one of relative consensus.

The book offers its own alternative periodisation of the development of postwar British politics and, by drawing on contemporary neo-evolutionary theories of social and political change, also introduces an original theoretical explanation of the main factors which have driven policy evolution. This provocative and challenging history of British politics up to the Blair government will be invaluable to undergraduates on courses dealing with postwar British public policy issues and the impact of the Thatcher and Major governments. It will also be important topical reading for academics in political science and public policy as well as historians.

Peter Kerr is Lecturer in British politics and political sociology at the University of Birmingham. He is co-author of *Postwar British Politics in Perspective*.

Routledge/PSA Political Studies Series
Edited by Michael Moran, University of Manchester

This series, published in conjunction with the Political Studies Association of the United Kingdom, aims to publish research monographs of the highest quality in the field of political studies.

1 Postwar British Politics
From conflict to consensus
Peter Kerr

Postwar British Politics

From conflict to consensus

Peter Kerr

London and New York

First published 2001
by Routledge
11 New Fetter Lane, London EC4P 4EE

Simultaneously published in the USA and Canada
by Routledge
29 West 35th Street, New York, NY 10001

Routledge is an imprint of the Taylor & Francis Group

Typeset in Baskerville
by Curran Publishing Services Ltd, Norwich
Printed and bound in Great Britain
by TJ International Ltd, Padstow, Cornwall

British Library Cataloguing in Publication Data
A catalogue record for this book is available
from the British Library

Library of Congress Cataloging in Publication Data
Kerr, Peter, 1962–
    Postwar British politics: from conflict to consensus / Peter Kerr
    p. cm. – (Routledge/PSA political studies series; 1)
    Includes bibliographical references and index.
    1. Great Britain–Politics and government–1945–
    I. Title. II. Series

JN231 .K47 2001
941.085–dc21   00–045945

ISBN 0–415–23275–9

This book is dedicated to
my parents
Peter and Marlyn
and my brother
Chris

Contents

Figures

Acknowledgements

This book is the product of my Ph.D. thesis, which I began in the Department of Government at Strathclyde University before moving to the Department of Politics and International Studies at Birmingham University. Throughout the course of this work I have accumulated an immense array of personal and intellectual (not to mention financial) debts to a number of friends, relatives and colleagues. The largest debt by far (particularly in financial terms, given that they have fallen victim on numerous occasions to my repeated attempts at emotional blackmail) is owed to my family – my parents Peter and Marlyn, my brother Chris and my grans Mary and Elizabeth – without whose help and encouragement over the years this thesis would never have been written. In a similar vein, I owe an immeasurable debt to Gayle McKerracher whose patience and support, particularly when I was often at my most frustrated and vociferous (i.e. ranting), has proved a real source of strength over the years.

Many of the ideas contained within the following pages are the product of numerous discussions which I have had over the years with friends and colleagues. As a result, I would like to extend my thanks to all the staff and postgraduates in the Department of Government at Strathclyde and the Department of Politics and International Studies at Birmingham who have offered me advice and constructive criticism during the many colloquiums and informal discussions which have helped to shape my views. These include: Jim Buller; Lorna Chicksand; Jim Johnston; Stuart McAnulla; Alex McDonagh; Fiona O'Neil; Martin Rhodes; Mathew Watson; Robert Watt; Roger Wicks and Daniel Wincott. I would also like to express my gratitude to all the members of the ECPR Joint Sessions Workshop on the 'Evolution and Transformation of the Modern State: Processes of Change' at Warwick University in March 1998 who provided me with invaluable comments and advice on an earlier draft of my main theoretical work. In particular, I would like to extend my thanks to Hugh Ward who helped organize the workshop and who has, at important times over the past few years, given me sound advice and encouragement, not to mention the original inspiration for introducing an evolutionary metaphor into my work.

In addition, I owe an immense debt for the help, encouragement, and invaluable insights I have had from my colleague Colin Hay. Since I moved to Birmingham the focus of my work has expanded considerably, and this is in no small part due to the enormous influence which Colin has had. Unfortunately, Colin has had to endure (which he has done with an enormous degree of patience) my stubborn proclivity for trying to provoke, at almost every opportunity, a 'lively discussion' (ie, arguing the toss) with him on his views on postwar British politics. However, it is Colin's work in this area, coupled with his highly innovative work on political change, that has provided me with the richest source of ideas, and from which I have drawn extensively.

I would also like to extend an enormous thanks to Andrew Gamble. I have admired Andrew's work on British politics for many years and have derived a great deal of inspiration from it. However, I have also been fortunate enough to benefit directly from his invaluable comments on my thesis and his very kind support and advice. This experience not only served to heighten my overall admiration for his insights into the subject area, but also reminded me of the substantial limitations to my own work.

My deepest thanks, however, are reserved for my thesis supervisor Dave Marsh. Dave's help and support date back to my final years as an undergraduate. Through his encouragement and guidance, Dave alone is responsible for helping me to get started on my thesis, and without his continual support and positive interventions I could never have come this far. Moreover, on an intellectual level, Dave's influence extends throughout this book. Many of the ideas contained in it are ones I learned from his lectures at Strathclyde and from numerous discussions which I had with him in my early days as a postgraduate student. Throughout the course of conducting my own research, I have consistently found that most of Dave's original insights have stood up to empirical examination and, as such, I have found few justifications for departing from them.

As anyone who has gone through the process of submitting a Ph.D. thesis will know, it is the final few months which inflict the biggest toll in terms of stress, anxiety, fatigue and sheer depression. As such, I owe an incalculable debt for the help and support which I received during this time and throughout the preparation of this manuscript from Bela Arora at the University of Warwick Business School, who has been everything that I could have ever wished for, the love of my life, best friend, dearest colleague and all this as well as being the best womble of all time! If Bela had not been *pargol* (the Scottish equivalent of this Indian word is, apparently, *eejit*) enough to come to my rescue on countless occasions, this study would simply never have been completed.

Finally, I reserve a special thanks to Mick Moran at the University of Manchester and to Craig Fowlie at Routledge for their support in helping me to have my thesis published as part of this prestigious series.

Peter Kerr

Preface

The aim of this book is to challenge the established narrative of the evolution of British politics in the postwar period. It presents a lengthy critique of the literature on both 'Thatcherism' and the 'postwar consensus'. I assert that conventional accounts of both periods are inherently flawed both in their empirical assumptions and theoretical explanations. In particular, they rely upon a static and oversimplified account of political change which fails to address the complex and multi-layered factors which continually converge to generate change. In contrast, this book proposes that the changes which have occurred in British politics in the postwar period can be better explained through the application of an 'evolutionary' perspective. As such, I elicit insights from contemporary evolutionary explanations of change in the social sciences and apply these to an empirical analysis of the evolution of the British state in the postwar period. Overall, I argue that postwar British politics is best characterised in terms of a gradual movement from conflict to relative consensus.

1 Introduction: what's the story?

The established narrative of the postwar period

Introduction

When we approach the study of the past half century of British politics, we are invariably drawn into a narrative which is both straightforward and pervasive. The story which is told is one in which two principal protagonists, the Labour government of 1945 and the Conservative governments under Mrs Thatcher, succeeded in their respective attempts radically to reconstruct the nature of the British state. Between these two periods, British politics is said to have been dominated by a long period of consensus and relative stasis during which government policy exhibited an overall degree of continuity.

The aim of this book is to take issue with the established narrative of the transformation of the postwar British state, and to offer in its place an alternative storyline. This is no small task, for, as we shall see, the assumptions which underpin the conventional story lie deeply embedded in the folklore of British political studies. Therefore, if we are to suggest that the established narrative does not offer an accurate reading of the evolution of the state in the postwar period, then we need to seek reasons as to why so many political scientists continue to reproduce it. Thus, throughout the book, I will engage not only with the established narrative of the period, but also with the methods and motivations of the storytellers themselves. The thrust of the argument which I will present is that political scientists and historians have largely misinterpreted the postwar period due to their normative desire to portray the Thatcher governments as radical and their proclivity to take the rhetoric of government actors at face value.

The purpose of this introductory chapter is to review very briefly some of the general themes of the overall book, outlining the main tenets of the established narrative before highlighting some of the weaknesses in the literature which will be discussed in later chapters. Specifically, I will highlight four broad problems within the literature:

- Most studies of the postwar period provide us with a blend of empirical evidence which is most often contradictory and complex. However, this complexity is rarely reflected in the overall simple storyline which is presented to us. As a result, while we can point to a number of objections to the established narrative within the literature as a whole, these have done very little to overcome the fact that one overarching storyline has tended to prevail.

- Much of the literature is the product of theoretical and conceptual hindsight. In this sense, our understanding of the transformation of the postwar British state has been shaped to a large extent by the experience of the Thatcher years. The perceived radicalism of the Thatcher administrations has served to obscure our perceptions of the comparisons which can be made between the pre- and post-1979 eras.
- The institutionally-directed focus of the discipline has tended to guide our focus towards visible influences on policy-making. This has led to a circumscribed definition of politics and power while generating a tendency to exaggerate the impact of governmental actors upon the structures of the state.
- The discipline suffers from the lack of an authentic notion of social and political change. This has meant that the established narrative of the postwar period has come to be dominated by a series of static representations which fail to provide a sophisticated understanding of the processes and mechanisms which have generated the evolution of the state.

Overall, I aim to demonstrate that these problems have translated them-selves into a pervasive misrepresentation of the postwar period and that we cannot understand how this has happened unless we come to terms with the subjective impulses which have generated the narrative of the period. In this sense, it is important to emphasise that the conventional storyline is not an innocent one. Rather, it must be viewed as a chronicle of events which largely reflects the normative assumptions of its authors as well as the rhetorical pretensions of government actors.

The established narrative: a parody of the period?

The conventional storyline of the period 1945–97 centres around the respective success of the Attlee and Thatcher governments in recon-structing Britain's political landscape. Essentially, the tale of the transformation of the British state is usually narrated as five main 'chapters' (see Figure 1.1). In the first of these chapters, the Attlee admin-istration, building on the experience of wartime, is said to have successfully forged a transformation of state–societal relations around a Keynesian, social-democratic agenda. In the next, this reconstruction is consolidated during a sustained period of policy consensus and state settlement. In Chapter Three, the consensus begins to crack amid a period of political instability and economic uncertainty. Thatcherism thus makes a grand entrance in Chapter Four, with a series of neo-liberal reforms which sweep aside the earlier state settlement, while John Major dithers into the last of these chapters to provide a further period of consolidation and settlement. The villain in this piece inevitably varies, depending on whether we are supporters of either social democracy or the free market. The hero throughout, though, appears to be the British political system, which reveals its essentially dynamic qualities and proves itself to be contingent upon the articulation of successfully constructed state strategies.

Some may object that this account presents a mere parody of a story

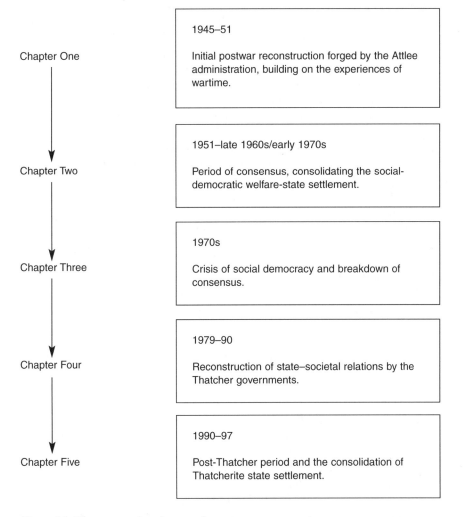

Figure 1.1 The conventional story of postwar reconstruction

which contains far more twists and sub-plots than is being acknowledged here. Others may object to the assertion that this narrative is as pervasive as the previous paragraph suggests. After all, three of the four chapters in the story have been subject to a large degree of both debate and revision.[1] For example, political and economic historians have recently begun to dispute the extent of change under both the wartime administration and the subsequent Attlee governments (see for example: Bartlett 1977; Barnett 1986, 1996; Tiratsoo 1991a; Mercer, Rollings and Tomlinson 1992; Fyrth 1993; Tiratsoo and Tomlinson 1993; Johnston 1999).[2] In a similar vein, many such authors have also begun to challenge the extent of both the wartime and postwar consensus (see for example: Pimlott 1988, 1989; Jefferys 1991; Brooke 1992; Rollings 1994; Marlow 1996, 1997; Kerr 1999). Likewise, the radical credentials of the Thatcher governments have also been open to a more modest, but no less significant, degree of scepticism (Jessop *et al.* 1988; Riddell 1991; Marsh and Rhodes 1992, 1995). The problem, however, is that these qualifications to each of the individual chapters of the conventional story have done little to dent the overall tale of the transition from a consensual, social-democratic state settlement to Thatcherism. As a result, they remain only as footnotes to the original story, for, as Chapter Two of this book will demonstrate, the prevailing view amongst political scientists, state theorists and historians alike, is that the Thatcher governments succeeded in reconstructing a political land-scape which was preconstituted by earlier postwar administrations and which was radically different from the one which they subsequently bequeathed to the Major government. In this sense, the Thatcher govern-ments have overwhelmingly been portrayed as having entered and reshaped a political terrain which had been previously mapped out by the Butskellite policy consensus. On the economic front, their strategy is assumed to have been a response to the prior failure of Keynesian and interventionist attempts at reversing Britain's long-term structural decline. At a cultural level, the Thatcherite cocktail of neo-liberalism and traditional Conservatism has been read as a reaction against the social-democratic ideals conveyed by earlier postwar political actors. In these ways, the idea that the Conservative governments after 1979 represented a fundamental and near absolute departure from previous practice has been held firmly intact.

Clearly then, the literature needs to be unpacked. As a result, the opening two chapters of this book will review the literature on both the Thatcher period and the earlier era of consensus respectively. As we shall see, most studies of these periods provide us with a contradictory blend of evidence. On the one hand, we are faced with the overriding assumption that the British state has undergone two significant and fundamental transformations since 1945. On the other hand, however, we are given many reasons to assume that the state has in fact exhibited more consis-tency and continuity than is generally acknowledged. This latter view is particularly prevalent within the literature on Britain's long-term economic decline, which most authors attribute to the overall lack of fundamental reform to Britain's political and institutional architecture. Yet, despite these contradictory appraisals (which are often given by the same authors), we are invariably confronted with only one overarching interpretation. It appears not to matter to the presentation of the overall story therefore that: 'few people now have any belief in the revolutionary intent or impact of the 1945–51 Labour governments'(Mercer, Rollings and Tomlinson 1992), or that there is an increasing awareness that the consensus 'is an illusion that rapidly fades the closer one gets to it' (Pimlott 1988). Likewise, the persistent claim that many continuities exist between Thatcherism and the earlier postwar period, appears to have been similarly unheeded. For the overwhelming assumption which pervades the literature on the period is that the Thatcher governments were successful in radically altering a state settlement which had been transformed by the impact of a social-democratic consensus.

In the following sections, and in the chapters which follow, I will argue that the established narrative of the postwar period presents a storyline which is overly stylised and ultimately misleading. Yet it is alluring because it serves the pejorative assumptions of both the left and right. As a result, the real parody of the period lies, not in the way the overall story has just been presented, but in the manner in which political scientists, historians and state theorists alike have oversimplified and related the complex series of events that have occurred in British politics since the end of the Second World War.

Narrating the period: insight or hindsight?

One of the most conspicuous features of the established narrative is the striking similarity which it bears to Mrs Thatcher's own interpretation of events (see Thatcher 1993: 3–15). We should consider this important, for, as Brendan Porter (1994: 249) points out: 'what we found confronting us in May 1979 was a Prime Minister with a very pronounced sense of history'. Here, it is crucial that we remain sensitive to the fact that Mrs Thatcher 'interfered shamelessly with our subject, telling us what we should think about a whole range of historical issues' (ibid.: 246).

One major reason why this should concern us becomes clear when we start to view the debate over Thatcherism. The earliest attempts at theorising the significance of Thatcherism pointed to the Conservative governments' ambitions of achieving a new type of political and ideological hegemony. In a neo-Gramscian sense, this 'hegemonic project' entailed capturing the hearts and minds of the electorate in order to promote new sets of 'common-sense' assumptions about the nature of political activity. Thus, Thatcherism was, from its inception, regarded by some authors as a potentially 'manipulative' project, designed to alter existing perceptions of political realities. Yet, as we shall see in Chapter Two, for the authors who proposed such ideas, very little reflexivity was paid to the way in which Thatcherite perceptions of postwar British politics could filter into their own analyses of the period. In this sense, most authors neglect any real consideration of the fact that Thatcherite common sense was built upon a set of ideological assumptions, not only about the nature of Thatcherism itself, but also about the historical context in which Thatcherism emerged. The result has been an outpouring of analyses which passively submit to Thatcherism's self-proclaimed radicalism and its narrow interpretation of postwar British history. It is arguable that an important element of Thatcherism's attempt to create its own common sense has been the willingness of political scientists and historians to bolster some of the core assumptions around which the Thatcher project was constructed.

As far as the Thatcherite view of history is concerned, the pinnacle of Britain's grandeur is to be found in the halcyon period of the Victorian Age. Here, the true spirit of British entrepreneurialism was believed to have been released amid a flourish of unbridled capitalist development. From there on in however, the story of the past hundred years or so of British history has been one of inexorable decline caused by the deleterious effects of creeping socialism. After 1945 this decline is perceived to have grown apace as the Attlee administration pushed the accelerator towards a more 'centralising, managerial, bureaucratic, interventionist style of government' (Thatcher 1993: 6). For her own part in this story, Mrs Thatcher cast herself as a modern-day Moses, endowed with a popular mandate to part the Red Sea of socialism, and deliver her nation to a promised land flowing with non state-sponsored milk and plastic money. Hand in hand with such prophecies went the self-fostered image that the Thatcherite staff of conviction would be waved against the evils of consensus.

In this sense then, Thatcherism was able to claim that it was presenting something new to the British political scene. Having illustrated the story of Britain's century of decline with a swathe of red brushwork, Mrs Thatcher and her followers could legitimately point to her own brand of Victorian values and economic liberalism as a distinctive response to Britain's decline. What should concern us here is the extent to which writers from both sides of the political spectrum have clamoured to avow the Thatcherites' self-proclaimed radicalism. The arrival of the Thatcher governments onto the political scene drew the attention of political scientists more than any other period in the postwar era. This point has been made by Marsh and Rhodes (1992: 1), who claim that: 'Margaret Thatcher's effect on British politics, or at least on British political scientists is clear; the study of Thatcherism became an academic and journalistic industry'. Inevitably, much of this literature was inspired by the apparent distinctiveness, in both style and substance, which the

Thatcherites brought to bear upon the policy-making arena. According to Kavanagh (1987: 288) for example: 'in terms of policy style and policies, there is something new and radical about the Conservative Party under Mrs Thatcher'. These types of unequivocal, and most often unqualified, statements are to be found scattered throughout the literature. One of the key aims of this book is to demonstrate that in casting a British government, which was wedded to the idea of limited state intervention and a traditionally monetary ethos, as a 'new' and 'radical' departure, politicians historians and political scientists have been equally involved in myth-making of significant proportions.

The charge being made here is that academics have been guilty of reproducing a narrative which concedes too readily to the rhetorical machinations of the Thatcher governments. This is not to suggest that Mrs Thatcher successfully engineered her own postwar history. However, it is important to emphasise that the vast majority of interpretative accounts of the period have been written in the context of the Thatcher years.[3] This point has been made by Catterall, who observes that:

> interest in the postwar era has been stimulated in recent years by the apparent challenge to the postwar consensus mounted by the Thatcher government. . . . In the process, the break it has supposedly made with the past has stimulated increasing interest in themes such as the postwar consensus or the practice of Cabinet government.
>
> (Catterall 1989: 221–2)

This eagerness to assess the impact of Thatcherism has led many authors to subscribe passively to a narrative which accords very favourably with the Thatcherite view of the earlier part of the postwar era. Of course, there are inevitable areas of dispute, particularly over the extent to which social-democratic interventions played a role in inhibiting British economic development. Yet despite this, the overall tale of Thatcherism railing radically against an earlier interventionist and collectivist state settlement remains intact, and as yet relatively unquestioned.

Consequently, when we come to view the transformation of the postwar British state, it is important to question the extent to which our understanding of the period has been the result of conceptual hindsight rather than true academic insight. While I do not make the claim that it is possible to escape the inevitable trap of reading history backwards, it is nevertheless important to retain a certain reflexivity about the dangers which it imposes. As I shall discuss in Chapter Three, this caveat is particularly relevant to our understanding of the postwar consensus thesis. The twin notions of 'Thatcherism' and 'consensus' gained an almost mutual ascendancy towards the end of the 1970s. What is significant here is the way in which the idea of consensus has been utilised by various authors in order to serve broader assumptions about both the Thatcher era and the earlier postwar period. As Rollings (1994: 184) points out, much of the debate over consensus has been based on: 'regurgitation of long-established positions and partisan assertions related more to participants' views of the present than to detailed historical analysis' (ibid.: 183; see also Butler 1993). According to Tiratsoo (1991b:1): 'the result, as Hennessey notes, is a situation where "ideological distortion distilled from prejudice and hindsight" all too often masquerades as real historical analysis'.[4]

This is not to dismiss the role of either earlier postwar governments, or indeed political scientists, in narrating their own account of the period. In his famous study, Samuel Beer (1965) had concluded as early as 1962, that the postwar era had seen the triumph of collectivism. Thus, as Catterall (1989: 221–2) observes: 'it would be wrong to conclude . . . that interest in the history of the postwar period is a recent phenomenon'. In many ways, we could say that when Mrs Thatcher began her ascendancy to power the prologue to her own version of events had already been written. The important point, however, is that the ascendancy of the Thatcherites to power provided the storyline with a sense of closure, and has in many ways resulted in the fact that the idea of a postwar social-democratic consensus is now more or less written in stone.

Parochialism and British political studies

The argument being presented here then, is that the established narrative is largely derivative from a tendency by political science to submit passively to the rhetorical pronouncements of government actors. To explore this point further, it is appropriate that we briefly consider the focus of the discipline in general and of the study of British politics in particular. In a sense, we may consider this a response to Marsh and Stoker's call (1995: 288) for political scientists to be 'more self-reflective in approaching their work'.[5]

As Page (1990: 449) has detected, current research in the field of British political science can be divided almost equally into three broad categories. On the whole, contemporary research concerns itself with analyses of political behaviour, institutions and public policy. This reflects a deliberate movement since the 1960s, whereby the focus of attention has been expanded to 'address issues of social and group behaviour behind formal decision-making structures' (Cox 1986: 157). As a result, research has been augmented to include a broad spectrum of input-output cycles of political practice. This point has been highlighted by Dowse (1986), who applauds the development which the study of British politics has made towards an approach which can be more broadly defined as political sociology rather than political science.

Despite these changes, however, it is important to remain sceptical of the extent to which political science has succeeded in departing from a traditionally circumscribed view of the 'political'. This point has been noted by Leftwich (1984b: 16), who attests that the discipline remains too closely 'confined to the public realm'. Indeed, the same theme emerges from various authors of contemporary textbooks within the field. According to Dearlove and Saunders for example:

> for most of the century, the emphasis has been on the liberal-democratic constitution and the formal institutions of Parliament, Cabinet and Prime Minister. More recently, political scientists have come to deal with the process of policy-making taking into account the significance of parties and interest groups. Yet despite this development a narrow view of politics and power has continued to prevail.
>
> (Dearlove and Saunders 1991: 7)

As a result, these authors advise their students to regard the British political system as a sphere of activity which is broader than the constituent parts of the formalised constitution. Essentially, they emphasise the crucial need to regard politics from an inter-disciplinary perspective, with particular emphasis being placed upon the wider social, economic and geographic influences which both constrain and facilitate political practice. This idea is predicated upon the view that government is:

> deeply enmeshed in a dense biomass of political life, and politics as a process involving, not merely the institutions of the state, but of the economy and civil society, and subject to a range of influences emanating from the global context of the state.
>
> (Kingdom 1991: 575)

Clearly it is never possible for any single study to incorporate such all-embracing holism. Nevertheless, it remains important to emphasise the need for political scientists to broaden the scope of their focus in order to achieve as global a view as possible. Yet, despite the efforts of the discipline to acknowledge these facts, the bulk of research undertaken in the field largely fails to deliver anything approaching the type of inter-disciplinary convergence shown by other social science subjects such as sociology, cultural studies and philosophy (Lekhi 1995b: 3).[6] As a result, the discipline has retained a broadly institutional bias towards political activity which is channelled through parties, elections and interest groups. Whereas broader societal influences are considered important to political practice, these are still on the whole examined through formalised constitutional behaviour.[7]

This point may be better illustrated if we consider the way in which mainstream studies of the Thatcher period have generally dealt with the concept of ideology. Any student introduced to the literature on Thatcherism soon becomes acquainted with Andrew Gamble's (1988) definitive assessment that the Thatcher governments embodied a contradictory tension between free-market liberalism and strong state conservatism. In this sense, Gamble's phrase 'The Free Economy and the Strong State' is often evoked to summarise the author's interpretation of the ideological basis of Conservative Party statecraft. However, while this expression is utilised by Gamble as the title to his main work on Thatcherism, it by no means reflects his overall thesis. Instead, the author presents the Thatcher governments as the embodiment of a new type of political hegemony that emerged throughout the Western democracies in response to a perceived crisis in capitalist accumulation. Despite this, British political science, in its interpretation of Gamble's work, has generally been content to strip the author's ideological assessment of Thatcherism down to the point where it relates only to the ethos of the British Conservative Party in the 1980s.

As this tapered-down version of Gamble's thesis demonstrates, it is possible to argue that the study of British politics, rather like the British political system at large, continues to display a parochial outlook which inhibits a rounded understanding of the events that it seeks to interpret (Norton and Hayward 1986; Kerr 1995). In this sense, the charge of parochialism can be used to refer not only to the lack of attention paid to the global environment, but also to the discipline's insularity from the concerns of other social sciences. For the purposes of this book, these criticisms are appropriate for an understanding of the weakness of the established narrative of the postwar period. For as we shall see, a restricted focus upon the narrow confines of institutionalised political practice has served to conjure up a simplified picture of postwar British politics which overstates the impact of governmental actors. Entrenched within a focus upon politicist behaviour, political scientists have inflated the force of political parties and their leaders in terms of their ability to imprint upon the structures of the state. Relatively few attempts are ever made to examine the broader sets of structural factors which constrain the successful implementation of political strategies, and which also serve to facilitate change beyond the control of government actors.

Attlee and Thatcher: dramatis personified

If we are to locate the manner in which the tendency to inflate the impact of political parties and key government actors has fed into our interpretations of the postwar period, then it becomes necessary to deconstruct the established narrative into its constituent parts. The following passage, by the journalist and biographer Kenneth Harris, allows us to see the essence of the conventional storyline in more detail. According to the author:

> two governments tower above all others in the history of Britain since the end of the Second World War: Attlee's between 1945 and 1951, and Margaret Thatcher's from 1979 on. These two administrations stand out from the others . . . [B]oth came to power promising positive

controversial and sweeping programmes intended not just to manage but to change society; both kept their promises.

(Harris 1988: 10)

This point is echoed in a similar passage, by Kavanagh and Morris (1994: 9) who note that: 'the most creative periods in postwar British politics can be associated with the Attlee and Thatcher administrations. These are the bookends, as it were, of modern British political history'. Moreover, Harris (1988: 11) goes on to add that: 'the existence of the long period of consensus, almost bi-partisan, politics is the paradoxical link between Attlee and Thatcher'.

In this sense then, we get a more precise anatomy of the period; for, as we can see from these accounts, the established narrative is constructed around two clear assumptions. First, we have the central premise that the Attlee and Thatcher governments provide our storyline with its leading dramatis personae. Indeed, far from being the bookends of the postwar period, it is these actors, more than any others, who have taken centre stage. Beyond these two pivotal characters, the remaining members of the cast have been consigned to mere supporting roles. When we consider the criticism that political scientists are susceptible, due to their institutional entrenchment, to becoming immersed in the dramas played out by governmental actors, this should not surprise us. In contrast to the glamour of the Attlee and Thatcher years, the consensus period is regarded as being marked by a succession of governments seen to be pursuing pragmatic rather than radical responses to economic and political decline. According to Hay (1996: 46), these governments are best described as 'state-accommodating' since they did not actively seek to: 'challenge the structures of the state inherited from the previous administration'. In direct contrast, however, the Attlee and Thatcher administrations appear at face value as 'state-shaping' since their ambitions were: 'to transform the very contours of the state itself, thereby imposing a new trajectory upon its evolution' (ibid.).

This point leads us into the second key assumption which underpins the literature. For it is worth noting the unreserved appraisal of success which the established narrative attributes to both governments. In this respect, the rhetorical pretensions of both these administrations have been affirmed almost without qualification. Each is widely perceived as having successfully embarked upon strategies which not only set in motion contrasting paradigm shifts in relation to Britain's economic decline, but also essentially altered the relationship between state and society. As Marsh and Rhodes (1992) point out in relation to the literature on Thatcherism, and as Tiratsoo (1991b) emphasises in his collected volume on the achievements of the Attlee administrations, these analyses rarely consider 'the full complex of constraints which shaped policy formation' (ibid.: 1). Accordingly, scant attention is paid to the extent to which the achievements of these administrations are 'more a product of rhetoric than the reality of policy impact' (Marsh and Rhodes 1992: 187). As a result, the established narrative not only equips us with two leading actors, but also applauds them for their star performances.

Consequently, an inherent problem here is the fact that the majority of political commentators conflate the rhetorical and purposeful machinations of governmental actors with the structural properties of the state regime. Little effort is made to separate government rhetoric from policy outcomes. Again, we can turn to the debate over consensus in order to illustrate this point. For, as I shall discuss in Chapter Three, it is assumed that the apparent pursuit of Keynesian demand management strategies and progressive welfare policies throughout the so-called consensus era provides us with enough evidence to identify a Keynesian, social-democratic welfare-state settlement. In this sense, the discursive commitment to Keynesian social democracy is invariably taken at face value. Few attempts have been made to question the extent to which the Keynesian, social-democratic rhetoric surrounding government policy was actually implemented, let alone the extent to which it was used successfully to transform the very nature of the state. Again, the concept that wider structural or environmental constraints may inhibit the successful implementation of government strategy is rarely taken on board.

Static representations of the period

If we continue our anatomy of the period further, then we can see that, beyond the avowed success of the Attlee and Thatcher administrations in reconstructing the state, lie a number of interpretative devices which have been employed by political scientists to describe the nature of the transformations which have taken place. The literature is infused with labels such as 'consensus', 'social democracy'. 'Keynesianism' and, of course, 'Thatcherism'. These idealised constructs pervade our understanding of the postwar period. In effect, they provide our narrative with adjectives which pay more homage to the success of the leading characters in impressing their ideas upon the structures of the state.

This book questions whether concepts such as these succeed in oversimplifying the complex realities of the postwar period. For, what is striking about these epithets is the remarkable fluency and consistency which they bestow upon the transformation of the state. The movement from 'social democracy' to 'Thatcherism' and from 'consensus' to 'conviction' and so on provides us with a storyline which has a comfortably smooth edge to it. In this respect then, the drama of the period is immersed in black and white contrasts, or 'binary oppositions', between the pre- and post-1979 eras (Kerr and Marsh 1996). The historian Kenneth Morgan, whose own account of the postwar period reveals a much more subtle and sophisticated analysis of change, aptly summarises the dominant view of the impact of the Thatcher governments:

more than any change of government since 1945 . . . Margaret Thatcher's election victory was taken as marking a decisive shift in the national mood, politically, intellectually, and culturally. Commentators across the political spectrum believe the fall of James Callaghan in the summer of 1979 signaled the end of an *ancien régime*, a system of corporatism, Keynesian spending programmes, subsidised welfare and trade union power.

(Morgan 1992: 437)

Clearly, the contrasts embedded in this type of view of the period could hardly be more consummate. Morgan's use of the term *ancien régime* is an appropriate one, as it evokes notions of a past dominated by a coherent set of political practices which differ radically to the contemporary era. By bolstering this mythical past with concepts such as 'Keynesianism' and 'corporatism', most authors can hardly go further in presenting the disparity of the pre- and post-1979 eras. This is a picture which invites us to consider contrasts rather than comparisons. It is a narrative which goes out of its way to reject continuity. More importantly, however, it is a storyline which reflects the desire of most authors to emphasise the impact of particular governments and, perhaps more accurately, governmental actors, on the policy-making arena.

Overall then, when we approach the study of the postwar period, we are confronted with a narrative which not only overemphasises the impact of governmental actors and political parties on the structural formation of the state, but also provides us with a series of static representations of the contrasts which can be made between the pre- and post-1979 eras. What is missing from such analyses is a sophisticated notion of the *evolution* of the postwar British state and the complex and constantly dynamic processes and mechanisms which have driven its evolution.

Conclusion: re-stating social and political change in postwar Britain

In examining the extent of social and political change in postwar Britain, this study purports to make a contribution to both the debates surrounding the transformation of the state in the postwar period and the analysis of political change more generally. The overall aim will be to move our understanding of the postwar period and of political change in general, beyond the stylised, static representations which have so far dominated the literature. In its attempt to transcend these depictions, much of this book will be influenced by some of the recent work of Colin Hay (1996; 1997; 1998; 1999) on the transformation of the state in postwar Britain and political change more generally. Hay's outstanding contribution to the literature has been to theorise the dynamic and evolving processes which have generated change in the postwar British state. In this sense, the author's work is firmly rooted in the state-theoretical tradition of authors such as Bob Jessop (1982, 1990a, 1992).

In a highly sophisticated and accessible account of the period, Hay's work continually emphasises the need to move beyond the static, or *synchronic*, analyses which have so far dominated the discipline's attempts to chart the state's trajectory. Instead, the author proceeds with a *diachronic* and evolutionary conception of the state which emphasises its essentially *dynamic* and *processual* nature. As a result, he continually asserts that:

> to 'fix' the state we must move towards a conception which allows us to 'follow' a constantly (and often rapidly) moving subject. In place of a series of instantaneous and static 'snapshots' we must seek to develop a 'panning shot' of the state *in motion*. This in turn must be premised upon an ontology of the state as an essentially dynamic subject and object.
>
> (Hay 1997: 6)

The purpose of the present study is to stress the need to take up Hay's challenge to view the state 'as a constantly moving subject' and to interrogate the processes which generate its trajectory. In this respect a key aim of the book is to develop this type of evolutionary conception of the state and to build upon Hay's diachronic analysis of change in postwar Britain, as well as some of his later work on the evolutionary nature of political change in general (Hay 1995, 1996, 1997). The theoretical basis for this is laid out in Chapter Four, where I emphasise that evolutionary theorising in social science has gained a renewed popularity in recent years, before eliciting the main insights which can be drawn from the current literature and outlining my own 'critical evolutionary' conception of political change. Overall, this chapter highlights the central theme of the book. This is that the major flaws within the established narrative can only be overcome through the application of an evolutionary approach which is sensitive to the temporality of political change, and to the complex and dialectical interaction between political actors' strategic adaptations and the strategically selective environment in which these are articulated.

Having outlined the basis for a 'critical evolutionary' approach to the period, the remaining chapters deal with a detailed application of this approach to an empirical analysis of the evolution of the state in the postwar period. This enables me to provide an alternative periodisation of change in postwar British politics which invokes a multi-dimensional explanation of the main processes which have generated the evolution of successive government strategies. Overall, I argue that we can only proceed towards a more sophisticated understanding of the period if we reverse the main assumptions of the established narrative. In this respect, this book forwards the thesis that, rather than viewing the evolution of postwar British politics as a movement from consensus to conflict, it is more appropriate to characterise it in terms of a gradual shift from conflict to relative consensus. In Chapters Five and Six, I argue that, throughout the course of the so-called consensus era, there was an overall failure by all governments and relevant groups of actors and institutions to agree on the main aims and the precise specificities of governmental strategy. Instead, strategic innovations consistently fluctuated, due to a whole range of cross-cutting pressures, between attempts to expand and contract the role of the state in social and economic affairs. Although policy-making in this period was underpinned by a coherent discursive commitment to social democracy, the reality was that, at the level of institutional reform and policy implementation, government strategy rarely approximated to any significant social-democratic innovations. Rather, attempts at restructuring the architecture of the state and the political agenda were continually thwarted by a fundamental conflict between social-democratic, progressive liberal and classical liberal views on the role of the state. This conflict, combined with the strategic selectivity of the institutional environment in which government strategy was played out, prevented any significant restructuring of the British state of the kind that is implied by the established narrative.

In Chapters Seven and Eight, I argue that the fundamental conflicts of the early postwar period, the lack of institutional change which these brought with them, combined with an overall crisis within both the international and domestic economic and political environments of the 1970s, provided the context and the overall basis for the emergence of Thatcherism, a political strategy which displayed a great deal of continuity with some of the central elements of previous government practice. The Thatcher governments' key task was to eliminate the remaining residues of the strategic conflicts which had dominated earlier postwar British politics. This endeavour brought the Thatcher governments into a series of often bitter confrontations with symbolic remnants of social-democratic and progressive liberal ideas, particularly throughout their first two terms in office. By the beginning of Mrs Thatcher's third term, however, Thatcherism had succeeded in overcoming the main pockets of resistance to its overall strategic vision. In turn, this helped to provide a relatively consensual environment in which the Thatcherite strategy, which had hitherto lacked an overall coherence and consistency, could take shape and begin to make a belated impact at an institutional level throughout the Conservatives' third term in office, and in particular, into their fourth, under the auspices of John Major.

In the concluding chapter, I return once again to an earlier point, which is that historiographers and political scientists must always 'consider the narrative dimensions of historical processes by recognising that the historiographic record is itself a product of narrative' (Hay 1996: 22). This is important, for as I will argue throughout, one of the key elements of Thatcherism was its attempt to impose its own narrative, not only of the crises and underlying problems of the postwar settlement, but also of the very nature of that settlement. In this sense, a crucial aspect of Thatcherism's attempt to construct an alternative common sense was its own ideologically distilled reinterpretation of the historical context against which the Thatcher governments emerged. This is a point which has been overwhelmingly ignored within the literature at the expense of analyses which fail to adopt a reflexive or critical approach to the Thatcher governments' continual claims to have represented a new and radical departure in postwar British politics. As a result, I argue that it is important for all academics interested in the study of the period to interrogate, as reflexively as possible, the core assumptions which the Thatcher governments used to underpin their historical narrative, and to question the extent to which our own accepted assumptions of the period have been constructed by the Thatcherites themselves upon an uncritical academic establishment.

2 Evolution, not revolution

The problem of explaining Thatcherism

Introduction

It may seem odd to begin an attempt to contest the established narrative of the postwar period with a review of the literature on Thatcherism. The most obvious starting point would be to try to erase some of the misconceptions about the earlier postwar era, so that we would then be in a better position to evaluate the literature on Thatcherism. However, it is important to note that the balance of the literature on the postwar period has been overwhelmingly weighted in terms of analyses of Thatcherism. It is the period of Conservative government in the 1980s which has most captivated the attention of those endeavouring to explain the overall transformation of the postwar British state. As this chapter will argue, this has had major implications for the way in which the period as a whole, including the post-1979 era itself, has been interpreted. In many respects, it is our perceptions of Thatcherism, with its supposed radicalism, that have had the greatest impact upon the way in which we have come to interpret the earlier postwar period.

The aim of this chapter is to interrogate the ways in which Thatcherism has been treated within the literature and to posit some initial views as to how we might proceed to a more satisfactory understanding of the period. I will point to three main problems within the existing literature. First, Thatcherism has most often been presented as a static concept which was radical and coherent in its impact from a very early stage of its development. In this sense, few authors take account of the temporality of the Thatcher project and the ways in which it was forced to evolve, adapt and change through time in order continually to redefine itself. Second, there have been few attempts to place the evolution of Thatcherism within the overall historical development of postwar British politics. Rather, Thatcherism has most often been dislocated from its historical context and treated as a phenomenon which was entirely new to the postwar political scene. Third, there have been very few attempts to examine the complex, multi-dimensional, factors which contributed to the evolution of Thatcherism.

Overall, these problems have meant that the Thatcher project has most often been treated as a static, uni-dimensional phenomenon devoid of any historical precedents. After examining each of these problems in turn, I will argue that, in order to advance our understanding of Thatcherism beyond the oversimplified accounts on offer, we must turn towards an evolutionary conception of political change and, of course, a re-evaluation of the historical context against which the Thatcher governments emerged.

The Thatcherite chameleon

Within the literature on Thatcherism it is difficult to find more than a handful of authors who can be said to share any fundamental agreement on what 'Thatcherism' actually entailed.[1] Although analysts from a variety of different quarters converged around the study of the Thatcher governments, the legacy of their research is a range of often disparate interpretations which offer us very little substantive convergence at all. The only thing which unites these different approaches is the idea that Thatcherism represented a *strategy* or, in the words of Stuart Hall (1979, 1988), the author who first coined the term, a *project*, to deliver something new to the British political scene. However, beyond this simple observation, few authors have been able to agree on how we should actually define the Thatcherite project.

For the majority, the key to explaining Thatcherism lay in an elucidation of the political dimensions of the Conservatives' strategy. These authors highlighted the reconstruction of political relations since 1979 with varying degrees of emphasis upon: the impact of Mrs Thatcher's personality and policy style (Riddell 1983, 1989, 1991; King 1985; Young and Sloman 1986; Jenkins 1988; Minogue and Biddiss 1987); the elimination of the central pillars of the postwar consensus (Kavanagh 1987, 1990; Dutton 1991; Kavanagh and Morris 1994); and the way in which Thatcherism recycled more traditional types of Conservative statecraft (Bulpitt 1986; Gamble 1988). Others, including Hall, emphasised Thatcherism's reconstruction of the ideological and discursive underpinnings to British contemporary life. For these authors, the radicalism of the Thatcher project lay in its ability to articulate an alternative 'common sense' ethos to that of social democracy and to permeate most levels of British society with its New Right discourse (Hall 1979, 1988; O'Shea 1984, Hay 1996; Philips 1996). For the remainder however, Thatcherism was to be seen as part of a wider international response to crises in capitalist profitability brought about by the exhaustion of Fordist modes of economic growth (Jessop 1988; Jessop *et al.* 1988; Overbeek 1990; Taylor 1992). To these authors, Thatcherism was merely the peculiar response by British governments to the more generic need for capitalism to re-regulate the conditions of future accumulation strategies. Overall, this diffusion, or indeed confusion, of different interpretations meant that the term Thatcherism came to assume the idiosyncrasy of a chameleon; lacking any precise definition it merely presented itself as a variety of things to different people.

Of course, this eclecticism in the explanations of Thatcherism could be attributed to the actual depth of the Conservatives' strategy itself. After all, the Thatcherites had sought definition for themselves at a number of different levels. Political conviction was to become the new creed, in response to earlier compromises which were perceived to have relinquished central autonomy to the demands of over-powerful interests. Competition and market forces were promised as an alternative to the discerned interventionist and demand-management economic strategies pursued by previous administrations. At a cultural level, individualism was offered to an electorate who were being expertly schooled in the premise that postwar collectivism had eroded individual freedom and stifled personal ambition. Thus, the Conservatives had, from the outset, spent much time and energy in reminding us of the sheer diversity of objectives which their own strategy encompassed. All in all, they vigorously proclaimed themselves to be engaged in a radical and fundamental restructuring of a multitude of political, economic and ideological practices which they saw as being responsible for Britain's long-term institutional malaise. It could easily be argued therefore, that the scope and complexity of the Conservatives' project made the academic confusion and ambiguity which characterised the study of the Thatcher governments almost inevitable. Clearly, if Thatcherism operated on such a vast scale, then it could be construed as overly optimistic to hope for any substantive academic clarity about its fundamental nature.

Such a standpoint, however, seems far from satisfactory, for it would be unduly pessimistic, even perhaps nihilistic, for political scientists to conclude that they are unable to develop explanatory frameworks which can incorporate the diversity and complexity characteristic of intense periods of political and social change such as the Thatcher years. Nevertheless, as several authors have pointed out, the literature on Thatcherism can, for various reasons, be shown to demonstrate precisely this failure (Jessop *et al.* 1988; Marsh and Rhodes 1992, 1995; Marsh 1994, 1995; Hay 1996; Kerr, McAnulla and Marsh 1997; Kerr and Marsh 1999). To each of these authors, the study of the Thatcher governments reveals an underlying weakness of political science explanations in coming to grips with the elasticity, and indeed the complexity, of the political, economic and social changes which have occurred since 1979. In different ways, these analyses locate the source of this weakness in the overriding tendency of most authors to evoke a circumscribed view of the contours and inherent characteristics of the Conservatives' project. Each highlight the fact that, although the Thatcherite chameleon assumed many different guises, most authors, having been captivated by one of its particular facets, were unwilling to focus their attention on its other relevant features. The result, therefore, has been an overall tendency by most authors to provide static and partial definitions of Thatcherism which in turn provide us with closed conceptions of the precise attributes and idiosyncrasies of the Conservatives' strategy.

The aim in the following sections is to elicit from the criticisms provided by these and other authors, some of the problems which have arisen from the tendency to provide a closed and static conception of Thatcherism. Specifically, I will point to three main related problems. First, by failing to recognise the crucial temporality of Thatcherism, few authors succeeded in highlighting the essentially contingent and often changing development of the Conservatives' strategy over time. Second, by dislocating Thatcherism from its historical precedents, most authors neglected a proper analysis of the longer-term conflicts and institutional compromises which contributed to both shaping and constraining the evolution of the Conservatives' strategy. Third, by binding their interpretations of Thatcherism to primary explanatory variables, most authors failed to provide a rounded and multi-dimensional approach to explaining the evolution of post-1979 Conservative strategy which could incorporate the complex range of dynamics which generated the Thatcherite project and contributed to its uneven temporal development.

The problem of explaining Thatcherism

Taking time out: the temporal closure of Thatcherism

According to Jim Bulpitt (1986), the Thatcher governments were able to manipulate popular perceptions of themselves by consistently constructing 'an image of governing competence'. This point remains one of the few insights into the Thatcher project which has managed to strike a chord with the majority of authors who have taken part in the debate. However, it is doubtful whether most considered the full implications of Bulpitt's thesis. For not only did the image of governing competence find resonance with the electorate at large, it could also be said to have had a subliminal effect upon the perceptions of those who sought to analyse Thatcherism. In this respect, most authors, in their attempts to assert the radicalism of the Thatcher governments, can be criticised for having placed too much face value upon both the rhetorical pretensions and the symbolic representations of competence which preceded the Conservatives' strategic interventions.

A central feature of the rhetoric of Thatcherism was its powerful adherence to the idea that the Conservatives had come to power with an informed blueprint for an extensive overhaul of the institutional practices responsible for Britain's long-term political and economic decline. The Thatcher governments entered office in 1979 with a stated commitment to dissolve previous practices and replace them with a new governmental philosophy. In order to reconstruct the political landscape they had to bulldoze their way through a number of the rhetorical and ideological pillars which had bolstered previous governments. Consequently, their distinctive rhetoric exuded an unprecedented degree of radicalism which centred around pledges to deliver something 'new' to the British political scene.

These rhetorical pronouncements relayed a symbolic image that the Thatcher governments had a competently worked out and coherent strategy for reducing the size and scope of the state sector through the introduction of market forces in the delivery of functions previously provided by the state itself. However, beyond these vague pledges to recharacterise the role of government, the Conservatives consistently remained relatively closed about both the extent to which this strategy should be implemented and, indeed, the means by which it could be achieved. Thus, from the outset, Thatcherism emerged as an open-ended strategy, held together broadly by a number of vague ideological objectives, but lacking any definitive substance at a policy and institutional level. Yet, few authors have acknowledged this point. Most, having fixed their attention upon the strategic nature of the Thatcherite project (reflected in the competent articulation of its vague objectives), appeared to assume prior knowledge (on the part of both the Conservatives and indeed, themselves) of what these objectives precisely were and of how they should be implemented in practice. This tendency above all led the majority of analysts to mistake the unity and coherence of Thatcherite discourse as evidence of a coherently worked out strategy on the ground.

The seminal work of Stuart Hall and his contemporaries played a significant role in shaping, albeit in a distorted fashion, much of the subsequent literature.[2] The early work which these authors produced on Thatcherism from the mid-1970s onwards, cast Thatcherism as an attempt to recruit the hearts and minds of the electorate into a common sense, anti-statist, discourse which could act as an antidote to the popular discontent with social democracy.[3] However, to Hall and his colleagues, Thatcherism, as a hegemonic project, was to be conceived of as a broad strategy which amounted to something larger than its substantive content. The radicalism which they had detected in the Thatcherite strategy extended beyond the particular set of policy options it contained. Yet this fact was largely ignored by political scientists, who, in their own early attempts to decipher the intricacies of the Conservatives' strategy, invariably sought to characterise Thatcherism as a set of radical and distinct policy outcomes. The result is that, from the outset, the terms within which Thatcherism could be interpreted became largely distorted. Whereas Hall's analysis saw the Thatcher project as a relatively coherent strategy at a discursive level, the vast majority of political scientists tended to explain its radicalism at a policy level.

As a result then, many of the conclusions which were initially drawn

about the nature of Thatcherism were made prior to the practical realisation of many of the key elements of the Conservatives' strategy. Thus,
Thatcherism was defined within the texts produced by political scientists
long before it found any definitive substance of its own. By reducing
Thatcherism's radicalism and coherence to the policy level, political scientists thereby ignored the crucial temporality of the Thatcher project and
the essential struggle which the Conservatives' had to engage in over time
in order to translate their deeper objectives into actual political outcomes.
What is missing from these accounts is a proper analysis of one of the most
defining features of Thatcherism: its inherent dynamism and elasticity as
the Conservatives continually reworked and redefined the parameters
within which their longer-term strategic objectives could be met.

As some of the more detailed studies of Thatcherite policies have
demonstrated, the Conservatives' strategy proved to be far more experi-
mental, pragmatic, and indeed, incoherent, than was obvious from their
more competently espoused ideological rhetoric (Riddell 1991; Marsh and
Rhodes 1992). Thus, although the Thatcher governments were remarkably
adept at articulating a relatively consistent vision of the direction in which
they wanted to go, many of their attempts to translate this vision into actual
policy outcomes were, in practice, significantly more haphazard. It was
only over the course of a considerable time, specifically into their third
term in office, that the Thatcher governments were able to achieve the
type of consistency and coherence which has been generally associated
with the Thatcher project as a whole. Thus, as various studies have shown,
it is possible to detect a heightened radicalism and sophistication in the
Conservatives' reforms as their strategy unfolded (Gamble 1988; Jessop *et
al.* 1988; Dolowitz *et al.* 1996; Hay 1996; Kerr, McAnulla and Marsh 1997;
Kerr and Marsh 1999).

Yet, despite this, the majority of authors have been content to view
Thatcherism as a singular, static and indeed unified, snapshot in time,
thereby excluding a proper recognition of the uneven development of the
Conservatives' strategy over a number of years. As a result, the radicalism,
and indeed the success, of the Conservatives in achieving their longer-term
strategic goals was most often presupposed. By way of recognising the
transformative potential of Thatcherism, most treated the transformation
of institutional structures to be axiomatic. The result then has been an
outpouring of often exaggerated appraisals of the achievements of the
Conservatives which give too much credence to the Thatcherites' own
bloated view of success.

The tendency to neglect a consideration of the temporal dimensions to
Thatcherism subsequently affected our ability to gain a proper assessment
of the development of the Conservatives' strategy under John Major (Kerr,
McAnulla and Marsh 1997). This is reflected in the relative dearth of literature available on the Major period. Whereas the Thatcher years gave rise
to an industry of theoretically informed academic debate, the Major

governments merely evoked a strange mixture of both indifference, and indeed indecision, concerning their precise relationship with earlier post-1979 Conservative strategy. Of the few authors who attempted to come to grips with the specificities of the Major period, most remained ambiguous as to whether or not later Conservative reforms could rightly be characterised as a continuation of previous Thatcherite strategy, or whether it was perhaps better to refer to Majorism as representing a distinct political phenomenon. Overall, the tendency has been to conclude, in a manner which can only be described as theoretically agnostic, that Major exhibited some types of continuity with his predecessor while demonstrating several peculiar characteristics of his own.

While it is by no means the intention here to deny this undoubted truism, it is nevertheless important to emphasise the vacuity of these sentiments owing to the fundamental absence of theoretical substance underpinning them. For what has emerged most clearly from the sparse amount of literature available is the notable absence of any real idea of how conceptually to link the strategy pursued by John Major with the temporal unfolding of the broader Thatcherite project as a whole.[4] When we consider that Major became Britain's third-longest serving postwar prime minister and that his position at the helm of the Conservatives' strategy lasted for more than a third of his party's term in office, this represents a significant gap in our understanding of how Thatcherism developed over time. The most worrying aspect of this however, is the fact that most authors, despite their often strenuous efforts to deny it, appeared to assume that Thatcherism represented a temporal conjuncture which can only be linked directly to Mrs Thatcher's own personal term in office. Clearly, this tendency to ignore the evolution of the Thatcherite project negates any real understanding of the ongoing processes of institutional change which not only emerged out of the Major years, but which will undoubtedly influence the future development of the policies and strategies of New Labour.

Thatcherism and its historical 'others': dislocating post-1979 Conservatism from its past

Just as the lines of continuity between Thatcher and Major have been largely ignored within the literature, so too have those which exist between Thatcherism and its historical predecessors. In this respect, there has been an overall tendency to take Thatcherism out of its historical context. Few serious attempts have been made within the literature to link the post-1979 process of reforms to the overall historical conflicts and institutional compromises which subsequently both shaped and constrained the development of the Conservatives' strategic choices.[5]

Of course, this point may be regarded as somewhat contentious, since a customary and oft-cited reference point within the literature was the

Conservatives' reaction to the period of postwar political consensus that was perceived to have emerged from the experience of the Second World War. The systematic dismantling of the main pillars of the so-called postwar settlement and the displacement of processes of consensual-style decision-making with a more determined movement towards conviction politics remains one of the key yardsticks against which the radicalism of the Thatcher governments has been measured. Clearly then, the majority of authors have, by way of noting Mrs Thatcher's opposition to the Keynesian, social-democratic discourse of the earlier postwar period, paid at least a partial lip-service to the historical background to the Conservatives' ascendancy to power. Nevertheless, it would be misleading to assume from these, often passing, references to the earlier postwar period that such analyses constitute a proper consideration of the historical forces which both shaped and constrained the evolution of the Thatcher project. On the contrary, the effect of this type of analysis was merely to detach Thatcherism from its ancestry and to ignore the important lines of continuity which have characterised the postwar period as a whole (Kerr and Marsh 1996).

It is worth noting that, again, it is possible to trace the source of this problem to the inclination of most analysts to take the rhetorical pretensions of the Thatcher governments at face value. As we noted earlier, the Conservatives proved remarkably forthright in their own attempts to demarcate the terms within which their strategic interventions should be understood. Above all, this led them continually to seek to distance themselves from the practices of their predecessors by espousing their opposition to almost every aspect of the earlier postwar era. In particular, the Thatcher governments consistently voiced their antipathy towards the inherent statism which they saw as the central feature of the Butskellite policy paradigm. Thus, an important element to the perceived radicalism of the post-1979 period was the fact that the Conservatives had ridden to power on the back of having constructed a series of successfully narrated 'binary oppositions' between their own ideological prescriptions for change and the supposed social-democratic parameters which framed the policy options of previous postwar administrations (McAnulla 1997, 1999). In many ways, this carefully manufactured historical dichotomy between the pre- and post-1979 eras enabled the Conservatives to construct a shrewd diagnosis of the past which was to prove far more incisive than their prognosis for the future.

The effectiveness with which the Thatcherites were able to penetrate the popular consciousness with their historical interpretations was reflected in the fact that even the most experienced and reputable academics began passively to accept the idea that the Conservatives' strategy represented a sea change in postwar political protocol. Political scientists overwhelmingly granted an uncritical credence to the Thatcherites' attempts to present themselves as pioneers of a new and radical agenda to halt Britain's long-term decline from empire. In their 'objective' attempts to assert the novelty of the policies pursued after 1979, the majority of those interested in British politics began to elicit the same diagnosis of the past as the Conservatives had from their own ideologically tinted historical speculations. Accordingly, the formerly popular 'adversarial politics' thesis, which blamed Britain's economic decline on the lack of bi-party agreement over government strategy, gave way almost overnight to the overwhelming view that Britain's postwar 'settlement' had been dominated by a 'golden period' of political consensus which was governed by a commitment to Keynesian and corporatist-style interventions in economic and social affairs. As the Thatcherite strategy, with its seeming commitment to uncoupling the state from the market, began to unfold, representations of the earlier postwar period began to jell into a picture of historical 'otherness'. In this sense, academics increasingly emphasised the role of previous Labour and Conservative governments in promoting an overwhelmingly active, consensual and social-democratic approach to managing almost every area of high politics.

What is interesting to note here is the enormous discrepancy between the accounts of those who attempted to demonstrate the radicalism of the Attlee and Thatcher governments, and those who have sought to analyse the reasons for Britain's postwar institutional decline (Nairn 1964, 1977; Anderson 1987; Ingham 1984; Fine and Harris 1985; Marquand 1988a; Cain and Hopkins 1993; Gamble 1994; Hutton 1996).[6] These authors' primary emphasis has been upon the notable absence of any fundamental restructuring of British institutional practices. They have emphasised the inability of all governments throughout the postwar period to create the institutional structures appropriate for an active, developmental state. Indeed, many have gone so far as to doubt the success of Keynesian ideas in penetrating the traditional Treasury ethos of fiscal conservatism.[7] Others, however, have pointed to the crucial constraints imposed upon all postwar attempts at active intervention by the enduring power of the City of London and the primary goal of maintaining the international status of sterling.[8] These analyses point to the important continuities between Thatcherism and the practices of earlier postwar political practice. In these accounts there are few historical 'others', merely a long dreary succession of 'sameness'.

Yet, these points have been rarely acknowledged within the literature on the Thatcher project. Most authors have created contrasting representations of both Thatcherism and the supposed consensus era which bestow an enormous favour on the Thatcherite interpretation of postwar political practice (see Figure 2.1). These analyses present a portrayal of the Thatcher project which could not go further in precluding any notion of continuity in government practice and state structures. By explaining Thatcherism in terms of a simple binary opposition between it and its presumed historical 'others' we have significantly failed to develop a

Pre-1979	Post-1979
'Butskellism'	Thatcherism
Keynesianism	Monetarism
Social democracy	Neo-liberalism
Corporatism/weak state	Free market/strong state
Consensus/conciliation	Conflict/conviction

Figure 2.1 Selected pre-1979/post-1979 dichotomies

proper conception of the evolution, and indeed stasis, of Britain's institutional structures between 1945 and the present day. Moreover, these types of oversimplification have also negated any real attempt to come to terms with the historical processes and mechanisms which have guided the evolution of the state from 'social democracy' to 'Thatcherism'.

Partial insight and holistic oversight: the prevalence of mono-causal explanation

The third key problem within the literature has been the tendency to preclude a comprehensive analysis of the essentially dynamic processes which have driven the evolution of the Conservative strategy over time. The author most directly associated with this criticism is Marsh (1994, 1995a), who has highlighted the inadequate level of illumination cast by the majority of interpretations on the highly complex and multi-dimensional factors that have been an inherent part of the Conservatives' strategy. Apart from a small number of authors who have attempted to provide inclusive explanations sensitive to the constant articulation between the political, economic and ideological dimensions of Thatcherism, the vast majority of those who sought to explain the Thatcher project simply succeeded in presenting the Conservatives' strategy as a uni-dimensional phenomenon which could be explained by reference to singular, mono-causal variables (see Figure 2.2).

The majority of these analyses attach an enormous degree of importance to intra- and inter-party politics. Much time is spent discussing the separate elements of Conservative philosophy and analysing the rhetoric of key political actors in order to assign primacy of explanation to the ideas, beliefs and intentions of individual politicians. Within such accounts global trends and wider social and economic dynamics are merely paid lip service. It is often acknowledged that similar patterns of policy can be detected throughout the advanced economies and that wider explanatory variables may have had an important impact; yet this point is most often pushed aside while the focus quickly returns to the central task of deciphering Conservative Party statecraft.

Type of explanation	Partial	Inclusive
Political	Thatcherism as electoral strategy and policy agenda. Emphasis placed upon Mrs Thatcher's political style, Conservative statecraft, attack on consensus, corporatism, welfare state. See King (1985), Bulpitt (1986), Kavanagh (1987), Crewe (1988).	Thatcherism as political response to domestic structural decline and global economic development. Emphasis upon: Thatcherite authoritarian state-craft, the use of ideology in hegemonic struggle, economic accumulation strategy. See Gamble (1988).
Ideological	Thatcherism as Neo-liberal strategy and populist discourse. Emphasis upon: role of New Right think tanks on policy, moral crusade and attack on collectivism. See O'Shea (1984), Wolfe (1991).	Thatcherism as hegemonic project. Emphasis upon: the narration of crisis around popular discontent, Thatcherite authoritarian state project backed by formation of new economic historic-bloc. See Hall (1979), Hay (1996).
Economic	Thatcherism as response to economic crisis and changes in global economy. Emphasis upon: the critique of Keynesianism and state inter-vention, bias in favour of particular class interests. See Coates (1989), Nairn (1981).	Thatcherism as accumulation strategy and response to changes in global capitalism. Emphasis upon: transition to post-Fordism, creation of 'two-nations' electoral strategy, partial hegemonic struggle. See Jessop *et al.* (1988), Overbeek (1990), Taylor (1992).

Figure 2.2 Partial versus inclusive explanations of Thatcherism
Source: Adapted from Marsh (1995a).

Clearly, the development of the Conservatives' strategy was propelled by a whole series of different inputs, ranging from the particular traits of the personalities behind it to the more generic institutional crises which have underpinned it. Moreover, the Conservatives' strategic aims were also driven as much by political and economic imperatives as they have were by ideological conviction. Politically, they were prescribed by electoral and statecraft concerns as much as, if not more than, ideological attachment. Economically, the Conservatives had to deal with the contradictions, on the one hand, of encouraging processes of market liberalisation to allow a transition to more flexible and global patterns of economic development and, on the other, of strengthening the ability of the state to oversee and encourage these processes. As a result, the Thatcherite strategy was provoked by a disparate range of factors, many of which pulled in different directions. Yet few authors have been willing to acknowledge this diffusion of generative forces. The majority of explanations tended to be divided crudely between structuralist and intentionalist accounts which privileged singular explanatory variables – political, economic or ideological – as the primary dynamic behind the Conservatives' reforms.

An important, though no less serious, adjunct of this problem has been the prevalence of ethno-centric approaches, derived from an overall neglect of the external factors which have both shaped and constrained the development of British politics since the 1970s. Throughout the literature, there have been few serious attempts to characterise Thatcherism as part of a wider, international, response to political and economic crises within the world system. This fact has meant that the balance of explanation remained firmly tilted towards an emphasis upon the political and ideological inputs which the Thatcherites themselves brought to bear upon the political process. The majority of analysts appeared happy to conclude that the combination of Mrs Thatcher's dominant personality and the Conservative Party's adoption of New Right ideas had converged to provoke an 'exceptional' conjuncture in British politics, and the fact that neo-liberal welfare retrenchment could be seen to spreading across the globe hardly seemed to impinge upon such an obviously spurious thesis.

Re-stating the problem of explaining Thatcherism

The three problems highlighted above have contributed to the fact that Thatcherism has most often been presented as a singular, static, 'snapshot' in time, dislocated from its historical precedents, while primary explanatory emphasis has alternated between ethno/agency-centred accounts of change or strict structural determinism. These analyses leave us with an inanimate picture of the development of postwar British politics, in which our understanding of the evolution of state structures and governmental strategies has been compromised by a series of static representations which merely caricature change and obscure important continuities. What is missing is a proper analysis of the complexity of change and the evolution of the state, through the dynamic and dialectical interplay between structure, agency and strategy.

However, what emerges more clearly from the literature is the overall lack of clarity and general confusion derived from the eclecticism in the approaches applied to explain Thatcherism. All in all, the study of the Thatcher governments presents us with a conceptual mire in which there appears to be little solid ground on which to find any theoretical foothold. As Marsh (1994, 1995a) has pointed out, the problem has not been that political science as a whole has failed to account for most of the discernible elements of the Thatcherite project. When we take the literature in its entirety, most of the pieces of the jigsaw required for a holistic perspective are clearly present. Yet, the challenge of linking these separate strands into a multi-dimensional approach has rarely been taken up. Most authors appear untouched by the need to develop a theoretical framework adequate to the task of elucidating the true complexity behind the Conservatives' strategy. As such, I will argue that the real problem in explaining Thatcherism lies not in the complexity of the Thatcherite project itself, but in the failure of political scientists to develop explanatory tools which can incorporate the complexity and intricacies of governmental strategy in general.

The root of this problem lies in the dualism between structuralist and intentionalist accounts of political change. Change resides in the constant articulation of structure, agency and strategy and, thus, any account which excludes an informed analysis of this dialectical interplay must necessarily negate any serious attempt to elucidate the full range of processes and mechanisms which contribute to the temporal unfolding of institutional change.[10] Yet, to focus upon the gulf between structuralism and intentionalism is perhaps to miss the target somewhat. As Hay (1997: 2) explains, the problem can be stated more broadly as an overall failure to explain change generally: 'political scientists in general, and anglophone political scientists in particular have tended to fail to develop a conceptual armoury adequate to the task of dealing with political change'.

If we take the point that political science has generally failed to come to grips with highlighting the complexity of political change, then it is possible to suggest that the problem of explaining Thatcherism needs to be restated as a problem of political science explanation more broadly. In this sense then, it is precisely the lack of any conceptual armoury sufficient to the task of elucidating the processes and mechanisms of political change which has resulted in the more specific failure to come to terms with Thatcherism.

If we are to account for the reasons for such failure, we may perhaps begin, as Hay (1997: 2–12) suggests, to look towards the bias which the discipline has retained towards a broadly empiricist methodology. Underpinning this approach has been the assumption, derived largely from natural science, that the 'rules of the game' governing political behaviour remain constant over time. This most basic premise can be considered to have fundamentally hampered political scientists' ability, and indeed their proclivity, to assess the fundamental concept of change. Instead:

> the pervasive tendency has been to extrapolate from evidence gathered and gleaned at a particular instant: a methodologically-prescribed propensity to frame and fix what is, essentially, a moving target – a contingently unfolding reality. Accordingly, orthodox political science tends *either* to have little to say about processes of change altogether, *or*, where it does, to seek to derive or impute processes of change from the counterposing or juxtapositioning of static snapshots.
>
> (Hay 1997: 7)

When we come to view the literature, we soon find that it is precisely such a juxtapositioning of static snapshots (between, for example, Thatcherism and consensus, Thatcher and Major, Keynesianism and monetarism) which has dominated our understanding, not only of the Thatcher period, but of the postwar era as a whole. These sets of binary oppositions, among others, have obscured a proper understanding of the processes of change that have governed the evolution of state structures before, during and after Mrs Thatcher's terms in office. As a result then, it is perhaps somewhat ironic that the most intense period of political, economic and social change since the Second World War should have inspired a myriad of interpretations, generally devoid of the ability to grasp the very concept of change itself.

Towards an evolutionary conception of Thatcherism

This leaves us with the question of how we can advance our understanding of Thatcherism, and, thereby, of the evolution of postwar British politics in general, beyond the types of simplified, formulaic understanding available. It would be somewhat vacuous to conclude that, by merely incorporating a discourse sensitive to the complexities of change, political scientists can automatically proceed towards a more sophisticated understanding of the multiple processes and mechanisms which generated Thatcherism. Clearly, the gulf which separates the various theoretical perspectives employed to explain Thatcherism represents a profound obstacle which cannot simply be overcome through a vague commitment towards the need for greater holism. The major problem is that current explanations, given their diversity and overall dislocation from each other, have failed to provide us with any concrete conceptual frameworks which can be employed for further empirical or theoretical research.

As Overbeek (1988: 87) explains, albeit in reference to explaining the postwar period as a whole, a proper conception of the complexity of change would need to give full weight to the fact that: 'what we are discussing here are superimposed dimensions of reality, where "facts" pertinent to one dimension only acquire their full meaning if they are considered against the background of the other dimensions'. However, the rigidity with which most authors have clung to an emphasis upon either the political, economic, ideological, structural or intentional factors that have generated the Conservatives' strategic calculations militates heavily against the attainment of the type of sophisticated analysis of the Thatcherite strategy required to satisfy this plea. Thus, the fulfilment of a multi-dimensional approach depends upon the ability of political scientists to extricate themselves from the narrow focus which they have traditionally retained for explaining singular dimensions to political behaviour.[11] This necessarily entails a movement towards a multi-disciplinary perspective capable of incorporating the insights of other social science fields of research. Thatcherism therefore, needs to be assessed in terms of its relationship to each of the dimensions – ideational, political, economic, historical, domestic and external – against which it emerged.

This means that Thatcherism must be seen as a particular British response to generic international crises of capitalist accumulation, as well as the specific manifestation of these crises and contradictory tendencies on a domestic level. Thus, any explanation of Thatcherism must account for the ongoing and dynamic interaction between the pressures caused by wider evolutionary trajectories within the international system, and specific adaptations to these as governments learn through time how to respond. More specifically, we need to account for what Jessop (1992: 232–6) refers to as the problem of macro-necessity versus micro-diversity, namely, the fact that wider international crises produce similar responses across all nation states, yet the specific articulation of these responses differs according to the specific circumstances of each individual nation and the inputs of the actors involved in the articulation of government strategy. This means that we need to develop an analysis of Thatcherism which is sensitive to the fact that the Conservatives' response to the crisis of the 1970s was conditioned by that crisis, yet dependent upon the Thatcherites' own interpretation of crisis and their adaptation to it.

Thus, the overall challenge is for political scientists to adopt a conceptual armoury which can help to incorporate the concerns of a wide array of rival theoretical traditions, without necessarily conceding the autonomy of their own discipline. While I would not advocate the dissolution of political-science attempts at analysing political change into the concerns of theorists whose main focus is, for example, the reproduction of capitalist relations, or the micro and macro dynamics which propel social change over time, we still need to remain sensitive to the concerns of these and other theoretical movements. This is no small challenge of course; yet it is one which needs to be taken up if we are to gain a proper insight into the complex and dynamic processes which contribute to periods of intense political, economic and social change such as the Thatcher years.

One of the principal aims of this book is to argue that the only viable route towards the attainment of a multi-dimensional approach is to be found in a complete reformulation of the theoretical tools that we can bring to bear upon the elucidation of past, present and future state strategy. In particular, the aim is to assert the usefulness of an evolutionary conception of political change, which emphasises the temporal unfolding of institutional change through a constant and dynamic process of strategic adaptation and learning in response to wider environmental pressures.

The prospects and potential of an evolutionary conception of political change

As I shall discuss in more detail in Chapter Four, the case for adopting an evolutionary approach has been strengthened in recent years by the redis-covery of the validity of evolutionary conceptions of change within a variety of social science sub-disciplines. Although this literature can be characterised broadly as 'evolutionary', it would be misleading to suggest that it is under-pinned by a firm, unified, theoretical discourse. Nevertheless, a central theme of this book is to argue that the recent wave of evolutionary theo-rising has produced a research paradigm which opens up an array of opportunities for political scientists to adopt flexible forms of explanation within a broader, less segregated theoretical conception of the complexity of change over time.

Of course, this is not the place to provide a detailed review of the liter-ature on evolutionary theorising; that task will be laid out in Chapter Four. However, here it is useful to very briefly outline the main elements of an evolutionary approach and the advantages which this can provide to an analysis of Thatcherism. First, however, it is worth reminding ourselves of the basic ingredients which would be required to satisfy a more rounded and multi-dimensional approach to Thatcherism. Here, I will emphasise five key elements:

- First, a proper conception of Thatcherism would need to include an appreciation of the temporal dimension of Thatcherism and a recog-nition of the fact that Conservative reforms evolved and gained a coherence over time. This necessarily entails an appreciation of the development of the Conservatives' strategy under John Major.
- Second, we need a proper assessment of the historical forces which shaped the development of the Conservatives' strategy. This means that we need to move beyond existing static accounts, which merely emphasise historical contrasts, and look instead at the long-term configurations of class compromises and institutional factors which played a key role in enabling Thatcherism to emerge.
- Third, we need a heightened sensitivity to the complex interplay between the political, ideological and economic dimensions of Thatcherism. This means that we need to move beyond viewing Thatcherism as a simple uni-dimensional phenomenon and emphasise instead the complexity and diversity of the Thatcherite project.
- Fourth, we need a proper appreciation of the dialectical relationship between structure and agency. This means that we need to move beyond reductionist accounts and seek to examine Thatcherism as the product of both structural and intentional factors.
- Finally, we need a commitment to analysing both the domestic and external contexts which constrained and enabled the Conservatives' strategic choices. This entails a movement away from ethno-centric approaches which emphasise Thatcherism's 'exceptionalism'.

As this book will attempt to demonstrate, an evolutionary approach can help us to satisfy each of these five ingredients of a multi-dimensional perspective on Thatcherism and the postwar period in general. Briefly, there are four key elements to an evolutionary account of change. These are:

- An inherent concern with the temporal dimensions of change. An evolutionary approach focuses our attention upon a variable, such as Thatcherism, which is changing over time (Nelson 1995: 54). As such, it diverts us away from a preoccupation with 'static' phenomena and directs us towards viewing change as a dynamic and ongoing process.
- A primary concern to explain the factors which generate change. The 'theoretical quest' behind an evolutionary approach is to examine the complex interaction of variables which contribute to making evolution occur (ibid.: 5). As such, primary emphasis is placed upon explaining complex change rather than merely simplifying and describing it.
- Change is perceived as occurring through a combination of both selective and adaptive processes. In this sense, evolutionary theory provides a heightened sensitivity to the environment in which variables evolve and that imposes selective pressures which favour certain types of change over others. In turn, the variables which are evolving can often adapt both themselves and, to a lesser extent, their environment, in order to increase their chance of survival.
- Change is seen as both path-dependent and contingent. It is path-dependent in the sense that a combination of environmental constraints and past adaptations shape the direction of future changes. In this sense, the changes which occur must inevitably display a certain continuity with past adaptations. However, because of the crucial input which goal-directed and purposeful actors bring to bear upon their environment, there is also a large degree of contingency involved in the process of change. Thus, the environment does not simply determine the direction of change; rather it provides the context in which actors can learn to adapt strategies in order to negotiate the constraints which they face.

The advantages of such an approach to an analysis of Thatcherism are abundant (see Figure 2.3). An evolutionary account of political and economic change presupposes a heightened sensitivity to the constantly changing relationship between strategic actors and the environment within which they are forced to operate. Change is conceived of here as being both contingent and path-dependent; in other words, as a conditioned response to environmental exigencies and crises filtered through the limited capacities and strategic heuristics of state actors. In this respect, an evolutionary explanation entails a proper consideration of the dialectical interplay between structure, agency and strategy by focusing our attention on the ways in which actors articulate strategies in order to negotiate the structural and strategic demands of the environment which they inhabit. It is this heightened sensitivity to the relational and contingent articulation of strategy which provides an evolutionary account with the explanatory depth required to elucidate periods of intensified political change such as the Thatcher years.

Problems of current explanations	Advantage of an evolutionary approach	Application to Thatcherism
Neglect of the temporal dimensions to the Conservatives' strategy. Thatcherism seen as a singular, unified snapshot in time.	Draws specific attention to the time span through which the development of the variable under scrutiny occurs. Thus, directs our focus to change rather than stasis and to the temporal compass along which this takes place.	Thatcherism viewed as a constantly changing and evolving phenomenon. Allows us to chart the development of Thatcherism from its early, tentative stages of reform to its maturation during the Conservatives' third and fourth terms.
Absence of an historical perspective. Thatcherism viewed in contrast to previous government strategy. No analysis of the lines of continuity between the post-1979 era and the earlier postwar experience.	Views change as 'path-dependent', i.e. past changes affect future adaptations. Thus, directs our focus to the fact that 'change' must exhibit a crucial element of 'continuity' with the past.	Thatcherism considered in the context of the historical forces and institutional compromises which constrained, enabled and provoked its development. Thus, viewed in the context of the crisis of social democracy and failure of Fordism.
Failure to link conceptually the political, ideological and economic dimensions to Thatcherism.	Evolution seen as the product of a multiplicity of different factors. The theoretical quest is to examine the complex interaction of dynamics which generate change.	Thatcherism viewed as evolving in response to a diffuse number of inputs, including: the personality traits of key actors, New Right ideology, Conservative Party statecraft, and crises in capitalist profitability.
Unequal consideration given to structural and intentional factors. Failure to view change as the product of the dialectal interplay between structure, agency and strategy.	Equal consideration given to the interaction between purposeful human agents and the selective 'environment', or context within which these operate. Thus, change is seen as both contingent and path-dependent, i.e. as the product of agents developing strategies to negotiate their structural environments.	Thatcherism viewed as the outcome of an evolving process in which the Conservatives attempted to implement their political, ideological and economic objectives within an environment which both constrained and enabled their strategic choices. Thus, consideration given to the ability of the Conservatives to adapt their strategic interventions and learn how to implement these over time.

Figure 2.3 The advantages of an evolutionary approach to explaining Thatcherism

(continued opposite)

Problems of current explanations	Advantage of an evolutionary approach	Application to Thatcherism
Prevalence of ethno-centred approaches. Thatcherism seen as an 'exceptional' phenomenon. Little attention given to the spread of similar policies across the globe and to the factors which provoked these.	Attention given to the full range of 'environmental' factors which shape evolution. Thus, directs our attention to the global as well as the domestic structures which influenced the development of Conservative strategy.	Thatcherism seen within the context of both the national-specific institutional environment in which it emerged, as well as the global factors which influenced its development. Thus, viewed as a response to generic crises within the international system, as well as the specific articulation of these on a domestic front.

Figure 2.3 (continued)

Thus, an evolutionary explanation of Thatcherism would, a priori, preclude the type of static, ahistorical, ethnocentric and reductionist accounts which have so far dominated the literature, by directing our focus to the inherent dynamism of the Conservatives' strategy, and to the multi-layered historical processes and mechanisms which generated, facilitated and constrained it. This also implies a proper consideration of the temporality of change, allowing us to view Thatcherism as a series of contingent interventions which unfolded and evolved through time.

The evolution of Thatcherite state strategy: a summary

Having taken up and developed these key themes in Chapter Four, I will proceed in Chapters Seven and Eight to provide an alternative periodisation of the evolution of the Conservatives' strategy. Here, I build upon the previous theoretical and empirical work laid out by Jessop *et al.* (1988) and Hay (1996). As these authors make clear, Thatcherism must be seen to have evolved out of the political and economic crises which emerged in the 1970s. On an international level, the ascendancy of New Right ideas across the globe have to be placed within the context of the weakening of US hegemony and the crisis of Fordist modes of economic regulation. This point remains relatively uncontested, if albeit largely ignored, within the literature. However, perhaps more controversially, I will argue that any analysis of the domestic conditions which shaped the Conservatives' strategy must take account of the failure of earlier postwar governments to create both a domestic consensus on Keynesian, social-democratic interventions and a stable, institutionalised, state settlement. As I will argue in more detail in the next chapter and in Chapters Five and Six, the historical context out of which Thatcherism evolved was one dominated by inherent conflicts and discontinuities in government strategy. Thus, Thatcherism, as well as representing a response to wider evolutionary trajectories within the world system, must also be read against the context of the earlier, fitful evolutionary trajectory of the postwar British state.

This previous evolutionary development significantly laid the foundations for the later emergence of Thatcherism, since it enabled crucial elements of the Thatcherite strategy to reside within the institutional architecture of the postwar British state. Thus, it is important to recognise the crucial constraints which were placed upon the so-called Keynesian consensus by the existence of a durable, long-term, previously institutionalised, consensus on the need to secure the interests of financial capital and the value of sterling, and to sacrifice active, interventionist strategies in favour of short-term fiscal prudence. Consequently, as well as viewing Thatcherism as a paradigmatic break with the ideological rhetoric of the postwar period, it is equally important to emphasise the crucial continuity of post-1979 Conservatism with previous political and economic institutionalised routines.

As we shall see, the period 1975/6 presented itself as a critical conjunctural moment for the emergence of Thatcherism as an active and evolving state project, as opposed to an innate property of the postwar British state. The failure of the previous Labour government to enact their domestic economic strategies, coupled with their appeal for help to the International Monetary Fund (IMF), played an important role in bringing to an end some of the fundamental conflicts of the earlier postwar period. In particular, it ended the conflicting selection pressures brought about by the need to maintain a domestic commitment to Keynesianism on the one hand, while trying to maintain Britain's status (and particularly that of sterling and the City of London) within a liberalised global economy on the other. The attempts by Labour to conduct the first real experiment with a Keynesian budgetary deficit revealed many of the contradictions and inherent conflicts of the so-called postwar settlement, and can be considered to have contributed, together with the events of 1978, to delegitimising the discursive commitment to Keynesian, social-democratic and corporatist strategies. It is throughout this period that the decisive moment for the selection of Thatcherism as an active state project occurred. The deepening problems of the British economy allowed the New Right to re-interpret Britain's postwar decline as a crisis of an 'overloaded' state caused by the social-democratic and statist interventions of earlier postwar political actors (Hay 1996). Thus, Thatcherism emerged initially as a determined critique of the (largely mythical) practices of the postwar period, a critique which political scientists, as well as the public at large, have been all too willing to absorb.

The Thatcherites' successful interpretation of the deleterious effects of 'socialism' throughout the postwar period, enabled the Conservatives to lay the foundation for a hegemonic anti-statist discourse, based around the false notion that social democracy had been successfully implemented and failed. However, it is important to emphasise that, beyond this simple but effective narration of the crisis of the British state, Thatcherism emerged after 1979 as an ill-defined and often incoherent (except at a discursive level) strategy. Thus, early Thatcherite policies reveal an overall lack of strategic direction, even though they remained held together by a very coherent, though highly abstract articulation of ideological discourse. It is this ideological discourse, or strategic vision, together with a cleverly-constructed electoral strategy, and the fact that Thatcherism faced a relative lack of conflict compared to earlier postwar governments, which enabled the Conservatives to gain the space to adapt to and learn from the environmental pressures which formed their strategic context. This enabled the Conservatives' strategy to become more consistent and developed through their successive terms in office, culminating in a rapid pace of policy change under John Major, a period I shall refer to as 'late-Thatcherism' (see Kerr, McAnulla and Marsh 1997).

However, as I will argue, the narrow articulation of an 'anti-statist', neo-liberal discourse, together with the satisfaction of short-term political aims, also proved damaging to the Conservatives' ability to formulate successful adaptations which could improve Britain's performance in the overall changing global climate. These problems contributed to longer-term troubles for the Conservatives which ultimately damaged their electoral fortunes under John Major, and revealed latent contradictions in the state settlement that emerged out of the Conservatives third and fourth terms in office (Jessop 1994).

Having adapted their strategic interventions to cope with the exigencies imposed by selective environmental pressures, the problem which the Conservatives faced is that, throughout their period in office, they were learning the wrong lessons. While crises and contradictions within their environment necessitated the re-regulation of the UK economy to cope with its strategic re-adjustment to changing global political and economic relations, the Conservatives consistently failed to respond effectively. Therefore, Thatcherism, although a dynamic and evolving process, emerged as an essentially flawed evolution because of the narrow conceptions which the Conservatives had of the types of crises which they faced and, indeed, the optimal solutions required to resolve such problems. Their dogmatic attachment to an anti-statist, neo-liberal ideology directed their attention away from the need to learn the appropriate means by which state mechanisms could be used in order to generate economic growth and successful accumulation. Instead, the Conservatives proved content merely to engage in an almost constant and ongoing process of learning how to satisfy their twin fetishes of welfare retrenchment and the depoliticisation of the very areas which could generate successful adaptation to the environmental crises brought about by the failure of Fordism.

Conclusion

The purpose of this chapter has been to interrogate the main problems in the literature on Thatcherism, and to suggest the utility of an evolutionary conception of political change in helping us to overcome these. Underlying the main themes explored here has been the suggestion that our general misinterpretation of the Thatcher period has also contributed to a broader misunderstanding of the earlier postwar period. In particular, the Thatcherites' attempts to narrate the crisis of the 1970s as a crisis of an overloaded state, caused by the consensual commitment amongst Britain's political elite to statist, social-democratic and corporatist strategies, has had a subsequent effect upon the perceptions which political scientists and historians bring to bear upon the pre-1979 era. It is to this theme that I will turn in the next chapter, where I will argue that the idea of a Keynesian, social-democratic and corporatist consensus (or settlement) has no real heuristic utility for our overall understanding of the evolution of postwar British politics.

3 Conflict, not consensus

The myth of the Keynesian, social-democratic state settlement

Introduction

As we saw in the previous chapter, the 1980s sparked a craze in academic circles for analysing the phenomenon of 'Thatcherism'. Inspired by the apparent distinctiveness of the New Right project, the vast majority of British political scientists clamoured to take snapshots of the idiosyncrasies of the Thatcherite agenda. From this, it was overwhelmingly ascertained that the Thatcher years marked an exceptional period in postwar British politics. Yet, this prevailing belief tended to be based less upon the success of the Thatcher administrations in implementing their own policy strategies than upon the variety of ways in which they contrived to uncouple previous ones. In this sense, Mrs Thatcher earned a degree of notoriety amongst her critics, not so much for her own policy achievements, as her part in killing off the 'postwar consensus' and the collectivist values around which this was supposedly constructed.

We also saw from the previous chapter, that the fad for analyses of Thatcherism became instantly passé as the rather less stylish John Major replaced his more glamorous predecessor. As a result, the 1990s evoked a shift in focus, with the glare of the academic spotlight turned increasingly towards a reappraisal of the earlier postwar period. Of course, towards the end of the decade the Blair administration emerged out of the shadows to capture most of the recent academic attention, but nevertheless the emphasis upon the historical dimensions of contemporary public policy has remained strong. Within this literature the idea that an era of consensus politics was replaced by the radicalism of the Thatcher years continues to be embraced by the vast majority of political scientists and historians alike. Indeed, as an analytical reference, the 'postwar consensus' has become as pervasive a term as 'Thatcherism'. As this chapter will demonstrate, this is no small point; for it is clear that many of the assumptions which have been made about both Thatcherism and the pre-1979 era have, to a large extent, been mutually constructed. The result, as I will show, is that both terms have assumed a mutual dependency. In particular, both have been utilised to overemphasise the transformation of the postwar British state.

The con which makes sense of it all

As Jefferys (1993: 297) has remarked: 'contemporary history grows apace'.[1] Clearly we should welcome this trend, for it provides us with an excellent opportunity to re-evaluate our original assessments of the postwar era. However, it would appear that this hope is perhaps overly-optimistic given the persistent tendency of most authors to reproduce an historical narrative with which we are all too familiar.[2] It seems that, although the period has been subject to more intense scrutiny of late, to most commentators the established narrative continues to hold its own fashionable appeal.

This appeal is perhaps best reflected in the continuing prevalence of the 'postwar consensus' thesis (see for example Marquand 1989; Kavanagh and Morris 1989, 1994; Lowe 1990; Dutton 1991; Kavanagh 1992; Butler 1993; Seldon 1994). Of course, it would be wrong to suggest that the thesis has been devoid of critics. A number of authors have questioned the extent to which policy in both the wartime and postwar periods can be considered the product of bi-party accord (see for example Pimlott 1988; Jefferys 1991; Brooke 1992; Rollings 1994). Yet, despite these efforts to revise conventional wisdom, the idea of the 'postwar consensus' still retains its status as a central chapter in the majority of attempts to narrate the trajectory of the state since the Second World War. As Butler (1993: 435) explains: 'recent publications regularly deploy the phrase, if somewhat more cautiously than hitherto, and it has by no means been purged from political debate'.

A key aim of this chapter is to argue that, if we want to explain the endurance of the thesis, then we need to look beyond its simple utility as a metaphorical device and seek to examine instead the aspirations of those who employ it. This point has been made by Butler (1993; see also Rollings 1994), who attributes the 'peculiar persistence' of the thesis to the fact that the majority of those who subscribe to it have a vested interest in keeping the idea 'alive and kicking'. To understand its appeal then, the author implores us to consider the normative dimensions of the debate, thereby taking into account: 'for whom, and for what purposes, theories of consensus are useful and interesting' (Butler 1993: 435).

Clearly, the idea of the postwar consensus remains 'useful and interesting' to most authors because it accentuates the belief that the Thatcher governments were successful in their attempts to reconstruct a state settlement which had been constructed by the Labour Party under Clement Attlee. In this sense, the consensus thesis provides, as Harris (1988: 11) notes, a 'paradoxical link' between the initial postwar reconstruction under Labour and the subsequent Conservative reform of the state after 1979. Thus, it effectively binds the established narrative together and thereby helps us to make sense of the period as a whole. Yet, this fact has tended to be obscured within the literature. For, as the following section will show, too much of the debate has thus far been bogged down in semantic squabbling over the meaning of consensus and pedantic altercations over both its depth and its timing. As a result, the wider implications of the consensus thesis have tended to be obscured by the seemingly banal terms in which the debate has been cast. We shall return to this point later. Here however, it is important briefly to clarify the basic tenets of the consensus thesis. As a result, the following section will sketch out the main contours of the debate in an attempt to provide what Butler (1993: 437; see also Pimlott 1988: 130) has termed: 'a photofit portrait of consensus narratives'.

Photofitting the consensus

The idea of a postwar consensus has successfully lured a vast number of authors, the overwhelming majority of whom have tended to subscribe to what Pimlott (1988) terms the 'accepted version' of the consensus thesis. This incorporates the belief that: 'for a period of about thirty years after the war the leaders of the Conservative and Labour parties were agreed on the fundamentals of a "postwar consensus", or "postwar settlement"' (Addison 1987: 5).

The key component of this thesis lies in Addison's assertion (1985: 2) that: 'Britain was reconstructed in the image of the war effort'.[3] In this sense, it is argued that the experience of the Second World War created the circumstances for the development of policies aimed at combating the deep divisions in British society. It is thereby suggested that a new agenda was forged around a policy convergence on the need for social security and welfare reforms. Much emphasis is placed upon the apparent pursuit of full employment as a primary ambition throughout the postwar era, coupled with rigorous fiscal and industrial policies. Most authors view four events: the 'Keynesian' budget of 1941; the Beveridge Report of 1942; the Education Act of 1944; and, the Employment Policy White Paper of 1944 as the cornerstones of the new consensus which is seen to have been consolidated by Labour under Clement Attlee and the Conservatives under Harold Macmillan.

To date, Kavanagh and Morris (1989, 1994) have provided the only comprehensive study of the specific areas of convergence. For these authors, the consensus consisted of two key elements. First, there was an adherence to a particular policy approach or style of government. This entailed the practice of institutionalised consultative arrangements between government and the major economic actors, akin to the 'corporate bias' identified by Middlemas (1979). Second, there was a shared commitment to a broad set of policies. This consisted of a bi-party accord in the areas of:

- *Full employment* underpinned by Keynesian demand management techniques.

- *The mixed economy* including the public ownership of basic utilities and core industries.
- *Active government* including a widening of the perceived responsibilities of the state and a move towards greater intervention in the economy.[4]
- *Industrial relations* entailing the conciliation of trade unions and their subsequent involvement in policy-making.
- *The welfare state* underpinned by Beveridge's ideas for universal national assistance.
- *Foreign and defence policy* entailing the maintenance of Britain's role as a nuclear power and membership of the Atlantic Alliance

Focusing exclusively on the cohesion which they detect in public policy, these authors conclude that:

> in this period, it is continuity rather than discontinuity that charac-terises the content of significant areas of public policy. . . . In no sense was postwar Britain a country without politics or without disagreement; our argument is that political disagreement took place within a broad set of shared assumptions about the goals – and the mechanisms – of government action.
>
> (Kavanagh and Morris 1994: 110)

Of course, it is the identification of a 'broad set of shared assumptions' which provoke these and other authors to posit the existence of a distinct policy convergence. Specifically, they emphasise that the consensus revolved around 'a set of parameters which bound the set of policy options regarded by senior politicians and civil servants as administratively practi-cable, economically affordable and politically acceptable' (ibid.).

Few authors have thus far disputed the origins of the consensus. Nevertheless, it is possible to detect differences in accounts of when the period ended. As Butler (1993: 439) points out, the years 1960, 1964, 1967, 1970, 1973, 1975 and 1979 have all been suggested as possible dates. However, the increased polarisation of the two main parties, coupled with the apparent breakdown of Keynesian economics and corporatist-style government, have led most to assume that the consensus gradually eroded throughout the 1970s, with Mrs Thatcher providing the final nail in its coffin.

This brief summary then, allows us to follow the broad contours of the consensus thesis. What is particularly curious, and indeed important to our understanding of the overall postwar period, is the extent to which this portrait has been so overwhelmingly incorporated into our political history. As Butler explains:

> Too many commentators find the rise and fall thesis particularly unde-manding. It helps them to agree on which subjects matter. Attention can be devoted to specific ideas, such as demand management or

public ownership, and to certain institutions, like the National Health Service, the BBC, or the NEDC. In this way the thesis inflates politicians' self-estimation and stifles intellectual curiosity.

Butler (1993: 445)

Here, the author provides us with one of the most perceptive interventions in the debate. For the ability of the thesis to 'stifle intellectual curiosity' has meant that the parameters within which subsequent revisionism has been exercised remain exceptionally narrow. In this respect, the vast majority of authors who have sought to interpret the evolution of the postwar period have eagerly acquiesced to the conclusions drawn by Addison and others. Of the few who have contributed to a 'debate' over the concept, most of these assume a position of qualified acceptance of the thesis, while only a small minority have chosen to reject it outright.

The debate over consensus

Semantics and pedantics: qualified acceptance of the consensus thesis

The vast majority of authors who have contributed to the limited debate have confined themselves to persistent squabbling over both the meaning and the subsequent depth of the consensus. Thus, while some authors refer to a convergence over policy, others argue that there was a deeper, more profound, commitment to a set of common beliefs, moral values and social aspirations (compare for example Ball 1981: 145–6; Warde 1982: 4–5; Punnett 1987: 25; Marquand 1988a: 18; Wright 1989: 209). The result, as Seldon (1994: 506) explains, is that various commentators stress 'different intensities of consensual expression'. For example, Turner (1989: 18) regards the situation after the war as involving: 'a *compromise* between hostile groups, not a consensus' (emphasis added). Likewise, Ritschel (1995: 270) remarks that 'while 'consensus' may be too strong a word, there did emerge during the war, if not an absolute accord, then at least *a widely shared agenda of social and economic reform*' (emphasis added).

Here, we begin to see the limited extent of the existing debate. It is clear that this type of discussion does more to entice us into a protracted exercise in semantics, than to resolve the complexities of governmental activity in the period under review. Indeed, it is interesting to note that the parameters of this debate become so circumscribed that even Addison (1987: 5; 1993) is able to concede that: 'the term consensus is open to question'. Given that Addison's work (1975) has been seminal in recruiting an army of academics to champion the idea of consensus, then this remark could be read by his contemporaries as a betrayal of the cause. At the very least, it should signal a breach in the defendants' camp. However, this is by no means the case, for the author's revised judgement still leaves him able to assert: 'by 1945 the areas of agreement within the Coalition were of more importance for the future than the party conflicts bubbling up from below' (Addison 1993: 93). In effect then, despite having made a key concession to his opponents, the constricted terms of the debate allow the author to emerge with a revision to his thesis which does absolutely nothing to alter its fundamental character.

Of course, this is not to say that the meaning and depth of the consensus remain the sole areas of dispute within this type of literature. Indeed, there are a number of broader concerns which various authors have been inclined to identify (for a review see Seldon 1994). While there is considerable agreement that the origins of the consensus lay in a cumulative process between 1940 and 1948, the question of when it ended continues to provoke a plethora of different opinions. Moreover, the issue of who shared in the accord has also sparked a significant degree of controversy, with answers varying throughout the literature. As Butler explains (1993: 438–9), different analysts tend to: 'pick and choose people – one minute we examine the population at large; the next we focus on parliamentary sentiment; then successive chancellors of the exchequer are in the frame, before we swing suddenly to "political elites"'.

It should be noted that much of the irregularity here has stemmed from theoretical inconsistency rather than any proper, edifying debate. As a result, these concerns do little to elevate the terms of dispute beyond a pedestrian level. In essence, they reflect a desire to amend the 'fine print' of the thesis, rather than any serious attempt to erase it (Seldon 1994: 507). Once we move beyond a semantic discussion on the applicability of the term consensus, we merely find ourselves involved in a pedantic dispute over who shared in it and when it existed. Overall, the consensus thesis emerges unblemished from this debate, with its main tenets quite firmly still in check.

A feeble barrage: outright rejection of the thesis

Of course, the type of objections outlined above have been raised by authors who, to a large extent, still accept that the postwar period was characterised by a significant degree of party accord. Recent contributors to the debate appear increasingly inclined to assume a more sceptical position (Pimlott 1988; Jefferys 1991; Brooke 1992; Rollings 1994). These authors concur more readily with Fraser's view (1987: 310) that: 'the real position was like that of two trains, starting off from parallel platforms at some great London terminus and running for a time on broadly parallel lines but always heading for very different destinations'.

The leading revisionist is Ben Pimlott (1988, 1989). For Pimlott (1988: 503): 'the consensus is a mirage, an illusion that rapidly fades the closer one gets to it'. In this respect, the author emphasises the fundamental ideological conflicts which divided the two main parties. He asserts that politicians throughout the postwar era were enmeshed in deep inter-party wrangles over a wide range of policies. In particular, he cites the Conservatives' inherent hostility towards universal welfare benefits, as well as Anthony Crosland's (1956) call for the left to oppose conservative ideas, as evidence of a fundamental lack of accord across both sides of the political spectrum. In addition, Pimlott argues that supporters of the two main parties were even more divided than the political elite:

> sandbagged in their electoral trenches, early postwar voters can be seen as the anonymous infantry of two implacably opposed armies in an era of adversarial politics, with the middle-way Liberals floundering in no man's land.
>
> (Pimlott 1988: 503)

It is important to emphasise that Pimlott's thesis has been widely regarded as a powerful and convincing polemic against the use of the term consensus to describe postwar British politics. So much so that Butler (1993: 435) acknowledges: 'those who have read Ben Pimlott's brilliant attack on the myth of British postwar consensus, may be surprised to find the idea still alive and kicking'. Moreover, his views have attracted support from, as Seldon (1994: 502–3) puts it 'an army of mostly younger historians . . . using documents at the Public Record Office and in party archives . . . to cast doubt on the existence of consensus in key areas of policy'. Seldon of course, is a firm supporter of the consensus thesis. Nevertheless, he concedes that the evidence collated by these authors suggests that: 'consensus might appear to have existed . . . when looked at from a very broad perspective. But when viewed from close to the ground, or the documents, the reality was very different' (ibid.).

Quite clearly, this approach does take us beyond the threadbare rejoinders to the thesis which have so far overwhelmingly dominated the debate. The aim of these authors, and of Pimlott in particular, is to undermine the consensus thesis by pinpointing the fact that it amounts to nothing more than a construct created by those who wish nostalgically to portray the postwar period as a mythical 'golden era' in British politics. Clearly though, however convincing their work may be, this task appears to have eluded them. For, although they do succeed in placing 'a more critical academic spotlight pointed on the consensus' (Seldon 1994: 502–3), the overall commitment to the thesis has remained resolute. As Seldon (ibid.: 503) explains in relation to Pimlott's own views: 'this high calibre pounding from the artillery of one of Britain's most senior contemporary historians in fact makes as little impression as the seven-day British barrage before the Battle of the Somme.'

As a result, these attempts to deny the idea of consensus altogether, have done little more to dent the accepted assumptions of the period than the majority of authors who persist in picking over the exact intricacies of the debate. Ultimately, the notion of consensus continues to pervade our understanding of the postwar period. Moreover, it does so in an almost unadulterated form, even in the face of adverse, and sometimes cogent, evidence.

Detecting the origins of the consensus thesis

This then, forces us to consider why the thesis has endured. To explain this, we need to link the consensus thesis to the pejorative motivations of those who apply it. As such, it is important to begin by considering its precise origins. This remains one of the most problematic, yet underdeveloped themes within the literature (although see Pimlott 1988). Here, I will emphasise that the recent interest in the thesis is mainly derived from the fact that the very idea of the postwar consensus is itself a relatively recent phenomenon. While it may appear to be somewhat old hat, the debate over consensus is in actual fact still very much in its infancy. In this respect then, the consensus thesis is, as Fraser (1987: 310) suggests: 'a myth of . . . recent origin'.

Of course, some may consider this point to be a contentious one as it is widely accepted that the term has a strong genealogical linkage to the phrase 'Butskellism' which was coined by *The Economist* (1954) to denote the apparent continuity in economic policy during the 1940s and 50s between Hugh Gaitskell and Rab Butler. However, as Rollings (1994) has reminded us, it is clearly wrong to assume, as most authors have been inclined to do, that the consensus is synonymous with Butskellism. For although we may recognise a manifest connection between both concepts, it is important to remain clear as to the obvious differences between them. Whereas the former refers to a broad spectrum of policy agreement, the latter relates only to a narrow convergence between the parties over their specific economic outlook. As such, the earlier term 'Butskellism' merely suggests the origins of one area of policy convergence. The origins of the broader consensus thesis lie in Paul Addison's work (1975), *The Road to 1945.*[5]

Most authors have been happy to cite Addison's thesis as the precedent for later references to consensus; however, few have expressed concern over its timing. This must surely then represent a point of considerable negligence. Certainly, it seems odd that few regard it as relevant that the emergence of the consensus thesis corresponded with the election of Mrs Thatcher as leader of the Conservative Party. This is even odder, when we consider that the consensus thesis has been more widely drawn upon to illuminate assumptions about the Thatcher period than the earlier postwar era (Marsh 1995b; Kerr and Marsh 1996). Moreover, if we add to this the fact that Addison's work did not impress upon subsequent literature until after 1979, then the overall neglect of this point becomes glaringly remiss.

Of course, this 'coincidence' has not been entirely overlooked within the literature; indeed, it was a key factor in provoking Pimlott's rebuttal of the thesis. In this respect, the author emphasises that the idea of the postwar consensus only started to jell when looked at in light of the bitter conflicts and party divisions which were characteristic of the late 1970s and early 1980s. Similarly, Marlow (1995: 16) makes this point when he contends that: 'with the advent of Thatcherism, the earlier years of the postwar era were thrown into starker relief and assumed a unity and coherence that had been previously less apparent'.

To these authors, the consensus thesis emerges as a product of attempts to re-arrange historical evidence to correspond with an outcome which is already familiar. Here, it is useful to draw upon an analogy which the historian Conrad Russell has used to illuminate the dangers which this imposes. As Russell (1976: 1) tells us: 'a historian is like a man who sits down to read a detective story after beginning with the last chapter'. In the case of the detective story, once we have read the conclusion, then the earlier clues which point to the identity of the murderer become so obvious that we wonder how they could ever be overlooked. Consequently: 'those who write the story remembering the ultimate conclusion may miss many of the twists and turns which gave it suspense along the way' (Russell 1976: 1).

Of course, Russell's point is related to a context far removed from the politics of consensus.[6] Nevertheless, his metaphorical allegory corresponds with the view expressed here, which is that political scientists and historians have been guilty of reinterpreting the past in order to justify their assumptions about the present. More specifically, both have utilised the consensus thesis as a crude means of underpinning their views about the Thatcher effect. Indeed, if we extend the author's analogy to the context of our present enquiry, it becomes clear that in this particular game of academic whodunit, both sets of authors have been primarily concerned about emphasising Mrs Thatcher's part in killing off the postwar consensus. Therefore, the consensus thesis has not essentially been about bi-party convergence in the period after the war. Instead, the vast bulk of the conclusions drawn about the consensus era have been made in the context of the Thatcher period in order to throw Thatcherism into stark relief. As a result, it is surprisingly difficult to trace a discernible literature on consensus per se. As we noted earlier, Kavanagh and Morris (1989, 1994) have provided the only comprehensive study of the period, and by the time they did so, the concept had already become taken for granted. Indeed, Kavanagh's (1985, 1987) original work on consensus, was in actual fact an analysis of Thatcherism. As such, it is imperative to emphasise that the contrasts made between Thatcherism and the consensus period have generally rested upon normative assumptions rather than empirical evaluation.

This point has been eloquently expressed by Marlow (1995: 7) who contends that the idea of the postwar consensus: 'remains something of an unexamined assumption'. Accordingly, the author states that: 'for such a taken-for-granted notion, it is . . . ill-defined, poorly explicated and inadequately analysed' (ibid.). In this sense, the literature displays many of the characteristics associated with the postmodernist concept of 'intertextuality'. This denotes a practice whereby an abstraction becomes defined through its repeated use within a variety of texts. When we trace the origins of the postwar consensus thesis, it becomes clear that, rather than finding a substantive literature on the concept, we merely discover: 'a universe of texts that collectively sanction the . . . thesis, by dint of their sheer persuasiveness' (ibid.).

As we saw in Chapter Two, the essential problem with the literature on Thatcherism, is the fact that the majority of political scientists concluded that the Thatcher governments were radical before such radicalism could be demonstrated to have taken place. In this respect, the notion of 'consensus' was used as a cast-iron way of organizing a contrast between the pre-1979 and post-1979 eras. By utilising the concept of consensus in order to locate Mrs Thatcher's achievements, political scientists were able to sidestep the awkward gap between rhetoric and reality which Thatcherite policies displayed. When we consider the recent origins of the idea of consensus, then we begin to get a better picture of the way in which most authors have used the twin notions of 'Thatcherism' and the 'postwar consensus' as mutually-supportive validations of each other.

The politics of the consensus thesis

What is particularly illuminating about the literature on consensus then, is the limited clarity which it bestows upon the period that is supposedly under scrutiny. The consensus debate offers us very little in the way of elucidating governmental activity between 1951 and 1979. Rather, it provides a static representation of the period that lends greater definition to the achievements of the Attlee and Thatcher administrations than to the so-called consensus era.

In this sense then, the thesis suits the pejorative assumptions of those who have utilised it. As Dutton (1991: 95) explains: 'both supporters and detractors of the present government have had good reason to exaggerate the extent to which 1979 marks a break with the past.' Its ability to organize a contrast between the pre-1979 and post-1979 eras and thereby define the extent of transformation in the period, has meant that the consensus thesis remains important to both the left and the right. As Marquand (1989: 2) explains, both groups' interpretations of the period can be seen as 'mirror images of each other . . . both say, in essence, that Keynesian social democracy collapsed because it was bound to collapse. It was a philosophy of the middle way, and there cannot be a middle way'.

To the New Right, the middle ground represented 'a slippery slope to socialism and state control' (Joseph, quoted in Letwin 1992: 83). It was thus 'dictated by extremists on the left' (ibid.: 84). According to Mrs Thatcher, consensus was the 'process of abandoning all beliefs, principles, values and policies . . . avoiding the very issues that have got to be solved merely to get people to come to an agreement on the way ahead' (quoted in Kavanagh and Morris 1994: 119). Paradoxically, the left believe that 'the consensus involved the abandonment of genuinely socialist goals and a too ready acceptance of a fundamentally capitalist system' (Dutton 1991: 95).[7] Here of course, the left are inclined to be much more cynical about the extent to which postwar Labour governments were successful in transforming the structures of the state. However, by utilising the concept of consensus in order to contrast with the Thatcher project, their endeavour to demonstrate this point becomes ultimately compromised. In their attempts to highlight the radicalism of the Thatcher governments in reconstructing state structures, these authors adhere to the same crude dichotomy between the pre-1979 and post-1979 eras as their counterparts on the right.

Consequently, it is important to emphasise, as Eatwell (1979: 158) explains, that much of the debate has been dominated by an 'attempt to engage in political myth-making'. The specific myth to emerge from the debate has been that the structures of the state were radically altered to create a social-democratic state settlement which was ultimately replaced by the Thatcher project.

Beyond semantics and pedantics: revising the consensus debate

So far, I have argued that the idea of the postwar consensus, and with it the implied claim that the structures of the state were fundamentally transformed in the immediate postwar period, is something of a myth created by those who wish to exaggerate the extent to which Keynesian social democracy became inscribed into the parameters of the state after the Second World War. In this section, I will contend that this myth has been successfully maintained through the highly selective information which most authors highlight in order to support their views. This selectivity in the information provided manifests itself in two different ways. First, the majority of accounts on offer provide us with a very circumscribed view of the 'political', thereby focusing almost exclusively on party politics to the neglect, or exclusion, of other key actors. Second, they also pay too much dividend to the power of particular ideas in shaping government policy to the neglect, or exclusion, of others.

Circumscribing the political: the overemphasis upon party politics

Throughout the literature on consensus, most authors focus, almost entirely, on an analysis of the behaviour of Britain's two leading political parties. Indeed, in many cases, the primary focus becomes the leading personalities within both parties. As a result, these analyses offer a narrow framework within which we might seek to view legitimate 'political' activity. In effect, they are implicitly driven by the idea that the 'power' to influence government policy rests primarily with government actors.

The problem however is that such accounts fail to appreciate both the subtleties and the complexities of the power relations which influenced the postwar political scene. In particular, they fail to acknowledge the complex interactions between class fractions, leading institutions, government and, indeed, the leading pressure groups, which *all* combined to influence policy in the postwar period. As I shall argue in the following sections, once we broaden our focus beyond the arena of party politics and personalities, we begin to get a better measure of the true dynamics within the postwar British state: the constant interaction and articulation of interests between politicians, unions, producer groups, financiers and leading institutions, such as the Treasury, the City and the Bank of England. When we consider the sum of these interactions, the picture which emerges is one of continual, and often fundamental, conflicts between the key actors involved in the formulation of policy, rather than of consensus.

Circumscribing the ideational: the overemphasis upon the power of particular ideas

There has also been a persistent tendency – and this relates to the problem just outlined – to overstate within the literature the impact of particular types of ideas throughout the postwar period. Most authors have been highly selective in emphasising the impact of ideas geared towards the implementation of 'statist' measures to promote economic growth, welfare reform and full employment. Particular, if not invariably almost exclusive, emphasis has been placed upon the role of both Keynes and Beveridge, and more broadly the role of social-democratic ideas in general, in helping politicians from both parties to formulate a coherent policy paradigm which could achieve these aims. The problem however, is that these accounts tend to exaggerate: the unity and coherence of the ideational paradigm around which the consensus supposedly revolved; the actual impact which statist ideas made upon the implementation of policy; and the extent to which the dominant ideas of the period differed from both pre-war and 'post-Keynesian' beliefs.

Overall, it has been easy for most authors to overstate each of these points. At the heart of the problem has been the way in which the definition of 'Keynesianism' has been widened within the literature to the point at which it has become synonymous with broader 'statist' ideas such as those we equate with Beveridge, corporatism and social democracy. Thus, the sum commitment to Keynesian, social-democratic, planned, interventionist strategies is presented as a unitary set of beliefs. No attention is paid to the tensions, contradictions and, of course, conflicts, both within Keynesianism, and between Keynesianism and other dominant ideas of the period. As Keith

Smith (1989: 182) explains: '(although) the "Keynesian" policy-makers have been condemned as full-scale interventionists . . . their belief in markets was scarcely less extreme than that of the monetarists'. The attempts to stretch the notion of 'Keynesianism' to include the ideas of corporatism and social democracy, fail to consider the crucial conflicts which existed between the commitments of Keynesian policy-makers to the promotion of 'statist', interventionist strategies on the one hand, and to more traditional monetary beliefs and non-interventionist policies on the other. More broadly, however, they fail to acknowledge the conflict which these ideas created between the desire to implement radical policy initiatives and the more conservative instinct to maintain the status quo.

As I will go on to demonstrate, the extent to which 'Keynesianism', in any form, let alone in the interventionist and radical guise which most authors assume, was ever fully incorporated into economic management is questionable. Nevertheless, this issue is most often sidestepped within the literature. By linking Keynesianism to such a broad church of political practices, the awkward fact that Keynesian ideas were often both inconsistent and indeed inconsistently pursued, becomes almost irrelevant and the false assumption that we can detect continuity based around a strictly 'statist' ideational paradigm is successfully maintained.

Separating rhetoric from reality

This then leaves us with the question of how we can advance the debate over the consensus in order to gain a fuller understanding of the evolution of the state in the postwar era. Here, I will argue that the only way to take the present debate forward is to move beyond it entirely and to re-direct our focus away from the question of consensus, to the key issue at the heart of the thesis; that is, the question of the extent of state transformation in the early postwar period. Once we start to examine this issue, it soon becomes clear that the concept of consensus, and with it the claim that the consensus brought about state transformation based around a coherent set of governing expectations and assumptions, has little resonance. For, as a review of the supposed planks of the domestic consensus clearly indicates, the aims of postwar politicians were invariably thwarted by the residual contradictions and tensions within those aims and by the overall conflicts which existed between the leading political and economic groups and key institutions of the period.

Keynesianism demand-management and full employment

To most commentators, the Keynesian 'revolution' in economic policy derived from the success of Keynesian ideas in penetrating the liberal orthodox 'Treasury View'. Traditionally, Treasury control over government finances stood as a powerful impediment to collectivist expansion. Driven by 'two powerful logics' – namely, the logic of tax-cutting and of fiscal responsibility – Treasury officials were: 'mainly restricted to the habit of saying no' (Cronin 1991: 12). Consequently, if Keynesian ideas had succeeded in piercing this monolithic arbiter of monetary vigilance, then we could conclude that they had become properly institutionalised.

However, it is essential to remain cautious as to how far the Keynesian ethos successfully penetrated, or indeed challenged, such liberal orthodoxy within the state. Throughout the postwar period, pre-Keynesian beliefs continued to dominate the Treasury, thereby serving as a major obstacle to the introduction of an effective demand-management strategy for achieving full employment. Consequently, many of the 'supportive' policies advocated by Keynesians during and after the war were ultimately sacrificed, leading to the development of a much more 'modified', or 'simple', variant of Keynesianism which displayed an overall degree of continuity with previous practice (Thompson 1984, Booth 1983). As a result, an 'oral tradition' in favour of sound monetary policies persisted within the Treasury and was reflected in the economic policies of all postwar governments (Bulpitt 1986).

Overall, the expansion of limited statist measures in the early postwar period designed to promote both full employment and welfare reforms, should be more readily seen as the result of a temporary loss of Treasury control, rather than as a fundamental conversion by the Treasury to Keynesian ideals (Cronin 1991). By 1947 this control had been re-established and the two 'political logics' of tax-cutting and financial rectitude took their traditional precedence in the minds of Treasury officials and, subsequently, politicians. Thus, by 1951 and the re-election of the Conservatives, the Keynesian 'revolution' in macro-economics had begun to assume: 'a pattern that bore a strong resemblance to the budgetary history of the interwar years' (ibid.: 208).

However, traditional Treasury orthodoxy and monetary concerns remained only one obstacle to the efficient use of Keynesian budgetary policy. The various attempts by all postwar governments to manage sterling and the exchange rate were a more crucial impediment. The attempts in the years 1957, 1960, 1964, 1966 and 1973 to protect the balance of payments meant that postwar governments were continually forced to throw their apparent commitment to Keynesianism, and with it major planks of their domestic policy, into reverse in the defence of sterling. These attempts at deflation rather than devaluation highlight the crucial fact that the 'consensus' on domestic policy was, in many ways, overshadowed by the persistent hegemony of the 'sterling lobby'. According to Blank: 'this lobby shared the belief that Britain's international position and responsibilities constituted the *primary policy objectives* and that the international role of sterling was vital to this position' (quoted in Grant 1987: 81, emphasis added). Thus the financial sector, with its ability to sanction governments by withholding investment, has played a crucial role in deflecting most postwar governments from the Keynesian policy of maintaining full employment.

Therefore, rather than extending the idea of Keynesianism to describe the institutionalised parameters of the state, it is more important to recognise that pre-inscribed institutional bias, within the state, coupled with conflicting policy objectives, served to hamper the full implementation of even the most basic Keynesian techniques. In particular, it is clear that the oft-cited consensus on 'Keynesian', interventionist, strategies, coincided with a rarely emphasised, often diametrically opposed and, indeed, primary, commitment to more traditional monetary concerns and an arm's length approach to economic management. This rival 'monetarist' ethos meant that macro-economic policy throughout the postwar era displayed an enormous degree of continuity with both pre-war and 'post-Keynesian' practice.

The mixed economy

The nationalisation programme, although viewed as a litmus test of the Attlee government's commitment to socialist transformation, reflected a more pragmatic commitment to dealing with short-term economic imperatives. Most of the industries taken into public ownership directly after the war were in vulnerable positions within the economy, facing either underinvestment, declining demand or fierce competition from both home and abroad. In this sense, the government had merely taken limited interventionist measures to secure Britain's core industries. Moreover, the provision of cheaper fuel, transport and communications services served, both directly and indirectly, to reduce the costs of private sector business and commercial interests (Thompson 1984: 89). Consequently, as Thompson (ibid.: 86) argues, the nationalisation programme: 'fitted into a strategy of moderately radical reform under conditions of support for the existing social structure and economic and political relations . . . *it did not mark a fundamental break with the previous set of state economic practices*'.

Although public corporations were formally responsible to ministers, in fact the ministry became merely a sponsoring department, and key decisions were left to boards and chairmen who enjoyed complete autonomy from parliamentary accountability. The relations between nationalised industries and sponsoring departments were characterised by tensions and mutual misunderstanding; as such, they were not fully integrated into the control of the state. Therefore, although nationalisation did represent a potential redefinition of the relationship between state and society which was consistent with a broadly statist policy paradigm, the reality was that there was little or no commitment to bringing these industries under state control. More importantly, from around 1967, most of these industries were subject to the investment rules and financial criteria of private firms. This effectively meant that they were: 'progressively integrated back into the market economy long before the question of their "privatisation" came onto the political agenda' (Thompson 1984: 91).

Of course, to an extent, these points are accepted by the majority of political scientists and historians. Nevertheless, the desire to demonstrate the radicalism of both the Attlee and Thatcher governments, and in particular their respective commitments to diametrically opposed policy paradigms, has meant that the bulk of literature on the postwar period has emphasised the contrast between nationalisation and privatisation, rather than stressing the crucial continuity in the structure of the state which has predominated.

Planned intervention and active government

As we have seen from our review of both Keynesianism and the national-isation programme, the commitment of postwar politicians, other leading groups and, indeed, key institutions within the state to implement statist measures in order to promote economic growth remained weak. Thus, the third plank of the so-called consensus, a broad commitment to active government, emerges as yet another myth within the literature. Certainly, it is possible to identify a broad coalition across the political spectrum in favour of greater intervention. However, this element of the dominant ideational paradigm co-existed alongside an even stronger commitment to arm's length government and an overall reluctance to institute radical reform.

On the few occasions when governments did reveal their commitment to intervene, they found that the tools which they could use to take supportive measures to aid industry were severely limited. Thus, they found themselves at odds with both the existing structures of the British state and the conflicting interests of other leading groups and institutions. In particular, the separation of the Bank of England and financial capital from the state, has effectively prevented all governments from having effective control over the flow of funds in the economy. Similarly, the Treasury has remained isolated from the coordination of industrial policy. This has meant that the views of industrial capital have generally been subordinated to the interests of the financial sector, and this remained so throughout the postwar period. Overall, these factors all combined to prevent serious attempts at planning up until the creation of the National Economic Development Council in 1962.

Between 1962 and 1976 it became increasingly clear to governments that the range of facilitative policies aimed at budgetary management required supplementary interventionist strategies. During this period, therefore, governments began to pursue more 'active' policies aimed at supporting industry. However, this change did not prove to be either fundamental, or indeed long-standing. The extent to which the government exercised 'control' over capital, even during this more interventionist period has been grossly overestimated. As a result, these initial attempts failed when, in 1966, in the face of a balance of payments crisis, the Treasury forced the abandonment of economic planning, and indeed full employment, in the defence of the value of sterling. Similarly, although the Labour government of 1974–9 came to power with a commitment to passing an Industry Act, which would provide for the establishment of 'planning agreements' between the government and the country's top firms, coupled with the creation of the National Enterprise Board, by the time the Act was passed it had become substantially de-radicalised in the face of major opposition from the Confederation of British Industry (CBI) and the City.

These points highlight the crucial need to distinguish between the statist, interventionist rhetoric, which underpinned both parties' policy choices, and the actual implementation of policy. It is certainly clear that, while a broad commitment to active government remained an important element of the paradigm governing postwar policy, this coincided, and indeed conflicted, with a more long-standing conservative ethos which sought merely to preserve the status quo. After 1962, when government did start to initiate limited interventionist strategies to promote industry, these strategies found themselves at odds with pre-existing institutional practices and the rival interests of the business and financial sector.

Industrial relations

There are two distinct (though related) myths often cited regarding the position of trade unions within the so-called consensus. On the one hand, it is argued that, throughout most of the period, the relationship between government and unions was a harmonious one. On the other, it is suggested that, within that relationship, unions enjoyed considerable power. Certainly it is possible to concede that a period of relative consensus did exist between unions and government between 1945 and 1966; however, thereafter this consensus was replaced by persistent conflict in which the balance of power was firmly weighted in favour of the state. Prior to the mid-to-late 1960s, the major reason for the relative accord between unions and government was the fact that unions were generally content to rely upon wage bargaining within a laissez-faire framework consistent with the practice of 'simple' or 'modified' Keynesianism described earlier (Marsh 1992). Ironically, rather than incorporating unions into the decision-making process, this model allowed them to preserve their autonomy and resist integration into any concrete consultative relationship with government.

The unions' devotion to voluntarism has meant that, for most of the postwar period, they have, contrary to popular belief, resisted direct involvement in the political sphere. Moreover, the increased union involvement after 1966 was the result of government, rather than union, initiatives (Marsh 1992: 56). In this respect, the politicisation of trade unions occurred primarily as a consequence of the political elite's search for a quasi-corporatist solution to the country's increasing economic malaise and, subsequently, as a direct result of the imposition of successive incomes policies. As Coates (1989: 50) explains: 'with the arrival of incomes policy, industrial relations were, so to speak, politicised at a stroke'.

Nevertheless, it is crucial that we do not lose sight of the extent to which union power throughout the postwar period remained 'overwhelmingly negative' (Dorfman 1979: 6). Any assessment of the relationship between government and unions throughout the postwar period needs to take account of the limited power over and, indeed, involvement with government which the unions had prior to 1979 (Marsh 1992). Even more crucially, most analyses of the political power of trade unions have neglected the enormous positive veto which capital has had over government in comparison to trade unions. As Hay (1996: 56) explains: 'far less visible, yet ultimately of greater significance were . . . the private and informal channels linking the City of London, the Bank of England and the Treasury'.

Overall then, much of the literature on the postwar period over-empha-sises the transformation which the 'consensus' brought about in the relationship between government and unions. While exaggerating both the extent of union power, and indeed of union involvement with government, most authors have also neglected to acknowledge the consid-erable influence which, compared to trade unions, the 'City–Bank–Treasury nexus' (Hay 1996: 56) had over successive postwar governments.

The welfare state

In contrast to the previous policy areas which we examined, the substantial package of welfare reform introduced by the Attlee administration indi-cates one area of the so-called consensus within which it is possible to identify significant structural transformation. The foundations of the welfare state settlement, which was to emerge in the aftermath of the Second World War, were laid down by Beveridge. Beveridge's plans for a radical restructuring of welfare based upon a national insurance scheme were accepted by both main political parties throughout the postwar era and, as Kavanagh and Morris (1994: 89) point out, remain: 'the most solidly implanted of all the planks of the domestic postwar consensus'. The essential ingredients of the welfare state were fourfold:

- The extension of existing social security provision
- The creation of the National Health Service
- The extension of a comprehensive education system
- The creation of a public housing service.

The creation of a universal welfare state system remains the least disputed of the achievements of the Attlee administrations. Indeed, for authors such as Barnett (1986), it remained the sole priority of postwar governments and, thereby, had a concomitant effect upon Britain's failure to adjust to the changing conditions of a restructured world economy. Of course, this is a contentious point within the literature. However, when we compare the achievements, and indeed the commitment, of postwar politicians in erecting, and then preserving, the welfare state system, with their lack of success in fulfilling most, if not all, of their other rhetorical commitments, then Barnett's point has some potency. Overall, the enormous successes in welfare reforms contrast starkly with the magnificent failures to implement radical reform in most other areas of the so-called domestic consensus. Ultimately, the welfare state emerges as a spectacular achievement compared to the efforts by postwar politicians to enact their other statist commitments.

Conflict, complexity and change in early postwar public policy

Having looked at each of the individual planks of the domestic policy consensus, we are now in a better position to assess which, and indeed whose, particular sets of governing assumptions and expectations succeeded in penetrating the institutional architecture of the postwar British state. Undoubtedly, there is no simple or easy answer to this question. Clearly, the answers vary from policy area to policy area. Thus, for example, the extension of the welfare state emerges as one policy area in which politicians successfully translated their rhetorical pronouncements on social democracy and active government into actual policy achievements. In this area we can see that significant structural transformation was brought about by a genuine 'consensus' amongst Britain's political elite. However, beyond the issue of welfare, once we start to examine the achievements in areas such as demand-management, nationalisation, industrial relations and support for industry, the picture which emerges is a somewhat more complex one. For example, it is clear that the limited efforts by politicians to implement measures to support industry were ultimately thwarted by conflicting pressures from key institutions such as the Treasury and the Bank of England and by the rival interests of the financial sector.

Moreover, the issue of locating any real continuity both within and between these distinct policy areas is further complicated by the fact that, in some areas, the direction of policy changed over time. Thus, for example, in industrial relations, it was the assumptions and expectations of trade unions which were primarily satisfied by government acceptance of voluntarism in the early postwar period. However, by the latter half of the so-called consensus era, the sudden interference in industrial relations by the state served to threaten the interests of the unions, while satisfying the broader aims of postwar politicians. Similar changes of direction in policy occurred with regard to nationalisation, when after 1967 nationalised industries were gradually integrated back into the market economy, and with regard to Keynesian demand management, when the initiative gained by politicians prior to 1947 was lost in the face of a resurgence of Treasury control.

The situation becomes no less complicated once we start to look at which particular *ideas* came to dominate the scene. Clearly, in the area of welfare, the liberal paternalism of Beveridge, coupled with a rhetorical commitment to social democracy, was in the ascendancy. However, in contrast, with regard to nationalisation we see a semblance of socialist discourse, giving way to pragmatism, before ultimately being replaced by an emphasis on market solutions. Similarly, in macro-economics the Keynesian policy of full employment was consistently abandoned in favour of traditional monetary concerns. Likewise, when it comes to planning, we are confronted by a commitment to active government, coupled with a concomitant commitment to laissez-faire.

Of course, it would be possible to go on highlighting more and more of the complexity of the postwar political scene without ever reaching any clear or firm conclusions. Yet this may not be a futile exercise, because it presents us with at least one clear conclusion: that it is more or less impossible to capture the complexity of postwar British politics utilising a simple, formulaic thesis. However, this is the aim, and the claim, of advocates of the consensus thesis. At the heart of the consensus thesis lies the assumption that postwar British politics can be characterised by an inherent continuity, both in policy, and in the governing ideas and assumptions which shaped policy. However, once we begin to get a measure of the true complexity of the period, the consensus thesis emerges as a heuristic device which has no real intrinsic heuristic value. The thesis diverts attention away from the inherent conflicts, tensions and contradictions which characterised British politics in this period. It 'selects' the ideas, such as Keynesianism and social democracy, which its adherents wish to emphasise, while at the same time neglecting and excluding others, such as the commitment to arm's length government and to traditional monetary orthodoxy. It also selects which groups we should focus upon, emphasising parties and leading pressure groups, while diverting our attention away from others, such as the financial sector. It chooses which institutions are important to look at, such as the nationalised industries or the NEDC, while neglecting others, such as the City of London or the Bank of England.

Overall then, we can only conclude that the postwar consensus is a harmful construct. It is harmful in the sense that it severely damages our understanding of the true dynamics behind governmental activity in the postwar period. As we shall see in Chapters Four and Five, once we begin to examine these it becomes clear that the real dynamic behind policy was the inherent conflicts which characterised the postwar political scene, between groups, such as politicians, producers, trade unions and financiers; institutions, such as the Treasury, the NEDC and the City of London; and ideas, such as Keynesianism, monetarism, laissez-faire economics and corporatism. The sum total of the interactions between these conflicting elements was a continual struggle between different groups, institutions and ideas to resolve the residual tensions and contradictions within the state settlement which each combined to create.

Conclusion

The postwar consensus thesis has been utilised by the majority of those interested in analysing the development of postwar British politics. However, as this chapter indicates, the concept of consensus has very little heuristic value in helping us to understand the complexities of governmental activity following the Second World War. Rather, its value to most authors lies in the fact that it helps to emphasise the impact of ideas such as Keynesianism and social democracy in bringing about the structural transformation of the state in the early postwar period, as well as highlighting the impact of Thatcherism in reversing these developments. However, once we begin to interrogate these assumptions, we soon find that the extent of state transformation brought about by the so-called 'consensus' was limited. Most importantly, the major reason for this is that too many conflicts and contradictions existed both within the aims of postwar politicians, and between the aims of politicians and other key actors. In other words, we can say that very little change occurred in the structure of the state in the early postwar period, due primarily to the overall lack of both coherence and consensus governing the implementation of policy.

In order to gain a better understanding of the complexities of postwar British politics, we need to abandon the consensus thesis altogether. In its place, we need to begin to re-appraise the dynamic and constantly evolving relationships and conflicts which structured the development of postwar public policy. This would enable us not only to develop a more sophisticated understanding of the earlier postwar period, but also to generate a better conception of the Thatcher years and beyond. It is to the question of how we may gain this type of perspective that we now turn.

4 Reconstructing our perspective

A critical evolutionary approach to political change

Introduction

Thus far, I have been concerned primarily with *de*-constructing the established narrative of the postwar period. In this chapter, it is time to begin to *re*-construct the pieces of our storyline by considering the ways in which we can respond to the problems identified earlier.

A key aim of this book is, of course, to explore the utility of an evolutionary explanation of political change in helping us to overcome the overwhelming tendency within the literature to exaggerate and caricature the changes which have occurred in British politics since the Second World War. Here, we will see that an evolutionary approach necessarily entails a proper consideration of the constant and complex dialectical relationships between: change and inertia; path-dependence and contingency; agents and their environments; material conditions and subjective interpretations of these; and selection processes and agency adaptation. By taking these various elements of an evolutionary approach as a starting point, I will outline the type of conception of evolutionary change to be used in the following chapters in order to provide a more sophisticated understanding of the evolution of the British state in the postwar period.

This chapter will divide into two main sections. In this first section, I will consider briefly the main contours of an evolutionary approach, as well as the distinction which can be made between formal theories of evolution and those which implicitly invoke an appreciative conception of evolutionary change. I will then proceed to examine in some detail two ways in which both formal and appreciative evolutionary theorising have been applied to analyses of political change. In the second section, I will elicit some of the insights which can be taken from these authors' work to put together my own 'critical evolutionary' approach to explaining political change.

Saved from extinction: the adaptive capacity of evolutionary theory in social science

Evolutionary thinking has a long, albeit checkered, history in attempts by social scientists to interrogate the processes and mechanisms of institutional change. The endeavours of early sociologists such as Comte, Spencer and Durkheim to apply evolutionary concepts to their analyses of societal development became the cornerstones of sociology as a discipline. Meanwhile, the work of economists such as Veblen (1898) and Marshall (1907) laid the foundations for what was to become an established tradition of introducing evolutionary metaphors into analyses of economic and organizational practice. Indeed, Marshall (1948: xiv) proclaimed that evolutionary theorising was the Mecca of economics and, for a while, during the late nineteenth and early twentieth centuries, as evolutionary theory gained popular appeal across both the natural and social sciences, it looked as if Marshall's prediction would remain true, not only for economics, but for the study of change in general.

However, this early optimism was soon proved misplaced, as the notion of evolution fell from grace amongst the social sciences during the first half of the twentieth century. The concept of evolution found itself struggling for survival in an environment in which social scientists were increasingly sensitive to the interpretive and subjective elements of social scientific enquiry. Apart from its brief re-emergence from the 1950s to the early 1970s, in the work of Talcott Parsons (1966, 1971) and other structural-functionalist theorists of that period, evolutionary thinking in social science remained largely discredited and its use has, until recently, been banished to the fringes of social scientific research.

One of the major reasons for its unpopularity has been the fact that evolutionary theorising in social science has been tainted by the popular misconception that its use was derived from crude attempts by social scientists to incorporate ideas drawn from biology into their analysis of social change. However, while it would be true to say that, through time, biological conceptions of evolutionary change have made a significant impact on the realm of social theory, it is nevertheless wrong to conclude that social evolutionism originated from a direct attempt by social scientists to emulate their natural science counterparts (Burrow 1966: 21; Nisbet 1969: Chapter 5; Hirst 1976: 19; Stzompka 1993: 125; Nelson 1995: 55). Evolutionary thinking in social science has retained a significant degree of autonomy from the theoretical and ontological assumptions of Darwinian biology. As a result, the connection between social theories of evolutionary change and Darwinian conceptions of biological and ecological development has always remained loose; indeed, it is only recently that some social scientists have made a much more deliberate attempt than their predecessors to produce a closer theoretical synthesis between the two (Stzompka 1993: 125).

Nevertheless, evolutionary theorising in social science has, for a long time, been damaged by its association with attempts within natural science to chart and explain the evolution of biological and ecological systems. This guilt by association has led many to reject evolutionary conceptions of socio-economic and political developments as callow, and sometimes even sinister, attempts to incorporate the 'objective' status of natural science reasoning into analyses of historical institutional change.[1] The major problem for evolutionary theorising in social science has been that, even though most of its advocates have avoided a direct link with Darwinian biology, they have nevertheless been unable to avoid this type of charge because classical accounts of the evolution of social and economic institutions have, in the main, attempted to uncover certain teleological principles of historical change. As a result, evolutionary theorising has been burdened with certain types of unfavourable theoretical baggage: an emphasis upon change as a unilinear path to 'progress'; a reliance upon functionalist explanation; a tendency to assert certain 'laws' of structural determination; and a failure to acknowledge the crucial role of human agency as a primary factor shaping historical development. Overall, these problems have meant that evolutionary theorising in social science has been exposed to a wide array of criticisms and, cumulatively, these have left it stripped of a great deal of its former credibility.

It would be wrong, however, to assert that these problems derive directly from attempts to incorporate the form of reasoning used in evolutionary biology into social science thinking. Whereas in biology 'evolution' has been recognised as a contingent process based upon certain 'chance' or 'random' factors, in social science the term has most often been used to infer certain types of historical 'logic' and 'pattern'. Ironically, then, evolutionary thinking in social science, rather than being handicapped by its association with Darwinism, actually suffered from its separation from the theoretical concerns of evolutionary biologists. In this respect, many of its chief proponents ignored the crucial elements of historical contingency and randomness which characterise the conception of evolution formed within the natural sciences, in favour of their own normative attempts to deduce logic and progress from the unfolding of societal structures.

If a modern evolutionary approach to explaining the development and transformation of institutions is to retain any form of legitimacy, it must shed itself of any former and unnecessary vestiges of historical determinism. What is needed is a fundamental recognition of the fact that the very concept of determinism lies beyond the broad compass of an evolutionary approach. Fortunately, this point is one which has been recognised in recent years by a whole new generation of theorists seeking to re-apply evolutionary conceptions of change within a variety of social science sub-disciplines. Foremost amongst these has been the attempts by various economists, organization theorists and sociobiologists to develop sophisticated theoretical models built upon insights derived from a variety of different sources including Darwinian and Lamarckian biology.[2] Meanwhile, less formal conceptions of evolutionary change have recently been employed within the fields of historical sociology and political economy, while even some political scientists appear to be showing a tentative interest in applying loose and often implicit evolutionary concepts to their analyses of political change.[3] Of these latter, admittedly tentative, attempts to incorporate an evolutionary conception of change into a political science discourse on the state, some of the most sophisticated work has come from state theorists and historical institutionalists.[4]

While these approaches differ markedly in the extent to which they employ a formal theory of evolution, they nevertheless share a rejection of teleological assumptions which infer an overall logic or pattern in the process of change.[5] Thus, as Stzompka explains, the basic novelty in the recent stream of neo-evolutionary thinking is:

> the rejection of determinism, fatalism, linearity and gradualness. In their place there are strong new emphases on chance, randomness, contingency, open-endedness of the process, qualitative thresholds, and the crucial role of human agency.
>
> (Stzompka 1993: 128)

In this respect at least, social scientists have turned more recently towards the general essence of evolutionary thinking in biology; that is that an evolutionary approach reasons negatively, by directing our attention to what is not likely to occur more than to what is likely (De Bresson 1987: 754). This 'form of reasoning' asserts that change is a 'process' which offers only potentialities and limits (Gould 1981: 330–1; see also De Bresson 1987: 754) rather than the gradual realisation of certain universal laws of development. Armed with this type of insight, recent evolutionary thinking in social science has been able to respond to damaging criticisms and re-establish its legitimacy.

What do we mean by an evolutionary approach?

It is difficult to discern a single, uniform conception of evolutionary change. Instead, what we actually find when we survey the enormous range of literature available is not a homogeneous theory of evolutionary change as such, but a very general framework of analysis, which has attained specific theoretical applications in different areas, such as sociology, biology and economics (Nelson 1995: 54). In this respect, evolutionary thinking represents an overall research paradigm; a heuristic explanatory device flexible enough to incorporate a wide variety of theoretical concerns (De Bresson 1987).

So what then are the basic elements of the evolutionary paradigm? Here we will examine four key elements which can be considered central to any evolutionary approach: a recognition of the dynamic and temporal dimensions of change; an emphasis upon the 'selection' of variables; a focus upon adaptive processes; and a recognition of change as a process which is both contingent and path-dependent.

A concern with both time and process

Nelson (1995: 54), provides us with a succinct summary of the starting point for any evolutionary analysis: 'the focus of attention is on a variable or set of them that is changing over time and the theoretical quest is for an understanding of the dynamic process behind the observed change'. As we can see then, an evolutionary schema offers a dynamic and processual account of change. In this sense, the variables under scrutiny are viewed in motion and, as such, the object of analysis is to interrogate and decipher the key processes which generate their movement. A related concern is to chart the temporal horizon through which change is perceived to occur. Thus, the issue of time, and the temporal compass along which the observed movement takes place, is considered central to any evolutionary schema.

Of course, this may seem rather obvious; or at least, it may appear at first sight to be the fundamental premise of any attempt to explain change. However, within mainstream political science this is far from being the case. The major problem has been the bias which the discipline has retained towards a broadly empiricist methodology (Hay 1997). Underpinning this has been the assumption, derived – perhaps somewhat ironically given our present concern – largely from natural science, that the 'rules of the game' governing political behaviour remain constant over time. This assumption has led many political scientists to present 'static' accounts of political practices which, by definition, preclude the very concept of change.

In order to elucidate this point, we need to distinguish between two different approaches to analysing change: synchronic accounts of static systems; and diachronic analyses of the processes and mechanisms which propel these. As Hay explains:

> Consider a system (such as the state) evolving through time from t_1 to t_2 to t_3. A synchronic analysis seeks to freeze this process of transformation at a particular moment in time (t, t, t, t) in order to elucidate, interrogate and describe the internal relationships (structural couplings, contradictions, crisis-tendencies, and so forth) which characterise that system at that instant. . . . A diachronic analysis, by contrast, seeks to capture the dynamism of the process of change itself, through an analysis and interpretation of the mechanisms of transformation, evolution and structural change.
>
> (Hay 1997: 37)

As we have already noted, within explanations of the postwar period the tendency has been to explain change by 'counterposing or juxtapositioning' a series of binary oppositions between for example: 'consensus' versus 'conviction'; 'Keynesianism' versus 'monetarism'; 'social democracy' versus neo-liberalism'. Here, change is presented in synchronic terms, as merely the differential outcome between one moment in time and another. In this sense, these approaches effectively 'freeze' change within a static, comparative framework which offers description rather than explanation. Moreover, the prevalence of synchronic analyses has meant that the majority of approaches to the postwar period can be criticised for their inherent failure to deal with both the temporal dimensions to change and indeed, the processes and mechanisms which govern it. Overall, these analyses demonstrate precisely the propensity of political scientists to exclude the very concept of change itself.

An evolutionary approach contends that a synchronic analysis of static variables is inadequate to the task of dealing with change. Rather, it implies the need for a processual, diachronic account of the historical development of whatever variables are under scrutiny. This entails viewing change as a continuous and ongoing process governed by a complex and unfolding array of different factors. As a result, an evolutionary approach, by definition, places the very concept of change and the factors which generate it at its core. It can be said to treat as its starting point Alfred N. Whitehead's famous dictum (1925: 179) that 'change is inherent in the very nature of things'.

A concern with processes of selection

As we noted earlier, evolutionary theory reasons negatively, by viewing change as being merely about potentialities and limits rather than any predetermined path to progress. The extent to which potentialities are achieved and limits imposed is viewed as contingent upon the processes of 'selection' which are at work upon the variables under scrutiny. Thus, evolutionary theory directs our attention to the fact that the process of evolution is heavily conditioned by factors which systematically act upon random variations (Nelson 1995: 54). However, it is important here to make a crucial distinction between the concept of evolution used in biology and the type of evolutionary analogy which is most appropriate for social scientific research. Whereas in evolutionary biology 'variation' can be considered to be essentially 'random', in processes of social and political change such variation is most often the result of goal-oriented actors, working within the parameters of strategic and ideological heuristics, who are deliberately seeking specific objectives. Thus, I will argue that it is more fruitful to suggest that selection processes act upon the strategies which these actors employ in order to achieve their goals.

We may consider two main types of selective pressures upon actors' strategies. First, attention should be directed towards the range of contextual factors which bring selective pressures to bear upon strategic interventions. In this sense, evolutionary theory directs our focus towards the 'environment' in which strategies are implemented and, in particular, to the 'constraining principles' that this sets upon actors goals (De Bresson

1987: 754). The idea that the environment shapes the type of variations which can occur within any given evolutionary process, and that all variations must exhibit a crucial element of continuity with the environment, remains central to any evolutionary schema. However, it would be wrong to conclude that the selective pressures which the environment brings to bear upon strategic interventions are entirely negative. Indeed, we may also say that the environment produces 'enabling principles' which have a positive effect in allowing the success of certain types of strategy over others.

The second type of selective pressure is that which is brought to bear upon strategic innovations by the actors themselves. Individuals or groups of individuals are not merely receptors of selection pressures which are exogenous to themselves. Instead, an evolutionary schema must entail a proper consideration of the fact that agents are continually active in ordering, filtering and thereby selecting for themselves the appropriate strategic responses to the environments in which they operate.

A concern with adaptive processes

Running parallel to the emphasis upon selection is an equal consideration of adaptive processes (Vromen 1995). In this sense, it is assumed that the objects subject to evolution must invariably 'adapt' in order to survive within a constantly evolving environment. Here again, it is important to make a clear distinction between evolutionary conceptions of change in the natural sciences and those used in social science explanation. As Giddens (1984: 233–6) explains, whereas in biology the notion of adaptation can be used in a fairly precise way, in the social sciences the meaning of the term has become 'irremediably amorphous' (ibid.: 234). In this sense, Giddens criticises conventional theories of evolutionary change in social science for their insistence that a direct analogy can be drawn between the adaptation of species within the natural environment, and the adaptation of societies, institutions or organizations within the social, historical or global environments in which they are situated. According to Giddens (ibid.: 233), an analogy of this type in the social sciences:

> can be shown characteristically to be either (1) vacuous, i.e., so wide and vague in its meaning as to be more confusing than illuminating, or (2) implicated in a specious and logically deficient claim to functionalist explanation, or (3) involved in the predication of dynamic tendencies in human societies that are demonstrably false.
>
> (Giddens 1984: 233)

Certainly, Giddens' arguments have a great deal of force as a criticism of the concept of adaptation in classical evolutionary sociology. Clearly, any explanatory framework which treated 'societies', 'institutions' or, indeed, 'organizations' as homogeneous entities which have the ability in themselves to evolve and adapt would indeed be guilty of such spurious reasoning. However, it would be equally spurious to suggest that Giddens' rejection of the specific use of the concept of adaptation in structural-functionalist sociology necessarily negates its utility outright. In fact, Giddens' criticisms are directed at a very broad use of the term, in which its meaning becomes either empty or involved in a form of reasoning which is, at best, tautological. Consequently, it is more fruitful to take Giddens' criticisms as a warning that, when employing the idea of adaptation, we need to be precise about what it is that is supposed to adapt.

Here, then, we can begin by directly refuting the idea that social 'populations', such as institutions or organizations, adapt and evolve as if driven by some hidden functionalist dynamic. To adopt such an approach would be to anthropomorphise social structures by implying that they are endowed with an immanent goal which pulls them in a particular direction (Elster 1983: 58–9; Ward 1997: 125). Rather, we must start by recognising that it is individual agents working within institutions and organizations which are the bearers of goals, not the structures themselves (Ward 1997: 125). Yet, to argue that it is individuals per se who adapt may not be constructive either, since this does not tell us much about how they adapt, or indeed about the processes which allow them to do so. As a result, I will argue that the notion of adaptation is best applied when it is used to refer to the *strategies* which individuals deploy in order to negotiate the environmental constraints and exigencies which they perceive themselves to face.

Such a conception of agents' strategic adaptation (whether wilful in the sense of purposive, goal-oriented action, or reactive, in the sense of a blind trial-and-error search for solutions to crises) within an evolving institutional context brings us closer, it could be argued, to Giddens' own views on structuration; however, it accords most favourably with the type of strategic relational approach to change proposed by Jessop (1990a) and others (Bertramsen 1988; Hay and Jessop 1997). In these state-theoretical attempts to explain processes of change, institutions such as the state are viewed as sites of strategic struggle in which competing strategies are employed within an institutional context which, in turn, imposes a selective bias.

A concern with viewing change as both path-dependent and contingent

Although evolutionary theorising is concerned primarily with analysing change, its basic premise is that change can only occur where the 'changes' that are imposed exhibit certain types of 'continuity' with both the environment and past choices. In this respect then, an evolutionary conception of change rejects the idea that the overall process of change is essentially 'random' (Nelson 1995: 55) It is this most basic premise that forms the crux of evolutionary theorising. However, this is not to say that change is necessarily pre-determined either. It would be equally misleading

to think of evolutionary theory as being principally about a series of tempo-
rally distinct stages along a unilinear, or indeed a multilinear, path to
progress.

Of course, it could be argued that these two statements inherently
negate one another; to do so, however, would be to enter a form of
reasoning which insists upon a dualistic relationship between random or
chance events and those which exhibit pattern or structure. It is precisely
this type of dualism which evolutionary theory seeks to reject. Early
attempts at evolutionary theorising in social science did, of course, retain
a heavy bias towards the idea that the process of change was, to a very large
extent, governed by the inexorable pull of 'progress'. However, as Nelson
(1995: 55) explains, this type of reductionist reasoning is entirely alien to
evolutionary theory and, as a result, such analyses must be considered to
be 'evolutionist' in their attempts to explain change, rather than essentially 'evolutionary' (Ward 1995: 15). The distinction here is important. In
'evolutionist' accounts of change, such as those often employed within
orthodox Marxism, it is assumed that change occurs through a sequence
of ascending stages towards some type of 'telos' or end (ibid.). However,
an 'evolutionary' account of change mainly avoids any prior assumptions
about the purpose of change and, as we have already noted, chooses
instead to enquire into the processes and mechanisms which propel
evolution (Van Parijs 1981: 51; Stzompka 1993: 114; Ward 1995: 15).

A proper 'evolutionary' conception of change therefore rejects any
notion of teleology and seeks instead to view change as 'probabilistic'
rather than deterministic (Stzompka 1993: 114). In this respect then,
evolutionary theory regards change as involving a dialectical and dynamic
relationship between changes which are 'path-dependent' and those
which are essentially 'contingent' or random (Ward 1995; Hay 1997). This
means that, although the process of change is often governed by chance or
random factors, once a particular evolutionary trajectory has been
embarked upon, the environment will begin to exhibit a 'selective' bias
which favours certain outcomes over others. However, although this bias
will necessarily preclude some types of action, this should not be taken to
mean that future changes are inevitably pre-determined; rather, it implies
that the environment will invariably help to 'condition' the course of
future changes by (*under*)-determining the success or failure of particular
forms of adaptation.

As a result, evolutionary theory regards change as a process which
involves a constant and dynamic struggle between innovation (whether
blind or wilful) and reinforcement. Moreover, it is insistent upon the
notion that this struggle is essentially an open-ended one in which it is
impossible to detect any form of teleogical logic. Thus, any attempt to
reflect upon the dynamic behind evolution, as well as the possible endings in sight, is not only fraught with danger, but also has no place within
an evolutionary paradigm. For, it would be wrong to view the 'causes' of

evolutionary change as static and essentially 'given' phenomena them-selves. The factors which generate change are viewed within an evolutionary schema as being as open to evolution as the changes which are being observed. Consequently, an evolutionary paradigm has, at its core, the underlying belief that it is these factors which are there to be speculated upon and elucidated within any particular situation.

Formal versus appreciative conceptions of evolutionary change

Although most rival conceptions of change may actively eschew the use of the type of metaphorical language that evolutionary theory draws upon, few would reject the basic theoretical premises which it has to offer when stripped of both its jargon and its reductionist pretensions. Perhaps the best example here is that of structuration theory as proposed by Anthony Giddens (1984), a staunch critic of evolutionary theorising. Giddens vocif-erously denies the utility of an evolutionary approach to explaining change. He regards evolutionary theorising in social science as a somewhat crude attempt by social scientists to emulate their natural science counter-parts by postulating certain universal laws or teleological principles governing societal development. As such, he argues that both the general concept of 'evolution', alongside the more specific notions of 'selection' and 'adaptation' must be consigned to the same dustbin as other postu-lates of structural determinism such as historical materialism.

What emerges most clearly from Giddens' attack on evolution (and indeed, with most criticisms of evolutionary theory) is the fact that he makes little, if any, distinction between evolutionary theorising in general and the altogether dogmatic and reductionist assumptions which inform an historical materialist conception of history. To Giddens both theories can be rejected on much the same principles. This serves to illustrate not only the detriment which classical theorists have bestowed upon the notion of evolutionary change, but also the fact that Giddens, alongside most other critics, carries a misconceived notion of what an evolutionary approach to change should properly entail. If we were to select each of the separate elements of the evolutionary paradigm which emerged from the recent stream of neo-evolutionary theorising, and compare these to the types of insight that structuration theory has to offer, then we would find that Giddens' own basic conception of change, would, if adapted, accord very favourably with the various 'forms of reasoning' which underpin an evolutionary approach.[6] In this respect, structuration theory, as with an evolutionary approach, asserts: the crucial temporality of change; a processual account of societal development; a heightened sensitivity to the various forms of 'conditioning' which the institutional context brings to bear upon agents' calculations; an equal consideration to the ways in which actors intuitively adapt and learn within institutional contexts; and, finally, that change should be conceived of as both 'patterned' and 'contingent'. Thus, although Giddens chooses to reject the formal use of notions such as 'selection' and 'adaptation', his theoretical conclusions do invoke a conception of change which is nevertheless implicitly 'evolutionary'. In this respect then, many of the objections which Giddens has about evolutionary theorising in social science can be taken to apply only to the type of 'evolutionist' accounts of change which most contemporary theorists of evolution would find equally objectionable.

As such, it is important to make a distinction between 'formal' theories of evolutionary change, and those which implicitly invoke 'appreciative' evolutionary conceptions of change when either describing or explaining social, economic or political phenomena (Nelson and Winter 1982: 46–8; Nelson 1995: 49–50). The argument here is that, even though most 'formal' theories may reject outright an 'evolutionary' logic, the type of reasoning which most employ when describing or explaining change is nevertheless invariably evolutionary. Most would agree that the 'environment' or 'context' in which problems are solved sets strict limits or 'selective' pressures upon the variety of responses which can occur. Similarly, most would contend that this forces individual actors or groups of agents to negotiate – and 'adapt' to – the context in which they are situated. Moreover, almost all sophisticated varieties of 'formal' theorising would agree that the primary analytical task should be to elucidate the factors which allow these selective and adaptive processes to occur. So, why then do we need an evolutionary account of change as distinct from any other type of theory?

The most obvious answer to this question is that a formal evolutionary conception of change renders more explicit ideas which are mainly implicit in other approaches to change; it provides us then with a more honest and direct commitment to our 'appreciation' of change as evolutionary. However, here, I will argue that the basic novelty within the type of research paradigm which has emerged from the recent stream of neo-evolutionary thinking lies in the way in which it helps us to approach the question of change. By offering a distinctive heuristic device which is 'flexible' to a variety of different concerns, yet underpinned by a broad set of explicitly labelled assumptions, an evolutionary conception of change provides a way of organizing the type of explanation we employ. First, it provides us with a full range of metaphorical language, which allows us to apply similar concepts across a very broad range of research projects, thereby enabling us both to utilise and to integrate insights from a multi-disciplinary field. Second, an evolutionary paradigm inherently points our attention towards examining a multi-dimensional array of factors which govern the process of change. By simply directing our attention towards the ways in which actors, through time, adapt strategies in order to negotiate the demands of the environment in which they are situated, evolutionary theory helps us to overcome a number of the problems which still pervade most attempts to elucidate political change. Essentially, it a priori helps us: to overcome the dualistic tendency to focus upon either contextual or intentional factors in the process of change; to avoid the temptation to invoke uni-dimensional explanations which stress political or economic or ideational variables; to come to terms with the complexity of the environment in which political action occurs; and to focus upon the crucial temporality of change and thereby avoid static, comparative description.

Having made these points then, it is now important to examine some of the insights which can be derived from the application of an evolutionary conception of change to the study of politics. Of course, thus far evolutionary theorising has largely remained solidly outwith the boundaries of a political science discourse, except in cases where it has been used 'appreciatively'.[7] However, in recent years there has been a limited number of tentative attempts to apply more formal and explicit notions of evolutionary change to analyses of both policy-making and state transformation. At the forefront of these attempts has been the work of Hugh Ward (1989; 1997; 1998), Colin Hay (1996; 1997; 1998) and Peter John (1998a; 1998b). My aim in the following sections is to elicit, from the work of these and other authors, some of the processes which might be considered appropriate to a specific analysis of political change. I will suggest that, given the major advances which theorists within other branches of social scientific research have made in updating and revising evolutionary conceptions of change, political science has a relatively untapped pool of theoretical insights which can be drawn upon to provide a much more sophisticated and 'post-disciplinary' perspective on change than it has hitherto achieved.

Towards a critical evolutionary conception of political change

In what is to follow then, I will examine the main contours of the evolutionary approach which will be used in the following chapters to elucidate the main processes and mechanisms which have impacted upon the evolution of postwar British politics. Specifically, I refer to this as a 'critical evolutionary' approach. There are three reasons why I have opted to label the approach as 'critical'. First, and quite simply, the term is used in its literal sense in order to imply that an evolutionary paradigm is being utilised here for the purpose of placing a critical spotlight upon the established narrative of the postwar period. Thus, the overall aim is not simply to provide a more adequate theoretical explanation of our conventional understanding of the development of postwar British politics; rather, it is to challenge orthodox interpretations and derive an alternative understanding and periodisation. Second, the term critical is used to denote the epistemological and ontological status of the conception of evolutionary change which I am seeking to advance. It implies that the methodological assumptions which underpin the approach are broadly in line with a 'critical realist' tradition which asserts that social realities are governed by deep structures of largely unobservable causal mechanisms, and that the primary analytical task must be to critique and interrogate these (Bhaskar 1979; Archer 1995). Critical realism also directs our attention to the fact that analyses of these causal mechanisms cannot be divorced from a consideration of the crucial power relations which have helped to construct them. Thus, the 'critical' aim is to highlight the centrality of power to the overall process of change. Third, it is used in order to distinguish between the purposes of my own approach and those of conventional evolutionary theories of change. Specifically, the aim here is not to provide any generalised conception of the nature of political change. In this sense, I remain deliberately agnostic as to whether evolutionary change is best conceived of as 'punctuated', 'iterative' or otherwise. Although some observations of this sort will inevitably be made in the following empirical chapters, my main aim is to use the evolutionary paradigm as a general analytical framework to interrogate the processes and mechanisms which have both generated and hampered the evolution of postwar British politics. As such then, the purpose is to develop an approach for critically evaluating and periodising the postwar era, rather than a general theory used for descriptive purposes.

As I shall argue, a 'critical evolutionary' approach offers two main advantages over conventional accounts of political change. First, by virtue of being grounded within an evolutionary paradigm, it places the concept of change and the complex interweave of different factors generating it at its core. Second, by virtue of being grounded in a critical realist ontology, it recognises the limits to empiricism and begins from the premise that the process of change is both shaped and constrained by relations of power, ideologies and structural mechanisms which are not always directly observable while making it a primary analytical task to interrogate and critique these.

In the following sections, I will examine the key assumptions that will guide our critical assessment of the evolution of postwar British politics. Specifically, I will assert that political change is best conceived of as the product of three main evolutionary processes: environmental conditioning and selection; agents' own selection of their strategic interventions; and, adaptive learning. As a result of the constant and dynamic interaction between these three factors, I will argue that institutional change emerges through time in the form of strategic adaptation and environmental elaboration. In sum, political change is presented here as the outcome of a contingent, yet path-dependent, dialectic struggle between actors and the selective environment in which they are situated. As purposive, intentional, yet rationally-bounded agents, these actors are conceived as constantly selecting strategies which will enable them to respond to environmental problems and crises as well as satisfy their own sets of goals and ideational heuristics. In turn, the environment poses a selective bias which effectively acts upon some strategies over others, while, at the same time, it is also transformed, as 'successful' strategies begin to impact upon pre-existing institutional practices and routines.

Environmental conditioning and selection

As we previously noted, the idea that the environment both conditions and exerts selective pressures upon the variables which are evolving, remains central to any evolutionary schema. As such, any informed analysis of political evolution must account for the inherent biases and institutional constraints that reside in both the global and the domestic environments in which state strategies are articulated. In this sense, we need to recognise that, when governments respond to environmental crises, they do so within a structured context which is itself the product of previously articulated strategies and historical processes and which will necessarily (*under*)-determine the success or failure of certain interventions over others. This point has been developed and applied to analyses of the state by theorists such as Jessop (1990b) and Hay (1997; see also Hay and Jessop 1997), who argue that the state imposes a 'strategic selectivity' upon agents' calculations, and by Ward (1997), who prefers the use of the term 'structural selectivity' to refer to the same type of strategic conditioning. Drawing upon the work of Claus Offe (1974) and Nicos Poulantzas (1978), these authors share the common assumption that 'particular forms of state privilege some strategies over others, privilege the access of some forces over others, some interests over others, some time horizons over others, some coalition possibilities over others' (Jessop 1990b: 10).

To conceive of this type of strategic selectivity is to concede the inevitable 'path-dependence' of political change. As Hay explains, once a particular evolutionary trajectory has been embarked upon, the selective pressures which this imposes upon future outcomes will invariably facilitate changes that are broadly in line with past choices. Thus:

> the order in which things happen affects how they happen; the trajectory of change up to a certain point itself constrains the trajectory after that point; and the strategic choices made at a particular moment eliminate whole ranges of possibilities from later choices while serving as the very condition of existence of others.
>
> (Hay 1997: 18–19)

However, as we have previously noted, this is not to say that the context in which strategies are implemented can be considered to be (*over*)-determining of the direction in which future change is likely to occur. Rather, it is to emphasise the strong insistence within evolutionary theory that change is an historically-specific process which is structured by past inheritance rather than entirely random or arbitrary design.

At this point, it is worth noting that I have chosen to replace the notions of 'strategic' or 'structural' selectivity with the broader term 'environmental selectivity'. The reasons for this are two-fold. First, it is arguable that the twin notions of strategic and structural selectivity, as they have been developed and applied by the authors mentioned above, are too narrowly state-centred in their appreciation of the context in which strategies are selected. In this sense, these terms have most commonly been utilised to refer to the specific bias which domestic state structures impose upon strategic calculation. Here however, I have opted for the use of the term 'environment' principally to imply that the terrain in which strategic selection occurs must be more broadly conceived to include selective processes which lie beyond the compass of domestic state structures. The second reason for invoking the idea of 'environmental' selectivity is to create an analytical distinction between the selective processes which lie outwith the control of the strategic agents under scrutiny, and those which are imposed directly by the agents themselves. Due to the active role which agents play in the process of adapting strategic interventions to meet environmental exigencies, it is important to reserve a notion of 'selection' to refer to the activities of individuals as well as structures. This is a distinction which is rarely made explicit within existing evolutionary conceptions of social and political change, and it is hoped that, by making it here, we may be able to provide a clearer elucidation of the dialectical interaction between structure and agency which the term 'evolution' implies.

In the following sections I will consider briefly the types of 'environment' which we need to examine if our aim is to chart the evolution of state strategies and institutional structures. Specifically, I will argue that it is important to assess the dynamic and dialectical interaction which occurs between both the global and the domestic environments in which state strategies are articulated. However, it is equally crucial that we examine both the constraints and opportunities which the overall discursive environment brings to bear upon actors' strategic interventions.

However, before we turn our attention to these various types of 'environment' in which selection processes can be said to occur, it is perhaps useful to consider further the concept of 'selection' itself. Here, it is heuristically appropriate to create an analytical distinction between two different types of selection; selection 'of' and selection 'for'. This distinction is made by Sober (1984: 100; see also Vromen 1995: 98) who argues that '"selection of" does not imply "selection for"'. In order to illustrate this distinction, the author considers the example of a toy which contains red balls of a relatively large size and green balls which are relatively smaller. If we imagine that the toy contains a filter with holes of equal size that are big enough to let green balls pass through but small enough to prevent the red balls, when the toy is turned upside down only the green balls can reach the bottom. In this sense then, the toy can be said to be operating a 'selection' mechanism.

This mechanism is forcing the selection 'of' green balls, however, it is not 'greenness' per se which is being selected 'for'. Consequently, when we are looking at selection processes, it is sometimes appropriate to be precise as to the traits which are being specifically selected 'for', in this case the size of the balls, and to distinguish between these and the selection of secondary traits, in this case the colour of the balls. As we shall see in later chapters, this distinction can enable us to gain a clearer understanding of the processes of selection at work in the postwar period. Thus, for example, we can argue that the political and economic crisis of the 1970s precipitated a movement in global relations in which state strategies aimed at improving economic flexibility and adaptiveness were selected 'for'. However, the accompanying selection 'of' specific forms of strategic intervention, such as privatisation for example, must be seen as being selected 'for' only by individual agents carrying specific ideological heuristics, and not by external circumstance. In other words, the 'traits' which were being selected for by environmental demands were those which encouraged economic flexibilisation and competitiveness; however, the selection of particular policies such as privatisation and de-regulation should be regarded as a by-product of this since these represented only one possible means of achieving this end. Having made this distinction then, it is now important to look at the various types of environment in which these type of selection processes might be said to occur.

Global environmental selection pressures

As we have already noted, one of the most pervasive problems with explaining political change is the overwhelming tendency for most authors to neglect a proper consideration of the relationship between processes of evolution and transformation on a domestic scale, and those which occur on an international level. This failure to include an analysis of the impact which global evolutionary patterns have had upon domestic structures, has been particularly prevalent in British political studies and has resulted in explanations which are often ethno-centric and which, by implication, invoke the idea of British 'exceptionalism' (Kerr 1995). Here, I will assert that, in order to overcome these problems and thereby provide a more sophisticated understanding of the full range of processes which contribute to the evolution of state structures and political practices, it is essential that we consider the crucial interaction which exists between global and domestic evolutionary trajectories.

There is perhaps no better author to remind us of the selective pressures which global political and economic structures bring to bear upon nation states than Immanual Wallerstein:

> it is futile to analyse the processes of societal development of our multiple (national) 'societies' as if they were autonomous, internally

evolving structures, when they are and have been in fact structures
created by, and taking form in response to, world-scale processes.

(Wallerstein 1991: 77)

Wallerstein and other world-systems theorists emphasise that the highly
integrated and competitive global environment exerts pressures upon all
nation states to accommodate themselves to the wider transitions and
crises of the world economy (Wallerstein 1974, 1980, 1983, 1989; Frank
1980; Taylor 1989; Hopkins and Wallerstein *et al.* 1996). At the core of
these analyses is the observation that capitalism and capitalist class relations have, from their very inception, been situated within a *global* context
and, as such, provide a 'systemic' environment to which all nation states
must respond. As Overbeek (1990: 3) explains: 'capitalism is not a social
formation located within the confines of a particular portion of the available global space, but it is a global social formation, with the historical
evolution of social forces tendentially also becoming global in character'.
More specifically, world-system theorists argue that capitalism has, since
the sixteenth century, evolved through regular cycles of growth and stagnation. These 'long waves' of capitalist development reflect shifts in the
character and spatial coordinates of capital accumulation and class formations, as individual nations are forced to strive for competitive
advantage within the hierarchical structure of the world economic and
inter-state system. Of course, this is not the place to begin to dissect the various intricacies of the debates which Wallerstein and other world-systems,
and indeed long-wave, theorists have provoked; nevertheless, it is important to emphasise the overall contribution which these types of analyses
make to our understanding of the links between global and national evolutionary trajectories. Although not explicitly evolutionary, these
approaches provide us with an important 'appreciative' conception of evolution which reminds us that the transition of the global economy through
developmental stages of capitalist accumulation forces 'systemic' selective
pressures upon nation states to adapt strategies which correspond with
global economic patterns.

Wallerstein's world-systems perspective on change is, of course, somewhat unfashionable in contemporary accounts of the state; however, many
of the fundamental insights that he and his contemporaries espoused have
been developed to form the basis of competing conceptions of the impact
that global patterns of economic evolution exert upon state strategies at
the domestic level. Foremost among these in recent years has been regulation theory (see for example Aglietta 1979; Lipietz 1987; Boyer 1990;
Jessop 1990a). Regulation theorists have highlighted the necessary co-evo-
lutionary tendencies which emerge between global technological
paradigms and national-specific strategic interventions. Here, the focus is
mainly upon the national (and sometimes local) specific configurations of
socio-economic and political structures, or regimes of accumulation,

which adapt in response to global technological paradigms. Accordingly, regulation theorists insist upon the need to 'periodise' capitalist development, focusing upon both charting and interrogating the major contours of the different types of technological paradigms that emerge alongside their accompanying modes of regulation. In contrast to Wallerstein, however, these authors emphasise the important element of contingency inherent in political change by pinpointing the variability of the national structures in which economic regulation is embedded. Nevertheless, they also serve to reinforce the argument put forward by world-systems theorists that, due to the exigencies which the global environment exerts upon all nation states, the overall direction of change within domestic political and economic structures is at the same time path-dependent.

Overall, these types of analyses provide us with important insights that are impossible to ignore when we come to elucidate the range of processes and mechanisms which govern political change. In particular, they direct our attention to the fact, to use Giddens' words (1984: 91), that: 'all actors move in situated contexts within larger totalities'. Thus, when assessing the state as an actor, it is crucial to examine the relationship that it has to the totality of economic and interstate relations which comprise its external environment, and to accept that this external environment does, to varying degrees, impose crucial selective conditioning upon national-specific strategic responses to crises. Moreover, these analyses also serve to remind us of the path-dependent nature of change given the range of global pressures which exist, while serving, at the same time, to illuminate the contingency and variability of the types of available responses to these.

Domestic environmental selection pressures

While it is important to consider the full range of external conditioning on strategic responses to crises, it is equally crucial that we recognise that global selective pressures do not exhaust the environmental factors which shape the evolutionary trajectories of state structures. Any proper attempt to elucidate processes of political evolution would, after all, still have to assess the selective pressures that are exerted by domestic institutional and historical processes. As Sanderson (1995: 15) explains: 'social evolution occurs both endogenously and exogenously, and neither of these can be causally privileged on a priori grounds'. To acknowledge this point is to concede: 'the dialectical unity of external and internal factors' (Overbeek 1990: 3). In this respect, we need to recognise that change can only occur through a constant and dynamic interaction between processes of selection within an environment which is both global and national-specific in character. Thus, although the global environment does clearly condition the trajectories of national adaptations to crises, these will still vary considerably given that governments are equally confined to act in accordance with environmental pressures that are unique to each individual state.

It is here that the insights of regulation theory and some branches of state theory have been most useful in illuminating the variability of the types of national response which emerge from global shifts in capitalist relations and accumulation. These types of analyses highlight the important point that, although the global environment does force systemic pressures upon individual nations, it is at the national level that political power and class relations primarily crystallize (Overbeek 1990: 13). Thus, the state must be viewed as a relatively autonomous site through which strategic struggles are operationalised (Jessop 1990b). Moreover, the outcome of these struggles will depend heavily upon the specific ensemble of class relations, balance of force and institutional bias residual within each individual state. This means therefore, that internal strategic struggles will invariably produce differential outcomes which will, in turn, force peculiar types of selective pressures and strategic responses.

Overall then, any informed analysis of political change such as the Thatcher years, must remain attentive to the complex interaction that exists between social forces and selective pressures which are essentially global in character and those which are nation-specific. To recognise this is to acknowledge that social relations appear almost contradictory in character, displaying a relative unity at a macro-level while showing a large degree of diversity at the micro-level of analysis (Jessop 1990b: 232–6). In sum, the evolutionary trajectories of each individual nation must be considered to be as equally conditioned by configurations of class compromises and institutional practices idiosyncratic to the historical struggles within those nations, as they are by their position within the global economic and interstate system.

'*Discursive' environmental selection pressures*

The third type of 'environment' in which selection mechanisms are at work, and which must be taken into account if we are to analyse properly the processes and mechanisms which generate change, is the 'discursive' terrain in which political action occurs. Of course, whereas both the international and domestic networks of economic and political power relations are, to a large extent, relatively concrete and identifiable, the discursive environment in which state strategies are implemented remains a lot more abstract and elusive. Nevertheless, this is not to say that its effect in conditioning and shaping policy outcomes is any less real.

The importance of 'discourse' to the study of social change has been widely acknowledged in recent years. Indeed, as Jessop (1992: 288) remarks, discourse analysis has become something of 'an academic growth industry'. The central tenet of discourse analysis is that all social realities are constituted by and mediated through, discursive and linguistic structures. However, here it is important to emphasise that to most discourse theorists the term 'discourse' implies something broader than actual language. Thus, according to Jabri (1996: 94) for example: 'discourses are social relations represented in texts where the language contained within these texts is used to construct meaning and representation'. Accordingly, discourse theorists recognise that, in making sense of the world, individuals draw upon shared meanings and interpretive schemes which are carried in discursive structures (ibid.). In turn, these interpretive schemes provide us with information which enables us to construct our realities. Thus, discourse acts as: 'a framework within which things are made meaningful' (Painter 1995: 14). However, as Potter and Wetherell explain:

> social texts do not merely *reflect* or *mirror* objects, events and categories pre-existing in the social and natural world. Rather, they actively *construct* a version of those things. They do not just describe things, they *do* things. And being active, they have social and political implications.
>
> (Potter and Wetherell 1987: 6)

The 'social and political implications' of discursive practices relates to the fact that relations of power are to be found embedded both in discourse and behind it (Fairclough 1989: 43). As Jabri (1996: 96) explains: 'structures of signification, seen in their institutional order in terms of symbolic orders or modes of discourse, are interlinked with structures of domination and legitimation'. In this sense then, the meanings and representations which are conveyed to individuals through discourse are constituted by particular sets of social relations. They represent attempts by dominant groups to impose their own ideologically distilled representations of reality upon others. Thus, 'discourses' must be considered to be highly manipulative, since they are active in helping us to incorporate other groups' conceptions of the world into our own 'common sense'. Moreover, following Gramsci, some discourse analysts assert that, through time, particular types of discourse may be successfully engineered to become hegemonic or 'totalising' in their effects (Laclau and Mouffe 1985).[8]

As a result then, we must recognise that 'discourse' provides an environment for strategic conduct which is inherently 'selective'. In this sense, dominant discourses help to 'filter' our understandings of the contexts which we inhabit and, indeed, of the range of interventions into that context which would constitute feasible or appropriate action. Thus, for example, as Hay (1996) has pointed out, the discursive construction of crisis narratives limits definitions of the legitimate forms of action which can be taken in order to deal with institutional contradictions and crisis-tendencies. Moreover, dominant discourses are, by nature, exclusionary; they help to forge constructions of identity around the identification of 'difference' and 'equivalence'. Thus: 'what an object *is* is a function of discursive structures that, like language, define it in relation to what it is *not*' (Martin 1998: 6). In this sense then, identities are forged through symbolic representations of non-identity; in Giddens' (1984: 43) terms, 'the constitution of the 'I' comes about only via the 'discourse of the Other'. Accordingly, the 'selectivity' of discourse is further enhanced by its ability to privilege the interests and participation of certain groups while excluding others.

As we saw from our analysis of the Thatcher governments, one of the most central aspects of Thatcherism was its ability to 'exclude' from the public agenda ideas associated with social democracy, corporatism and Keynesianism. The primary means by which this was achieved was through the application of a discursive critique of the postwar period which associated Britain's decline with the implementation of these ideas in the early postwar era. Thus, Thatcherism assumed an identity through the discursive construction of symbolic 'others'; in particular, it created a series of binary oppositions between, for example, conviction versus consensus, neo-liberalism versus social democracy and strong government versus 'ungovernability' (McAnulla 1999). By permeating the public consciousness, via media manipulated representations of the deleterious effects of socialism and the left, with the 'common sense' that there was 'no alternative', Thatcherite discourse was able to impose a 'selective' bias favouring New Right ideology which continues to haunt the Labour Party even in power.

As a result then, it is important, when examining the evolution of state strategy, that we assess the role which particular types of discursive formation play in providing an 'environment' that both constrains and enables the implementation of future strategic interventions. Through discourse, representations of material practices are distorted and manipulated. By stating this, however, it is important to emphasise that I am adopting a different ontological position from most discourse theorists. For, it is common for discourse analysts to assume that there is no independent material reality which exits beyond discourse. Thus, as Martin (1998: 7) points out: 'discourse theorists reject the idea of a pre-social "positive essence", that is, an objective "presence" prior to its signification'. This does not mean that they reject the idea of a material reality outright; rather, it implies that material relations can only be recognised and defined through discourse. However, this is perhaps to overstate the decisive role which discourse can play in shaping material relations. Instead, throughout this book, discourse will be regarded as only one factor in the context of a constant and evolving dialectical relationship between the objective conditions of political practice and subjective interpretations of those conditions. In this sense then, recognition will be paid to: 'not only the role that discourse plays in making things real, but also the role that material practices play in enabling or constraining discourse' (Painter 1995: 14). As such, as well as providing a 'selective' environment of its own, discourse exists within wider institutional environments, which, in turn, impose their own 'selective' pressures upon particular types of discursive formation.

Agents' own selection of their strategic objectives

Having stressed the importance then, of retaining an emphasis upon the types of environmental selective pressures brought to bear upon strategic responses to crises, it is equally important to stress the processes of selection which actors themselves impose upon the formulation of strategy. Any analysis which retains a singular emphasis upon the environmental conditioning of political and economic strategy, would run the inevitable risk of falling into a strict reductionism. If we were simply to assume that strategic responses to environmental exigencies were invariably automatic, or indeed, entirely congruent with these, then we would be guilty of employing the type of crude functionalist logic which has hitherto dogged evolutionary theorising in social science and stripped it of its former credibility. As a result then, it is important that we consider the very active role which human agents have to play in the process of evolution and, in particular, their constant ordering and selecting of their own strategic objectives. For, as Layder (1997: 203), eloquently puts it: 'the human being is not a simple plaything of social forces operating in the social stratosphere, beyond the reach of human agency'.

Although evolutionary theorising in social science has, in the past, failed to deal sufficiently with the understanding that it is through the actions of individuals and groups of individuals that evolutionary change occurs, it is important to emphasise that these type of analyses have been guilty of providing a false notion of what the process of evolution entails. For, as we have already noted, any explanatory framework which grants sole, or indeed primary, attention to environmental selection as a factor in the process of change, cannot be considered to be in essence evolutionary. More precisely, a proper, informed conception of evolutionary change must consider the dual interaction which occurs between knowledgeable and purposive agents and the environment in which they are situated. Fortunately, this is a point which the recent wave of evolutionary theorists have been quick to emphasise. As Ward (1995: 14) explains, evolutionary theories 'do not squeeze out human agency from social theory'.

In evolutionary biology, selection is assumed to occur on random mutations. Of course, this analogy can also be usefully employed in social theories of evolutionary change. Thus, with regard to political analysis for example, we can argue that, due to the bounded rationality of individual policy-makers, policy is often blind and random and, therefore, 'successful' policies are those which more or less accidentally accord most favourably with the selective pressures brought to bear by environmental exigencies (Ward 1997). However, while this type of argument does have a great deal of utility in helping to explain some types of political outcome, it is nevertheless important that we do not present an explanatory framework which invariably treats human agents as passive dupes who are always merely 'groping' for solutions to crises. Much of the recent stream of evolutionary theorising in social science acknowledges this point and, thereby, argues that variation is not always blind and random; rather, it can be the result of purposeful design. Therefore, it is 'willful in the sense that human beings are goal-oriented and constantly engaged in the search for strategies or behaviours that are in some sense superior to old ones' (Lopreato 1984: 247; see also Burns and Dietz 1992).

Thus, we must take account of what Giddens (1984) calls 'human knowledgeability'. As the author states: 'human agents or actors . . . have, as an inherent aspect of what they do, the capacity to understand what they do while they do it' (ibid.: xxii). Actors are never passive creatures in the formulation of strategy; rather, they will invariably insert their own sets of meanings and objectives into their strategic interventions. In this respect, we need to consider the fact that agents both extrapolate meaning from the information they receive from their environment and interpolate their own intentionality into their strategic responses.

There are at least three main considerations which can be emphasised here. First, although the environment exerts pressures for particular types of solutions to crises, actors' bounded rationality will invariably prevent them from gaining full knowledge of what these might be. As a result, the agents' limited awareness will inevitably force them to elicit and insert their own interpretations of the types of strategic interventions which are appropriate to the environmental crises which they detect. Second, and relatedly, strategic actors carry their own sets of goals and strategic heuristics. Thus, political actors are not merely bounded actors: they are also intentional, motivated, agents who have their own selection criteria. As a result, responses to environmental crises are mediated, filtered and, thus, selected, through the ideational and subjective processes of purposive, goal-oriented and strategic agents. Third, and importantly, environmental crises themselves cannot be narrowly conceived as objective properties of the system; rather, they are essentially contested constructs which reflect the subjectivity and intentionality of the actors who narrate them. Thus, before responses to crises can be made, actors must extrapolate (through their own biases and strategic heuristics) from their environment, information about the types of crises and contradictions which exist; moreover, they will, in turn, interpolate their own intentionality into their strategic responses.

Adaptive learning

The third main process that is important to an informed analysis of political evolution is that of adaptive learning. Here, I will contend that strategic responses to environmental crises evolve in part through processes of reflexive monitoring and strategic learning. The idea of strategic or policy learning has become particularly prominent within the recent stream of historical institutionalist literature (Skocpol 1992; Hall

1993; Pierson 1993; see also Hay 1997). These authors have helped to high-light the fact that, through time, policy actors reflexively monitor both their actions and the effects of those actions and indeed, of the evolving environment which they inhabit. Moreover, adaptive learning has similarly been acknowledged within economics as an evolutionary mechanism which must be considered distinct from exogenous selection processes (Vromen 1995: 116–20). Thus, for example, Simon (1982, 1983) regards the process of learning as taking the form of a selective trial and error search. In this sense,

> if a human agent is trying to solve a problem, the agent's attempts to do so are assumed to be informed 'negatively' by past failures (errors) to solve it (if there have been previous attempts to solve it), and to be informed 'positively' by successful attempts at problem solving.
>
> (Vromen 1995: 117)

Accordingly, 'rules of behaviour that so far have yielded satisfactory results are retained while rules that failed to do so are dropped' (ibid.: 205). In the latter case, actors will be forced to 'search' for further solutions. This idea, of a 'selective search' by individuals for solutions to problems, inher-ently contradicts the notion in evolutionary biology that 'mutations' are invariably produced blindly before being filtered by exogenous selection mechanisms. Instead:

> In adaptive learning, the 'mutation' mechanism does not operate independently of the 'selection' mechanism. 'Mutations' spring from search efforts which in turn are enticed by dissatisfactory results of using 'old' rules that so far have yielded satisfactory results.
>
> (Vromen 1995: 117)

In this sense, adaptive learning is likened, by Vromen (1995: 118) to Van Parijs' (1981) notion of reinforcement. According to Van Parijs, rein-forcement can further be likened to what behavioural psychologists term 'operant conditioning'. This refers to the process of: 'artificially rein-forcing (by an experimenter or an owner of a pet animal, for example) a certain way of behaving by rewarding it. As a result, a behavioural pattern may emerge' (Vromen 1995: 118).

Importantly however, Vromen (1995: 120) insists that to recognise adaptive learning as an evolutionary process distinct from exogenous selection mechanisms is to concede the crucial element of intentionality and subjectivity involved in evolutionary change. Thus, although indi-viduals may learn on the basis of receiving beneficial results from their actions, these are never objectively prescribed by environmental exigencies. Thus: 'in natural selection, "beneficial" refers to "objectively useful", whereas in adaptive learning it relates to "subjectively gratifying or rewarding"' (ibid.). For this reason then, the concept of adaptive learning cannot be used to support a valid functional explanation since it inherently 'implicates both intentionality and recognition' (ibid.).

Taking these points into consideration, we may say that 'feedback' mechanisms can be posited to occur as political strategies unfold which allow the relative success of previous interventions to be monitored. An important consideration here is the inherent inertia which resides within institutional structures, and the rigidity of organizational routines and existing institutional practices. Thus, initial strategic interventions will invariably prove unsuccessful in meeting desired outcomes, and the evolution of state structures is heavily dependent upon governments' persistence and their ability to respond and adapt to previous failures. For this reason, if we are to explain the evolution of the state, then it is equally crucial that we focus upon the evolution of agents' awareness and knowledgability, since: 'adaptive learning typically implies changes *within* individuals' (Vromen 1995: 115). Through time, agents must be conceived as being as open to transformation as the environment which they seek to effect, as indeed are both their beliefs and goals. Thus, in the process of action, agents themselves are transformed, as they become increasingly more aware of their relationship with their evolving environment. In this way, as Margaret Archer (1995; see also Stzompka 1993: 200) has pointed out, the morphogenesis of agency must be considered to coincide with the process of environmental elaboration, as the outcome of strategic interventions impact upon both the agents themselves and the context which they inhabit. Over time, this constant process of adaptive learning within a structured environment will inevitably allow the agent to become more informed of the type of strategic interventions which are appropriate to achieve the bounded and narrowly conceived objectives that they seek.

If we acknowledge this point, we thereby recognise that the formulation of strategy has a crucial temporal dimension. As Jessop *et al.* (1988: 9) emphasise: 'the relationship between objectives and actions across different time horizons is crucial to strategic calculation'. Thus, as we shall subsequently highlight in more detail, strategy cannot be conceived of as a static variable. Rather, it has to be viewed as a dynamic and constantly evolving process, which is worked out and adapted over time by purposive agents who are themselves involved in: 'adopting trial and error techniques, learning by doing, and changing along with circumstances' (ibid.: 8).[9] Again, it is worth emphasising that such a schema places the crucial role of agency in a central position within the evolutionary process. Here, agents are seen as very purposively 'selecting and ordering objectives; deciding on a pattern and sequence of actions deemed appropriate to attaining these objectives; monitoring performance and progress; and *adjusting tactics and objectives as strategic interaction proceeds*' (ibid.: 9).

Strategic adaptation and environmental elaboration

Having considered very briefly then, some of the key processes which may be appropriate to an informed analysis of the evolution of political strategy and state structures, we can now turn our attention to a consideration of the eventual outcomes which these processes are likely to produce. Since change is perceived here as a constant, dynamic and contingent process, it is of course most appropriate to conclude that there are no real endings in sight. However, what we can say with certainty is that evolution leads to further evolution. According to Sanderson (1995: 15) then: 'social evolution is itself a process that evolves'. In this respect, we must consider the product of evolutionary change to be merely a changed context which will inevitably condition the shape and direction of future changes. Given our concern with the process of political change, it is crucial to examine the way in which processes of selection and adaptive learning contribute to strategic adaptation and environmental elaboration.

What is meant here is that, through time, partly in response to environmental conditioning and partly through the active interventions of human agency, strategic responses to crises will 'adapt' to meet the exigencies of the environment in which they are situated and the overall intentionality of the agents who enact them. Moreover, it is equally important that we consider the impact which these adaptations subsequently have upon the immediate environment. This dual process of strategic adaptation and environmental elaboration will inevitably provide the changed context in which future selection processes and adaptive learning will occur. To Archer (1995; see also Sztompka 1993: 200), this process is best conceived of as:

> [a] 'double morphogenesis . . . in which the elaboration of both structure and agency are conjoint products of interaction. Structure is the conditioning medium and elaborated outcome of interaction: agency is shaped and reshapes structure while reshaping itself in the process.
> (Archer, quoted in Stzompka 1993: 200)

In this respect then, it may be appropriate to postulate, for the purposes of analysis, the existence of a constantly moving equilibrium towards which evolution is drawn. This point of equilibrium is a point at which strategies are 'optimally' adapted to meet environmental exigencies. Within such a heuristic evolutionary landscape we could also postulate the existence of 'local' points of equilibrium at which strategies are 'more' or 'less' well adapted than at others (Elster 1989; Ward 1995). This allows us to plot the various stages of adaptation through which political strategies evolve, thereby enabling us to chart the evolution of, for example, Thatcherite state strategy, as the Conservatives continually strove to adapt strategies which would transform Britain's institutional structures to meet the demands of the transition from a 'Fordist' regime of accumulation to more flexible forms of regulation.

Of course, this is not to say that it would be appropriate to attempt to determine what these points of local and global equilibria may be. Clearly, given the crucial element of subjectivity involved in the formulation of strategy, these will vary depending upon the strategic heuristics and motivations of the actors involved. Moreover, it would also be inappropriate to assume that 'optimal' solutions to crises are necessarily achieved due to the fact that the environment in which strategies are implemented is itself constantly changing, as well as the problems which it produces. As Nelson explains:

> frequent or continuing shocks generated internally as well as externally, may make it hazardous to assume that the system will ever get to an equilibrium; thus the fixed or moving equilibrium in the theory must be understood as an 'attractor' rather than a characteristic of where the system is.
>
> (Nelson 1995: 49)

In addition, a further obstacle to 'optimal' adaptation is the fact that selection mechanisms can only work upon the specific (and most often flawed) inputs which rationally bound agents have to offer. Thus, given that human understanding is inherently limited and that no one is in possession of the knowledge of how to adapt 'optimally' to their environment, most interventions are likely to fall significantly short of the requirements for optimal adaptation. This point is also acknowledged within Darwinian natural selection. As Vromen (1995: 96) explains:

> natural selection works on existing genetic material and this material need not include the optimal genetic 'program'. If the optimal program is not available, natural selection cannot lead to optimal adaptation. The outcome of natural selection cannot be better than the genetic material that it works on.
>
> (Vromen 1995: 96)

Overall then, the process of evolution is continually 'attracted' towards the point at which strategies can be best adapted to meet the problems which reside within the domestic and global environments in which they are located. However, each new adaptation creates its own sets of problems and selective pressures which further enhance the need for future adaptations. Thus, as Nelson (1995: 49) asserts: 'the actors should be regarded as searching for a best action, as contrasted with actually finding it'.

Conclusion

In this chapter, I have noted that the broad contours of an evolutionary paradigm are: an emphasis upon change as a set of 'processes' unfolding through time; a concern with the 'selection' of variables; an emphasis upon 'adaptation'; and an emphasis upon the dialectical interaction between 'contingency' and 'path-dependence'. From this then, I have proceeded to outline the main contours of my own 'critical evolutionary' approach. Specifically, I have argued that any informed analysis of political evolution needs to remain sensitive to the ways in which the global environment exerts 'selective' pressures upon all nation states to respond to the wider trajectories of international economic and interstate system. However, these pressures are also cross-cut by selective bias imposed by the configuration of institutional compromises and historical conflicts peculiar to each nation state, and by the particular types of dominant discourse which pervade the institutional settings in which political action occurs. While these types of 'environmental' selective pressure must be considered to 'condition' and (*under*)-determine the types of political response which can be made, it is equally crucial that we acknowledge the selective pressures brought to bear upon strategic interventions by agents themselves. As motivated and knowledgeable actors, agents both extrapolate meaning from their environment and interpolate their own intentionality into their strategic responses. Moreover, through time, the knowledgeability of political actors increases as they engage in a constant process of reflexive monitoring and adaptive learning. This enables them to adapt their strategies in order to respond more successfully to, and impact upon, the environment which they inhabit. Thus, through time, political change can best be conceived of as the product of both strategic adaptation and environmental elaboration.

5 Go . . . stop . . . go . . . stop!

The fits and starts of government strategy, 1945–76

Introduction

So far, I have assessed the major empirical, theoretical, and methodological problems in the established narrative, and outlined an alternative theoretical framework through which, I have argued, we can gain a more sophisticated understanding of the evolution of postwar British politics than the often crude and exaggerated accounts already on offer. The next step must be to provide an alternative periodisation; one which can help us to move beyond the comparative, static and often uni-dimensional analyses that have so far dominated the literature. The purpose of this chapter therefore, is to present a periodisation of the years 1945–79. Here, I will argue that, during these years, government strategy oscillated between respective attempts both to expand and to contract the role of the state. Thus, rather than viewing the period as one which was dominated by consensus, stasis and continuity, it is more appropriate to emphasise the fundamental conflicts and changes of direction which contributed to making the early postwar era as dynamic, if not more so, than the Thatcher years.

Periodising the postwar era

At the outset, we need to distinguish between what is meant by simply chronologising as opposed to periodising a particular time frame. According to Jessop *et al.* (see also Hay 1996: 146–7):

> chronologies are essentially one-dimensional, focus on temporal coincidences and adopt a narrative approach. . . . Thus, a chronology orders actions and events in a unilinear, calendrical time; classifies them into successive stages according to their occurrence in one or other time period . . . and thereby gives the basis for a simple narrative.
>
> Jessop *et al.* (1988: 13–14)

In contrast:

> periodisations operate in several time dimensions, focus on conjunc-
> tures and presuppose an explanatory framework . . . a periodisation
> orders actions and events in terms of multiple time horizons; classifies
> them into stages according to their conjunctural implications . . . for
> different social forces; and, since both these procedures involve
> consideration of how actions and events are generated as a complex
> result of multiple determinations, they operate with an explanatory
> framework as well as providing the basis for a complex narrative.
>
> Jessop *et al.* (1988: 13–14)

Given this definition, it is not strictly accurate to say that this book has
so far taken issue with existing periodisations of the postwar era, since the
bulk of the literature within which the established narrative is embedded
merely outlines a chronology of events rather than offering a proper theo-
retically-informed periodisation. To be more specific, the literature
exhibits two different types of approach: an historical narrative approach
that orders the various stages of postwar political development into a
simple chronological sequence, more often than not separated by governmental spells in office; and what I shall term an historical categorisation
approach that offers a simple characterisation of different stages of development without any accompanying, multi-dimensional, framework of
explanation.

Within the former approach, used primarily by historians, it is normal
to encounter detailed analyses of the Attlee governments from 1945–51
followed by a description of the Conservatives in power from 1951–64 and
then the Wilson administration of 1964–70, and so on. This type of simple
historical narrative offers no real selection of data and is rarely accompanied by any complex explanatory framework. On the other hand, the
latter approach, found particularly within the political science literature,
orders analyses according to the dominant system of characterising the
postwar period; namely, a consideration of the era of so-called postwar
consensus is followed by an examination of Thatcherism. Although this
type of approach does take us a step closer to a formal periodisation as
defined by Jessop, through its selection of historical data and its emphasis
upon categorising distinct time frames, these analyses still err on the side
of chronologising events since they most often still rely upon a simple
narrative without offering any complex explanatory model. As Jessop's
definition shows, the problem of providing a multi-layered explanation of
events that highlights distinct causal relationships is central to any attempt
at periodisation and, as a result, explanation must be given primacy over
description.

The aim of this chapter is to chart and periodise the evolution of the
early postwar period. As in Chapter Seven, when I examine the development of Thatcherism, the basis for the periodisation will be a focus upon
the various types of strategic adaptation that have dominated the postwar

political scene. In this sense then, each of the different periods that I look at will be defined in terms of changes, or more precisely adaptations, to the basic underlying thrust of government strategy. In this chapter, I will argue that early postwar government strategy evolved through five main temporal stages: liberal-welfarist expansion, 1945–7; liberal-Keynesian retreat, 1947–62; liberal-corporatist expansion, 1962–6; liberal-corporatist retreat, 1966–72; and Keynesian-corporatist expansion, 1972–6. In the following sections I will examine each of these in turn, before proceeding in Chapter Six to offer a multi-dimensional explanation of the main processes and mechanisms that drove this fitful evolution.

Liberal-welfarist expansion, 1945–7

A great deal of time and energy has been devoted within orthodox accounts of the postwar period to eulogising the achievements of the Attlee government in creating a radical momentum of policy implementation directly after the war which set in place the primary conditions for future strategic interventions. However, as I have argued and will show in both this and the following sections, this type of narrative tells only a partial story. First, it largely fails to acknowledge the fact that the momentum achieved during the early years of Labour's term in office was one that had been set firmly in motion during the wartime plans for reconstruction. In this sense then, the Attlee administration, in embarking upon its early frenzy of legislative reform, merely followed an evolutionary path which had, to a considerable extent, been previously mapped out for it. As I shall demonstrate, the major problem for Labour, and indeed the fate of social democracy, in postwar Britain was that the Attlee government failed to create any real momentum of its own. Second, and perhaps more important, although Labour did set the fundamental precedents for future policy interventions, these were largely laid down after the series of reforms that had created the structures of the welfare state and the nationalised industries. Thus it was in the latter half of the Attlee administration, during which Labour retreated from its former radicalism and implemented a series of crisis management measures rather than any coherent informed strategy, that the primary policy objectives for the remainder of the postwar period became established.

Labour's 'lost victory'

There can be little doubt that the early years of the Attlee administration did represent a period of rapid policy change otherwise unmatched in the history of postwar British politics. As Hennessey (1989: 35–6) explains: 'it was a period of unprecedented legislative activity' in which 'the Bills rolled in and the Acts rolled out as if on a parliamentary production line'. From the time of its election, the Attlee government acted quickly to fulfil its key manifesto pledges. Between 1945 and 1947 the government successfully set in place the main structures of the welfare state. Although not formally established until 1948, the National Health Service had been legislated for by the 1946 National Health Service Act. Meanwhile, in the same year, the National Insurance Act had been passed to establish a universal system of social security benefits and pensions. In housing, 188,000 new homes were being constructed by the end of 1946, rising to one million by the end of Labour's term in office, while in education the government ensured the successful implementation of the 1944 Education Act passed by the wartime Coalition. Moreover, throughout the same period, Labour also fulfilled its commitment to a comprehensive programme of nationalisation. By the summer of 1947 measures had been taken to bring the Bank of England, Cable and Wireless, civil aviation, coal, electricity and road and rail transport under the ownership of the state, with the further nationalisations of gas and iron and steel scheduled to follow in the next three years. As a result of such heightened parliamentary activity, the years 1945–7 do stand out as a remarkable period of legislative reform in which new institutional structures were established through the implementation of a determined and relatively coherent governmental strategy. However, it is important here to ask how we might characterise the seemingly sweeping changes that Labour implemented. In doing so, we need to assess the radicalism of the policies that the Attlee government introduced in terms of both their design and relative impact.

At the time, most people believed that the reforms introduced by Labour amounted to nothing less than a 'silent revolution' (Dorey 1995: 34). To many of its supporters, the Attlee administration was embarking upon a Parliamentary road to socialism and the eventual transcendence of capitalism. While this ambition was never actually the aim of the Labour Party leadership, there was nevertheless a strong rhetorical commitment amongst their ranks to altering radically the direction of British politics by steering a middle way between socialism and capitalism. However, there are numerous reasons for rejecting the idea that Labour's reform programme amounted to anything other than a limited set of measures designed both to protect capitalism and to sustain the status quo in Britain's existing power relations (Johnston 1999).

First, many of the reforms, particularly with regard to welfare, were merely built upon existing policies and pledges (Howell 1976: 150). In this sense, the Attlee government had, to a large extent, been fortunate to be handed the opportunity by the electorate to implement policies which had already been conceived under and agreed by the Coalition government. Thus, for example, the Beveridge Report, published in 1942, had paved the way for the establishment of the welfare state, and it is generally agreed that the strong likelihood is that its recommendations would have been implemented regardless of which party had entered office directly after the war. Similarly, the commitment to full employment had been presaged by the White Paper on employment published in 1944. Consequently, as Dorey (1995: 35) argues: 'it can be said that the 1945–50 Labour government took the credit for the pursuit of major policies which had actually received cross-party support during the war'.

Second, and related to this point, is the fact that the Attlee government had: 'merely confirmed a trend towards collectivism and a more active state which had been gathering pace long before the outbreak of the Second World War' (ibid.; also Middlemas 1979). This long-term trend in British politics had involved a supporting role for central government in economic affairs alongside agreement from other governing institutions such as trade unions and employers' associations. Parallel with this trend had been the gradual development of welfare policies since the end of the nineteenth century. The origins of the welfare state can be traced as far back as the 1870s, when the Conservative government led by Disraeli introduced measures to improve the living conditions of the poor, while the 'peoples budget' introduced by the Liberal government in 1906 provided benefits for old age, sickness and unemployment.[1] As a result, it is important to place the 'active state' policies introduced by Labour into the context of the overall evolution in the growth of the state that had been taking place throughout the early part of the century.

Third, and most important, once we move beyond the area of welfare and examine the content of the rest of Labour's strategy, it is difficult to discern anything other than a moderate and relatively conservative reform package which left the core structures of the state and existing power relations completely intact. As Gamble explains:

> the war marked a sudden alteration in Britain's world status and the balance of its internal politics, but there was no similar discontinuity in the formal organization of the state itself. The general character of Britain's institutions was little changed. . . . The fundamentals of the education system, the House of Lords, and the civil service all remained – although all had been major targets for reform in the past.[2]
>
> (Gamble 1994: 102)

Thus, it could easily be argued that the most important reforms were the ones which were *absent* from Labour's strategy. Apart from the creation of welfare institutions, the Attlee government did little either to create new state structures or, indeed, to dismantle old ones. At no point did it take steps towards effective central planning, nor did it disrupt the stranglehold that institutions such as the Treasury, Bank of England and City of London had traditionally held over policy. Although the nationalisation programme did offer an enormous potential for a significant alteration to Britain's institutional settlement and internal power relations, most authors concede that its actual impact was at best marginal. Indeed, not only did the nationalisations fail to alter the relationship between state and society, they also did little to alter the structure of, or indeed, the personnel behind, the industries themselves. As a result: 'the government ensured that the management structure of nationalised industries served the general needs of capitalism and did not offer any element of workers' control that others might want to emulate' (Cliff and Gluckstein 1996: 221; also Hall 1986: 70). Moreover, one of the major reasons why the Conservatives had chosen not to vehemently oppose the nationalisation programme was the fact that the industries that were taken under the ownership of the state were ones which had been non-profitable, yet central to the rest of the economy. Consequently:

> nationalisation of these industries was vital for the expansion of the profitable industries that remained private. It strengthened the private sector by freeing it of the burden of industries which demanded heavy investment and were essential to the running of the economy.
>
> (Cliff and Gluckstein 1996: 221)

Thus, despite the initial enthusiasm that Labour would somehow usher in a radical new phase of pseudo-socialist reform, the reality was that by the end of its legislative frenzy the structure of British capitalism and the class relations that accompanied it remained relatively unaltered. Britain retained virtually the same constitutional and institutional settlement that it had when it entered the war, while the governing principle of main-taining a relatively unfettered economy was left intact.

Finally, a further reason for disputing the alleged radicalism of the Attlee administration is the fact that, directly after the war similar policy trends began to take shape throughout the Western economies. The fundamental principles of Keynesianism, alongside measures to increase welfare provi-sion and ensure a more dirigiste role for the state, were being actively pursued throughout Europe and North America, often with more vigour than in the United Kingdom. This is a point which is almost universally and conveniently overlooked within the literature, given the emphasis by most authors upon stressing the 'exceptionalism' of the policies pursued by the Attlee administration. However, some of the more sophisticated studies of the postwar era do point to the crucial need to place British postwar devel-opment within the overall context of changes within the international political and economic system (Jessop 1980; Hall 1989; Taylor 1989; Burnham 1990; Overbeek 1990; Gamble 1994; Johnston 1999). To these and other authors, the evolution of British politics after the war can only be understood against the backdrop of the spread of similar ideas across nation states in response to international pressures, and changes in the balance of global power relations. Thus, in order to gain a more balanced perspective on the policies initiated by the Attlee government, we need to consider the way in which Labour's strategic adaptations were designed to accommodate 'selective' pressures from both home and abroad.

Overall then, we may say that Labour's reforms, which were broadly in line with developments in other parts of the globe, had failed – indeed arguably were never intended – to bring about the radical restructuring of state-societal relations that most authors assume. As Coates explains, by the end of the government's period in office:

> power had not shifted between classes. Qualitative social transformation had not come. Nor was it any nearer for six years of office. In essence, the Labour Government of 1945–51 had not created a socialist commonwealth, nor even taken a step in that direction. It had simply created a mixed economy in which the bulk of industry still lay in private hands, and the six years of its rule had only marginally altered the distribution of social power, privilege, wealth, income, opportunity and security.
>
> (Coates 1975: 49–50, quoted in Dorey 1995: 38–9)

Although it is virtually universally accepted that the Attlee government neither succeeded with nor even attempted serious socialist transformation, there remains nevertheless the common belief that its strategy was generally underpinned by some variant of socialist principles. More specifically, the period directly after the war is invariably regarded as a conjunctural moment in which social democracy had triumphed over a traditional liberal capitalist governing ethos. In this respect, 1945 is seen as a watershed in which the twin pillars of Keynesianism and social democracy became inscribed within the institutional architecture of the state. It is further suggested that this particular policy 'paradigm' helped shape the formulation of government strategy throughout the remainder of the early postwar period. The problem is, however, that when we examine Labour's strategy in more detail, there is very little evidence to suggest that it was guided by any hint of socialism, even in its reformist, social-democratic, guise. Indeed, what is clear is that there is no real hint of any distinctive Labour strategy at all.

It is perhaps more accurate to characterise the changes implemented by the Attlee government as a particular stage in the overall evolution of ideas throughout the twentieth century towards a progressive form of liberalism which equated social justice and egalitarianism with increased state intervention in order to create a fairer redistribution of wealth and the elimination of poverty. Beyond the issue of welfare, there was little else in Labour's reforms that could be characterised as either social-democratic or even distinctive from the broad context of ideas that had been floated around before and during the war. Although much focus has been placed upon nationalisation and Keynesian demand management, neither of these represented any type of radical strategy on the part of the Labour government. As Mercer (1991: 71) explains: 'while this focus is natural, there was little in these policies that was distinctively Labourite. Even the party's manifesto argued for specific nationalisations on empirical grounds almost identical to those outlined in Harold Macmillan's *The Middle Way.* Beyond these limited measures, Labour 'had little in the way of clear policy guidelines for the conduct and role of private industry within the mixed economy, and lacked the theoretical basis to formulate one' (ibid.: see also Coates 1975: 54–5; Lereuz 1975: 61–2; Morgan 1984: 130). As a result, Labour's strategy for intervening in the economy virtually began and ended with the limited process of nationalisation, a policy instrument that allowed them absolutely no effective control. Although Labour demonstrated an interest in using state machinery to effect an industrial strategy (see Tiratsoo and Tomlinson 1993), in the end they did little or nothing to enhance the capacity of the state to intervene in order to achieve this. Ultimately, as Dutton (1991: 27) explains: 'the most that the government aspired to was a loose partnership with industry – one in which the forces of capital and the market would remain supreme'.

As a result then, the best way to characterise the changes that occurred in the years immediately after the war is to describe this as a period of liberal-welfarist expansion, in which progressive liberal ideas that had been developing throughout the early twentieth century, and used to a limited extent to inform earlier attempts at social reform, found their full practical expression in the creation of a comprehensive programme of welfare provision. Clearly, these initiatives did represent a key moment in the development of British politics. As Hay (1998) argues, the Attlee years must be regarded as a period of 'punctuated evolution' in which the pace of change dramatically increased and the responsibilities of the state expanded. Nevertheless, given the overall paucity of Labour's ambitions beyond the provision of welfare, the qualitative impact of the changes which occurred has been grossly exaggerated. The legacy of these years was one of Labour having missed a real opportunity to effect genuine transformation. Its programme fell spectacularly short of its proclaimed intention of creating 'New Jerusalem' and, with regard to its rhetorical commitment to achieving a middle way between capitalism and socialism, all it had succeeded in doing was to pull capitalism out of crisis while retaining the traditional liberal principle of a relatively unfettered economy.

Liberal Keynesian retreat, 1947–62

The year 1947 proved to be a turning point for Labour's reform programme. As Dorey (1995: 29–34) explains, it was a year in which achievements turned to atrophy. Throughout its term in office, Labour found itself beset by a series of economic crises.[3] Three of these converged during 1947 and resulted in the government retreating from its hitherto reforming zeal, a retreat which lasted until the end of its term in office and which was later consolidated by the Conservatives after 1951 (Jefferys

96 Government strategy, 1945–76

1997). As a result, the period of welfarist liberal expansionism, which had lasted only two brief years, was to give way to a long phase of crisis-management and relative stasis, governed by a vacuum in government strategy and a virtual return to economic orthodoxy.

Labour's retrenchment

The factors affecting Labour's crises of 1947 were both short-term and long-term (Cronin 1991: 162). The main long-term problem was the mounting shortage of dollars with which to pay for imports. In the years immediately following the war the United States had become virtually the sole supplier of food and raw materials, both of which had been depleted on an almost worldwide scale. Sterling's inconvertibility into dollars, combined with the fact that British exports were not sufficient to earn enough dollars to cover the balance of payments, meant that payments had to be met using Britain's gold and dollar reserves (Cairncross 1991: 28). By the early half of 1947 it was clear that the 'dollar shortage' represented a financial crisis for the government, which had been forced to use up a substantial amount of the nearly four billion dollar loan that Keynes had negotiated from America towards the end of 1945. It was the combination of balance-of-payment difficulties, the dollar shortage and the conditions of the American loan which combined to create the second long-term problem, resulting in a crisis for the government during the same year. As part of the conditions of the loan agreement, the US had insisted that sterling should become freely convertible into dollars within one year. Although the terms of the loan were largely unacceptable to British Ministers, they were nevertheless forced reluctantly to concede. However, by 1947 neither the Chancellor Dalton, who was 'unduly optimistic' about how sterling would fare during convertibility, nor the Treasury, had taken steps to ensure that the conversion would be a smooth one (Cronin 1991: 162). As a result, in the weeks after the date for convertibility Britain suffered a massive run on sterling that eventually resulted in the process being suspended: 'much to the chagrin of the Americans and the detriment of the government's reputation' (ibid.).

The third major crisis – this time the result of short-term factors – was a massive fuel shortage during the first two months of the year. 1947 had begun with a terrible winter that was recorded as the most severe since 1880–1. Given that fuel stocks had been depleted by the war, the winter placed a heavy burden on remaining fuel supplies, eventually forcing the government to place restrictions on the use of electricity. As a result, industrial output dropped by 25 per cent, resulting in a temporary loss of two million jobs and an overall £200 million in exports (Dorey 1995: 31). Since the government's attempts at restoring economic stability were heavily reliant upon increasing exports, this crisis, amid the other related problems it was facing, brought Britain close to financial calamity and prompted a significant change of direction and strategic emphasis.

Although most commentators are agreed that Labour had handled these crises relatively successfully, its subsequent handling of its longer-term strategic objectives proved to be very poor indeed. In fact, in the midst of 1947 and throughout the following years of its term in office, the government appeared to abandon any further attempt to impose its former strategic vision upon the institutions of the state. As Cliff and Gluckstein (1996: 230) argue, in the face of the financial crisis 'the Attlee government panicked. A new financial policy was put forward, with dire implications for the entire thrust of Labour's reforming strategy.' Although further nationalisations did occur after that year, by 1949 the government's enthusiasm for the policy had exhausted itself, and conflict arose over whether or not subsequent proposals for public ownership should be included in the next manifesto (Hall 1986: 70).

The immediate response to the crises suffered during 1947 was the introduction of an austerity budget designed to 'balance the books' (Dorey 1995: 31). Although Dalton's budget was aimed at achieving this age-old Treasury obsession, enshrined within years of economic orthodoxy and proposed through the familiar themes of deflation and cuts (this time in basic rations), it has been subsequently deemed to have been a 'revolutionary' development in Britain's economic history (Cronin 1991: 162). The reason for this is that the 1947 budget was the first to have been: 'shaped with the explicit use of Keynesian techniques and consciously designed to control inflation by dampening demand, especially for imports' (ibid.). What is particularly interesting here is the fact that the so-called Keynesian 'revolution', rather than, as most authors insist, ushering in a radical new direction in British politics, actually signalled an end to the erstwhile period of innovation and state transformation. In effect, the adoption of Keynesian demand management merely presented postwar governments with a different means by which to pursue orthodox economic targets.

This reconversion back to dealing with traditional economic concerns was perhaps best symbolised by Dalton's successor as Chancellor, Sir Stafford Cripps. It has been widely recognised that under Cripps Labour's strategy collapsed into a series of austerity measures, including cuts in the housing and welfare programmes and proposals to impose prescription and dental charges. More importantly however, the adoption of Keynesianism in 1947 finally killed off any remaining hopes that the government would take further steps towards creating the mechanisms to allow serious economic planning. As Hall explains:

> the Government began to dismantle the unpopular system of controls used to supervise the flow of goods and funds within the economy during the war. . . . These moves were significant because the industrial controls assembled during the war were powerful instruments that might have put teeth into a system of economic planning.
>
> (Hall 1986: 72–3)

This move away from a more social-democratic inspired attempt at allowing the state to take the type of dirigiste stance in economic affairs pursued by countries such as France was again symbolised by Cripps' term at the Treasury. Under his chancellorship:

> the Ministry of Economic affairs, which had not yet been institutionally established, in fact became a department of the Treasury. In this way industrial policy was subsumed under monetary policy, which consoli-dated the restored domination of the Treasury over government policy.
>
> (Overbeek 1990: 121)

As a result then, the year 1947 must be seen as the beginning of a restoration of Treasury control and a long phase of a very liberal variant of Keynesian thinking in which the tools of economic policy had been modified but the overall objectives remained little changed from the interwar years.[4]

The Conservatives' wasted years

By 1951, Labour's term in office had fizzled out and 'the actual experience of government had proved to be a "graveyard of doctrine"', in which a clear 'barrier had been erected between the Labour Party and the economic theories of Marxism' (Dutton 1991: 26; see also Harris 1982: 452). As a result then, it is perhaps easy to conclude that the relatively high degree of bi-party consensus to have emerged during the 1950s, was the product of the fact that Labour had reconciled itself more to the progressive liberal ethos of the Conservative Party than the Conservatives had to the so-called social-democratic sway of the Labour Party. Thus, the Conservative governments after 1951, who, as Ingham (1984: 206) points out, 'were intent on restoring market capitalism', were responsible for the consolidation of the narrow strategy of liberal Keynesianism embarked upon by the Labour administration after 1947.

The period of the Conservatives' thirteen years in office from 1951–64 has been neglected within the literature. However, a recent study by Jefferys (1997: 6) has concluded that, on detailed examination: 'the picture which emerges . . . is that of a nation uncertain of its economic future, less consensual and more socially divided than often assumed'. Thus, although the degree of inter-party consensus was relatively high, it would be wrong to suggest, as Addison (1985: 198) does, that: 'in their different ways the two main parties lacked ideological purpose'. While in power, the Labour government had prompted a 'neo-liberal backlash' within the Conservative Party and the new government, led by Churchill, was composed of a balance of forces between corporate and classical liberals (Overbeek 1990: 130; Ingham 1984: 209–10). Although the eventual promotion of Macmillan to Prime Minister did help to restore the balance in favour of a more corporate-liberal ethos, these tensions were never ultimately resolved.

Moreover, during the early 1950s, the left of the Labour Party appeared to have rallied again and seemed to have recovered from the 'acute exhaustion of ideas' (Dalton 1962: 370) which had formerly hampered the Attlee government while in power. Although this recovery was temporarily halted with the subsequent election of the right-wing Hugh Gaitskell as leader in 1955, such conflicts were again never far from the surface, and provided a dynamic to the evolution of ideas and policy throughout the postwar period which is rarely acknowledged within the literature. To most commentators these areas of *dis*-sensus were less important than the overall continuity of emphasis between the party elites. While this is to some extent true in terms of the impact which the disputes had upon the main aims and objectives of both parties, and the actual implementation of policy, this is nevertheless to miss the point somewhat, since the areas of disagreement remain crucial to our understanding of the evolution of postwar British politics. What is important here is the precise terms of the dispute. Essentially, these revolved around the definition of what the broad parameters of economic and social policy should entail.

As we have already discussed, the adoption of Keynesianism in Britain reflected a very liberal interpretation of what the precise role of the state should be in relation to the operation of the market. In this sense, the Keynesian ethos which emerged after 1947 was one which envisaged only moderate adjustments to the level of demand, and which was, to a large extent, broadly consistent with the long-term goals of the classical liberal tradition of sound monetary financing and non-direct interference in the economy enshrined within the Treasury. As Peden explains:

> the main advantage of demand management was that it allowed the government to appear to be in control of the economy even after the range of physical controls had been reduced. It is not at all clear, however, that the policies which were adopted from 1951 were 'Keynesian' in every respect.
> (Peden 1991: 158; see also Tomlinson 1987; Rollings 1988)

Thus, unlike countries such as France, where Keynesianism incorporated a more dirigiste stance towards private industry, in Britain the use of Keynesianism was restricted to demand-management (Hall 1986: 76–80). Since this did not involve any direct controls on either capital or labour, this type of minimalist intervention became fully acceptable to both financial and industrial capital, and to their representatives in parliament (Jessop 1980: 29). Moreover, throughout the period, and particularly under the Conservatives, the application of Keynesian techniques was used primarily for purposes other than the attainment of full employment (Hall 1986: 76–80; Cronin 1991: 205–8). The principle concern for policy-makers proved to be the recurring problem of balance-of-payments difficulties. This instigated a frequent series of deflationary measures and attempts to maintain budget surpluses, driven primarily by the obsession to secure Britain's international prominence in the financial markets.

The second priority under the Conservatives was the desire to cut taxes. This had also been a long-term logic within Treasury thinking and, combined with its traditional concern of maintaining 'fiscal responsibility', these considerations took precedence in the framing of budgetary policy (Cronin 1991: 208). As a result, the combined effect of these three factors meant that a succession of budgets granted: 'steady, if minor tax relief while restraining government spending. *It was a pattern that bore a strong resemblance to the budgetary history of the interwar years*' (ibid.; emphasis added). Only three main factors differed from this period: first, the liberal-corporatist rhetoric used to legitimate policy; second, the levels of taxation and public spending inherited by the Conservatives, which were enough to allow tax reductions without any serious damage to Labour's welfare programmes; and, third, the favourable international environment, particularly the growth in world trade which enabled Britain to sustain economic growth 'whatever the policies adopted by the British government' (ibid.).

It was precisely the terms of this broad definition of government economic policy that the main disputes of the postwar period centred around. While liberal Keynesianism during the 1950s appeared to satisfy the main leaders of the two parties, conflict arose beneath the surface over whether or not the policy should be sustained. Within the Conservative party, this conflict was continually expressed at the highest levels and was perhaps best symbolised in 1957 when the Chancellor, Peter Thorneycroft, and two junior Treasury ministers, Enoch Powell and Nigel Birch, resigned over disagreement about public expenditure. At the time, Macmillan's government had allowed a limited expansion of state welfare expenditure financed by reductions in defence and later by an overall increase in public spending (Overbeek 1990: 131). This had been the first real move that the Conservatives had taken towards a positive commitment to the direction taken by the Attlee government. However, this trend incurred almost instant opposition within both the Cabinet and the Treasury from those who desired deflationary policies to stem inflation and avert devaluation of the pound. Although Macmillan was able to resist, these conflicts were to persist within the Party and ultimately were to signal the beginnings of the gradual resurgence of classical/neo-liberal ideas that were to gain an ascendancy within the Party throughout the 1960s.

Within the Labour Party, the traditional conflicts between right and left, and between the leadership and the rank and file, were sharpened in the early 1950s, although these had admittedly died down in the latter half of the decade with a decisive victory for the right. Nevertheless, the areas of dispute were again important for our understanding of the direction of state strategy and the constraints imposed upon state expansion.

Essentially, the left, led primarily by Bevan, had rejected the moderation and bi-partisanship of the leadership. As a result, they called upon the party to commit itself to further nationalisation, an extension of comprehensive education, the phasing out of all private schools and the abolition of health service charges (Dutton 1991: 50).

Although these disputes within the right and left of both parties were temporarily contained by both leaderships, and although they were not properly to surface until the following decade, they do represent one of the most neglected, but important, features of the postwar political scene; that is, the tenuous nature of the so-called consensus and the evolving dynamic of conflicts shaping economic and social policy-making. At the heart of these disputes was a growing dissatisfaction with the content of policy between those happy to maintain liberal Keynesianism, those wishing to return to a more explicit commitment to an orthodox approach that would overtly prioritise inflation, the value of sterling and tight controls on public expenditure, and those who wanted to extend the definition of Keynesianism to include expansionist and corporatist ideas more directly in line with social democracy. Until the beginning of the 1960s these conflicts had made little impact on the actual output of policy, other than to force a compromise situation in which the façade of active government and social democracy was maintained throughout a long period of arm's length government and strategic atrophy.

Liberal-corporatist expansion, 1962–6

Towards the end of the 1950s the growing dissatisfaction with existing policies had heightened amid signs that Britain's long-term economic stability was under threat. Although the economy was growing faster than it had since the 1870s, publications such as Andrew Shonfield's *British Economic Policy Since the War* (1958) and Michael Shanks' *The Stagnant Society* (1960) were pointing to evidence of Britain's relative economic decline. Moreover, inflation had been steadily rising. All in all, Britain's infamous postwar stop-go cycle had assumed a pattern in which the periods of go were getting shorter and the periods of stop more frequent.

With the Treasury becoming more entrenched in its hardline stance towards public spending, Macmillan, towards the end of the decade, was becoming more sceptical about its 'dogmatic liberalism' and its 'primitive faith in the efficacy of market mechanisms free and unrestrained' (Cronin 1991: 223). His response, after 1962, was to move towards the type of indicative planning that was being used effectively in France. These moves towards promoting economic growth through a limited expansion in state institutions were to become the dominant characteristic of policy-making throughout the end of the Macmillan era and the first half of the Wilson administration. However, while they did take Britain closer to the type of active government that most authors associate with the postwar period as a whole, they were to prove ultimately ineffective and short-lived owing to the inability of both administrations to change the essential priorities of governmental policy and to disrupt the prevailing central power of Britain's leading institutions. Overall then, the steps towards planning were never institutionalised, and the whole experience further highlighted the total absence of any real attempt to transform either the prevailing structural characteristics of the British state or the essential traditional content of economic policy.

The move towards planning

The recognition by the Conservatives and others that economic growth needed to become a governmental priority meant a subsequent evolution in the rhetoric surrounding policy. '"Growthmanship" became a pervasive discourse' (Cronin 1991: 227). However, beneath the emerging consensus on growth and the renewed emphasis upon planning there were disagreements about the reasons why the British economy was failing to grow in relation to other countries. Two main arguments were put forth (ibid.: 226–7). Some believed that the major obstacle to growth was rising inflation resulting from excessive wage increases and the subsequent impact that this had upon the balance of payments. In contrast, others argued that Britain's problems lay at an institutional level, in the civil service, the machinery of government and the British establishment. While these did not dispute the importance of controlling inflation:

> what they found objectionable was the way the battle against inflation took precedence over other objectives and how a preoccupation with inflation led almost automatically to policies concerned to bolster foreign confidence and support the balance of payments and the exchange rate.
>
> (Cronin 1991: 228)

One of the major problems for the subsequent development of policies aimed at growth was the fact that these disputes were never properly resolved. As a result, the debate over Britain's economic difficulties produced very little of actual substance since much of the focus remained centred on the economy as a whole, or on central government and national institutions, without much real attention to the types of specific policies needed to address the problems of specific industries or increase 'micro' level productivity (ibid.: 227). Nevertheless, the response of the government was to take steps towards addressing both concerns by creating new institutional structures that would enable them to plan for industrial growth while keeping a tight control on inflation. The response came in 1962 in the form of the National Economic Development Council, or Neddy for short, established as a tripartite forum for consultation between government, unions and industry. In addition a National Economic Development Office was created to contribute to longer-term plans, while the NEDC established a number of Economic Development Councils (or 'little neddies') at the sectoral level following the same tripartite pattern.

This strategic adaptation towards indicative planning was not prompted by any change of direction in the ideology underpinning governmental strategy. First, the reforms were broadly in line with the corporate liberal ethos of Macmillan which had gained a temporary ascendancy within the Party towards the end of the 1950s. Second however, the impetus for reform had actually come from outside the government, specifically from the private sector. In 1960 the Federation of British Industry held a conference in Brighton which: 'endorsed proposals for closer cooperation between government and industry in the formulation of longer-term economic plans' (Hall 1986: 86). The state's general reluctance to engage in direct manipulation of the market was reflected in the actual direction that the implementation of planning procedures took. As Hall explains in relation to the central planning institution, the NEDC:

> first and foremost it was a tripartite forum for consultation between government employers and unions rather than an arm of the state charged with the preparation of an economic plan. . . . Thus, the council perpetuated a voluntaristic tradition according to which the state left matters of industrial reorganization largely up to the private sector rather than try to impose its own plans.
>
> (Hall 1986: 87)

Moreover, the twenty-one Economic Development Councils set up by the NEDC were equally ineffectual. These were used almost exclusively as consultative bodies for the exchange of sectoral level information rather than as agents for reform.

The major problem for these new institutional structures was that they had merely been tacked on to existing institutional arrangements, rather than being fully incorporated into the policy-making process. As a result, the creation of basic planning procedures was not accompanied by any formal restructuring of the state apparatus. Thus, the Treasury, with its long-term opposition to state expansion and hostility to increases in public expenditure, remained in full control over policy, thereby thwarting the ambitions of the planners and ignoring most of their recommendations while imposing 'its priorities of balance of payments and reserve position' (Overbeek 1990: 132; Jessop 1980: 39–40).

Overall then, these seemingly expansionist measures served merely as a smokescreen for the pursuit of a continuation of the government's passive role towards the private sector. Indeed, even more significantly, the tripartite arrangements were further used as a tool for the age-old concern of keeping a tight rein on inflation rather than as a means of harnessing any type of control over the economy. After the late 1950s, it had become clear to policy-makers that Keynesian demand management had no inherent mechanism for controlling inflation (Hall 1986: 80). Moreover, this fact, combined with the discovery by A. W. Phillips of the trade-off between inflation and unemployment, had persuaded the government to find alternative means to tackle inflation. By the end of the 1950s the most favoured alternative was the introduction of incomes policy. The first of these came in 1961. However, by the following year the new tripartite arrangements for planning agreements were seen as an alternative effective means of incorporating the unions into wage restraint. As a result: 'what appeared therefore, as an institutional innovation aimed at over-coming bureaucratic conservatism was in reality intended as a device by which bureaucrats and politicians could get their way with the unions' (Cronin 1991: 231). Overall then: 'planning had come to Britain, not under the auspices of Labour and as part of an effort to intervene in the economy, but with the sponsorship of the Conservatives and officials seeking a forum for working out an incomes policy' (ibid.).

Wilson's modernisation strategy

The push towards planning was given a fresh impetus with the election of the Labour government in 1964 led by Harold Wilson. Promising to embrace the 'white heat of technology', Labour entered office with a 'tech-nocratic vision of socialism' which instilled the virtues of industrial modernisation through the use of planned growth (Hall 1986: 88). Like the Conservatives, Labour's aim was to incorporate both perspectives in the debate over growth. In this sense, they were committed to structural reform while ensuring a tight control over inflation. As such: 'Labour moved both to restructure the apparatus of policy-making and to control incomes' (Cronin 1991: 232). The most visible aspects of this policy were the creation of a new Department of Economic Affairs, which was allocated the role of devising a National Plan and given responsibility for long-term economic performance, and the creation of a Ministry of Technology to administer research and development funds and supervise four high-tech industries (Hall 1986: 88). Overall, the DEA, with its focus on long-term growth in the economy, was expected to act as a counterweight to the Treasury's dominance over short-term economic policy. However, ulti-mately, what was supposed to work as a 'creative tension' between the two departments turned into a dismal failure since: 'the relationship between the DEA and the Treasury was never clarified, and the new department never wrested control of the key instruments of policy from the Treasury' (Cronin 1991: 232). As Ingham explains:

> such rationalist interpretations amazingly failed to grasp the essential point that the Treasury–DEA conflict which emerged simply represented

the historical fissure which had developed within British capital over a period of two centuries . . . there was no *prima facie* reason to suppose that balance of payments crises and the Treasury's deflationary responses would suddenly disappear . . . or that the Treasury as controller of the public purse would benignly fund the DEA's operations in the expansion of the economy.

(Ingham 1984: 214)

As a result, Labour's moves towards further corporatist expansion were to be thwarted by the refusal of the government to alter either the fundamental priorities of economic management or the institutional hegemony which the Treasury–Bank–City nexus had over policy (Jessop 1980: 38–47; Ingham 1984: 214–17; Overbeek 1990: 132–7). According to Ingham (1984: 216): 'the government seemed unable to perceive that profound changes in sterling's role and the City's domination of the economy were required if the industrial strategy were to succeed'. While Labour's plans for industrial modernisation were supposed to halt Britain's continual cycle of stop-go, the dominance of the Treasury–Bank–City triumvirate over policy, combined with Labour's attempts to pursue a strategy of 'governmental competence' by protecting the value of sterling and controlling inflation, meant that the expansionist drive was halted by a series of short-term deflationary measures (Ceadel 1991: 272; Hall 1986: 88; Ingham 1984: 215; Overbeek 1990: 134). Moreover, a further obstacle to Labour's strategy for growth was the fact that planning was to be indicative and voluntary (Jessop 1980: 41; Overbeek 1990: 134–5). This meant that there were no real policy instruments which could ensure compliance with growth targets; instead, the success of these targets relied upon the active cooperation of unions and industry, the so-called 'social partners'. The problem however, is that in Britain: 'the 'social partners' of government in the management of the economy are weak, decentralised and fragmented' (Jessop 1980: 41).

Amid these constraints then, Labour's strategy finally failed in 1966 when the government took steps towards defending sterling by introducing a package of deflationary measures. This effective departure from attempts to inspire growth meant that the government was left without any real governing strategy (Ceadel 1991: 273). As a result, the period of liberal corporatist expansion ended without having made any real impact on either the essential nature of the policy-making apparatus or the actual content of macro-economic policy. Although Labour did have a limited degree of success with the creation of Mintech and the Industrial Reconstruction Corporation, its key policy instruments in the search for growth, the DEA and the National Plan:

were dismal failures, partly because they were never equipped with the tools required to enforce their proposals, and partly because unremitting pressure on sterling forced the government into a series of deflationary measures that vitiated their overly optimistic plans.

(Hall 1986: 88)

Even if Labour had provided itself with a degree of breathing space by devaluating and deflating upon entering office, and even if the overall international environment had been more favourable, it is still unlikely that planning would have been any more successful (ibid.; Ceadel 1991: 272). As Hall explains:

> the DEA would still have lacked the means to implement its plans, since it had no microeconomic instruments of its own and was locked in battle with a Treasury that continued to control the direction of macroeconomic policy, [while] the National Plan itself entailed no more than the promulgation of hastily conceived and wildly ambitious targets for growth that bore little relation to the actual trajectory of industrial sectors.

(Hall 1986: 88)

As in the period 1945–7, a relatively ambitious strategy of state expansion had failed to: enhance the role of the state in relation to the market; disrupt the hegemony of existing power relations within the state; and, transform the essential character of Britain's prewar institutional arrangements. This period, in which government strategy had been adapted to alter the nature of Britain's postwar settlement, was to be followed by yet another phase of atrophy, and a further descent into the as yet uninterrupted traditional patterns of liberal governance.

Liberal-corporatist retreat, 1966–72

Labour's abandonment of its strategy for growth amid attempts to deflate the economy and protect the value of sterling was finally hit by a humiliating blow when in November 1967 the government was forced into a 14.3 per cent devaluation of the pound. At the time, this 'set the seal' on a whole series of problems for the government: the closing of the Suez Canal during the six-day war between Israel and Egypt had threatened damage to British exports and caused further vulnerability to sterling's position; Britain's application to join the Common Market had been vetoed by France's General de Gaulle; problems had been mounting in Rhodesia and Nigeria; and Britain's economic performance was steadily worsening (Morgan 1992: 276). Overall, confidence in the government appeared to be waning, while Labour appeared devoid of any coherent strategy for dealing with its diffi-culties. As a result, the years following 1966 were marked by another period of retrenchment and retreat in which Labour dismantled its strategy of expansionism in favour of a more concerted attempt to prioritise inflation, this time by focusing upon restrictions on wage increases and reducing trade union power. This assault upon the unions, consolidated by the Conservatives in the early years of the Heath administration, combined with the commitment to withdraw the state from the hitherto limited corporatist attempts to modernise industry, became the dominant feature of British politics until Heath's famous policy U-turn in 1972. As we shall see, the period between 1966 and 1972, following on as it did from the second major attempt at state expansion in the postwar era, almost directly mirrored the years after the Attlee government's initial attempts at state transformation. Governed primarily by austerity measures, a slackening of the commitment to Keynesianism and an ever stronger commitment to economic orthodoxy, this period further highlights the overall failure of postwar governments to effect any fundamental change in either Britain's institutional structures or the actual direction of policy.

Labour's U-turn

Labour's initial reaction to devaluation in 1967 was to adopt tough deflationary measures aimed at consolidating the devaluation and restoring the balance of payments. The new Chancellor Roy Jenkins promised 'two years of hard slog' (Morgan 1990: 276) and subsequently imposed 'restrictions not experienced since the grim days of the Korean War' (ibid.: 27). These included budget cuts of £500 million followed by substantial increases in taxation (Cronin 1991: 234). According to Morgan (1990: 279), this represented: 'the most severe deflationary package of any postwar budget. Instead of stop-go, it would be stop-stop, at least for some time'. Despite such draconian measures, however, Britain's poor economic performance continued apace. The deflationary package failed initially to prevent a worsening of the balance of payments, and it was not until the autumn of 1969, aided by changes in the international environment, that clear signs of a recovery emerged (ibid.: 279–81). Moreover, signs of a continued loss of confidence showed in an accompanying outflow of £183m of private capital investment from the economy. As a result then, what had begun as an enthusiastic attempt to expand the British economy through policies to promote industrial growth, was ending in a sharp increase in the spiral of economic decline.[5]

Labour's longer-term response to these crises was to turn its attention towards imposing restrictive measures on the activities of trade unions. The first of these had come in July 1966 as part of the failed attempt to avoid devaluation, when the government broke with its hitherto voluntarist approach to incomes policy by announcing a six-month statutory freeze on wage increases. This was followed by a further six months of 'severe restraint' which 'had sufficed to drive a wedge between the government and the unions' (Cronin 1991: 234). As we have previously noted, the use of incomes policy to control inflation had become a dominant theme of policy-making since the early 1960s. With the election of the Wilson government this policy had continued. At first it secured the support of the unions on the basis that Labour's plans for growth would bring longer-term benefits to industry, but with the subsequent abandonment of the government's modernisation strategy and its imposition of a twelve-month statutory incomes policy, resentment between government and unions heightened. Moreover, these tensions became sharper when, after 1967, the government restricted pay settlements to a maximum of 3.5 per cent, thus provoking the TUC decisively to turn against Labour's hardline deflationary measures.

The second part of Labour's offensive against the unions came in the form of the White Paper *In Place of Strife*, published in 1968. This represented a direct attempt to tame what Labour saw as excessive union power. The White Paper ignored the recommendations of the Donovan Report, published the same year, that the voluntarist tradition of industrial relations should be strengthened; instead, it opted for legislative reform which would impose statutory curbs on union activity. The proposed measures, regarded by the unions as a major threat to their bargaining position given the excessive powers bestowed upon the Employment Secretary to intervene in trade union affairs, only served to heighten union resentment. Moreover, the unions also attracted support from within the Parliamentary Labour Party when fifty MPs voted against the document and forty abstained. Although the leadership initially pressed ahead to implement the proposals, they were finally forced to back down after the TUC and government had: 'waged the most intense negotiations that any government ever had with a producing group since government first took up peacetime management of the economy in 1945' (Dorfman 1979: 35).

There is of course a glaring irony here, in the sense that the Wilson government had initially embarked upon a strategy of tripartite negotiations with producer groups in order to achieve voluntary agreements over policies aimed at generating economic growth through industrial modernisation. After having abandoned its half-hearted attempts to implement this strategy, the government was by now devoting all of its energies to bipartite consultations designed to coerce only one half of industry's representatives into accepting major restrictions on their affairs. Here was one area of economic management where the government was at last showing a great deal of enthusiasm for interventionist measures to enhance the capacity of the state to manipulate market forces.

This period reveals therefore, perhaps more than any other in the postwar era, some of the fundamental flaws in the established narrative of the so-called consensus era. First, it highlights the overall lack of consensus over the main aims of governmental strategy. There was clear disagreement between: producer groups committed to industrial intervention and cooperation in order to stimulate domestic growth and foreign exports; financier groups (and state institutions such as the Bank of England and the Treasury) committed to traditional economic priorities such as reducing inflation, controlling public expenditure and maintaining a high value for sterling; and politicians, who appeared to have little firm commitment to any discernible strategy other than to do what the dominant mood of the day was telling them.

Second, the period also highlights the myth that throughout the postwar era the trade unions had been incorporated into some kind of harmonious and close partnership with government. It was not until 1962, and the establishment of the NEDC, that the unions were invited into any kind of consultative role with government and, as we have seen, this was primarily driven by the idea that the consultation process could be used as a means of securing wage restraint. Thus, the move towards strengthening cooperation between government and unions coincided with the growing tendency, in the early part of the decade, to present the unions as the 'scapegoats of economic decline' by blaming Britain's poor economic performance on excessive wage levels and the growing number of unofficial strikes (Taylor 1993: 1–15; also Dorey 1995: 70; Marsh 1992). By the end of the decade, this theme had become the primary preoccupation of government, and the fallacy of a close partnership between government and unions had been starkly exposed.

Third, the period also highlights the determination of all postwar governments to pursue orthodox economic goals above all other priorities. The early debate over economic growth was dominated by two distinct visions: one which asserted that the principle obstacle to growth was inflation, and another which maintained that major institutional reform, involving the abandonment of the traditional short-term obsession with inflation, was required before growth could be achieved. Although both the Macmillan and Wilson governments attempted to incorporate both visions, by the end of the Wilson administration the idea that inflation was the primary evil was dominant. The established narrative emphasises the attainment of full employment and the stimulation of demand as constituting the main goals of economic policy. Yet the reality, throughout the postwar period, is that the suppression of demand in order to control inflation, even at the expense of unemployment, clearly dominated macroeconomic management. Although the growth of the economy throughout the 1950s had enabled the Conservatives to preside over full employment while maintaining a stable rate of inflation, the period from the mid-1960s onwards, when economic growth had turned to decline, revealed the political elites' tenacity to cling to prewar assumptions about economic policy which had never, in truth, been rejected.

All of these factors then, point to long-term residual tensions and conflicts in Britain's so-called postwar settlement. From the mid-1960s onwards these had become more apparent as the gap between the left and right of both parties began to widen. Within the Labour Party, the government's overt assault on the trade union movement helped to crystallize a resurgence of left-wing rebelliousness (Ceadel 1991: 273–4). Between 1966 and

1969, the leadership was defeated thirteen times at conference, reflecting a growing unwillingness by the trade unions to use their block votes to defend 'the platform' (ibid.; Cliff and Gluckstein 1996: 296). Moreover, the growing gulf between the party's national executive and conference was further reflected in a rift between the executive and government and in divisions amongst Labour MPs. After Labour's defeat in 1970, the left achieved an ascendancy within the party, eventually winning control of the NEC. Meanwhile, in the Conservative Party throughout the 1960s, 'a major revival of liberal political economy' had developed as the New Right began to assert themselves on issues such as inflation, immigration, law and order, trade unions, social security abuse and permissiveness (Gamble 1994: 138).

It was amid this resurgence of liberal political economy that the Heath government came into power, determined to 'change the course and the history of this nation' by pursuing a strategy of free market liberal economics (ibid.: 122).

Heath's market strategy

The basis of the Heath government's strategy was worked out in January 1970 when the Shadow Cabinet met at the Seldon Park Hotel in Surrey to finalise agreement on the range of policies that the Conservatives would take into the next general election. The package of proposals that was agreed upon included: a commitment to reducing state intervention and restoring the free role of the market; a pledge to withdraw state subsidies for unprofitable industries; a tougher stance on law and order, immigration and social policy; and greater selectivity in the allocation of welfare resources (Dorey 1995: 109). According to Gamble (1994: 122), this strategy of reform, widely perceived as the precursor to Thatcherism, was, at the time, the most 'radical attempted by any government since the war'. While this is to a very limited extent true, in the sense that the government's break with the rhetorical pretensions of earlier postwar administrations was more decisive and deliberate than any that had gone previously, it would nevertheless be wrong to regard the 'Selsdon Man' strategy as anything other than a continuation of the overall direction taken by the Wilson government. In this sense, Heath's strategy of non-intervention and disengagement, coupled with a further attack upon trade unions, merely followed the same evolutionary path as the policy of retrenchment and retreat embarked upon by Labour after 1966. Moreover, it also mirrored the natural tendency of postwar politicians to tackle inflation and balance of payments problems by restricting public expenditure and reducing the role of the state during periods of economic instability and slow growth. In this narrow sense then, the policies pursued by Heath in the early half of his term in office were no more 'proto-Thatcherite' than the majority of the crisis-management measures implemented by all of his postwar predecessors.[6]

Nevertheless, it is true to say that the main difference in the policies implemented by the Heath government was the fact that they were specifically aimed at generating economic growth. Whereas in the past deflationary measures and state retrenchment had been used as instruments to prevent expansion in the economy, this time they were regarded as positive measures that would increase the competitiveness of British industry by making it leaner and fitter.

Overall, Heath's strategy had four main elements. First, severe cuts were to be made in government expenditure. In 1970 a mini-budget was announced which cut free school milk and subsidies for council house rents, while dental and prescription charges were both increased. Plans were made for public expenditure cuts of £330 million in the next financial year, rising to £900 million by 1974–5 (Dorey 1995: 112). Second, the government continued the trend of liberal corporatist retreat by loosening government support for industry. The Prices and Incomes Board, the Ministry of Technology and the Industrial Reorganization Corporation were all dismantled, and in their place the Department of Trade and Industry was created and given a 'low-profile' (Jessop 1980: 44; Overbeek 1990: 158). Meanwhile, government subsidies were removed from 'lame duck' companies while profitable parts of the nationalised industries were 'hived off' and sold to the private sector. Third, following the Wilson administration's failed attempt at reforming industrial relations, the government committed itself to a further attack on union strength. This had been developed during opposition and was eventually enshrined within the proposals set out in the Industrial Relations Act 1971. The main provisions of the Act were that: closed shops would be made illegal; all unions would be made to register; legal immunity for secondary action would be removed; and emergency powers should be given to the Secretary of State for Employment to apply for a sixty-day 'cooling off' period to be imposed if industrial action was deemed to be damaging to the economy. Fourth, and most significant in the long-term, the government gave a firm commitment to entering the Common Market. This policy confirmed Britain's acceptance of its reduced status in world affairs, and also reflected a re-evaluation of the long-standing connection with the United States.

Despite this one success, the other three elements of Heath's strategy were spectacular failures. Inflation soared to an all-time high in postwar experience and was accompanied by rising wages. Moreover, unemployment rose sharply alongside inflation, thereby sending the economy into 'stagflation'. Meanwhile, the policy of withdrawing subsidies to loss-making companies ended almost as soon as it had begun, when the government had to step in to extend help to both Rolls Royce and the Upper Clyde Shipbuilders. At the same time, the idea of 'hiving off' parts of the nationalised industries to the public sector was similarly abandoned (Overbeek 1990: 158). The greatest problems however, at least in the short-term, were encountered in the area of industrial relations. Initial opposition to the Industrial Relations Act had come from within the Conservative Party itself, with several MPs expressing reservations about the threat which the Act made to the voluntarist tradition of industrial relations, and about the likely efficacy of its proposed measures. Moreover, it was also opposed by leading sectors of private capital, and by Campbell Adamson, the President of the CBI, who denounced the act because of the damage it would bring in relations between employers and unions (Overbeek 1990: 160). Ultimately of course, the Act produced bitter resentment from the unions, and in March 1971 the TUC urged its members to boycott the legislation. This was followed in 1972 by confrontation between the government and the railworkers and dockers unions. As we shall see in the next section, this heightening of tensions between the Heath government and the union movement was the start of a series of conflicts that eventually proved fatal to the government's reputation and its tenure in office.

In the meantime though, the net effect of these early policy failures was to force the government into a major reorientation of its strategic objectives. From 1972 onwards Heath abandoned his erstwhile market strategy, and embarked instead upon an expansionist course based around a more active industrial policy. This 'U-turn' in policy did not just mark a departure from the 'Selsdon Man' strategy, it also represented a break from the period of state retrenchment that had been taking place since the mid-1960s. Throughout this period, the state had been consistently uncoupled from any form of direct intervention in the economy, and even the commitment to liberal Keynesianism had been seriously weakened.

Keynesian-corporatist expansion, 1972–6

As we have already noted, the overall experience of the 1960s demonstrates the remarkable lack of consensus over policy. Strategic adaptations in this period had mirrored the deep divisions amongst the political elite and dominant institutions over whether the role of the state should be extended to include greater intervention in economic affairs, or whether public expenditure should be curbed and the state's role reduced in order to restrict direct manipulation of market forces. Inherent in these divisions were arguments about the level of priority that should be given to inflation and the international role of sterling. Should government policy be driven by short-term pressures on inflation and sterling, even at the expense of full employment and welfare expenditure, or should the government's focus be centred on longer-term issues such as industrial modernisation and restructuring?

By the mid-1960s the real priorities of economic management were starkly exposed. Full employment policies, spending on welfare, attempts at increased state intervention and even the government's relations with producer groups had all been compromised to varying degrees, amid attempts to satisfy the demands of the financial institutions that inflation should be curbed and the value of sterling protected. In effect then, the struggle over policy had, in fact, been 'settled' in favour of a firm commitment to an orthodox mix of liberal economics and political conservatism, the building blocks for what was later to be known as 'Thatcherism'. The first two years of the Heath administration had seemingly confirmed this victory. However, as we shall see, by 1972 the victory had not yet been absolute, for there was one more final attempt at state expansion and industrial modernisation during the latter half of the Heath administration and the early part of the subsequent Labour government's term in office. To some extent, this period of attempted Keynesian-corporatist expansionism could be characterised as exceptional in the evolution of postwar British politics, since it represents the first real commitment by the Keynesian policy-makers to extending the scope of the state, and increasing public expenditure during a period of rising inflation and economic instability.

Heath's U-turn

Heath's reversal of strategy in 1972 had been prompted by a whole series of economic and political difficulties: the attempt at industrial relations reform had failed to keep wage increases down; inflation was rapidly rising; unemployment was starting to spiral; investment in industry was slow; industrial unrest had heightened; and the government's electoral popularity was suffering (Gamble 1994: 124). The major problem for the government was that, rather than having to adapt its strategy – as other postwar administrations had done – in order to deal merely with rising inflation, it now also had rising unemployment as a key concern. As a result the government had to find a way of dealing simultaneously with both unemployment and inflation.

Heath's response was to embark upon an economic strategy which was 'exceptionally expansionary, arguably more so than at any time since the war' (Britton 1991: 13). The government's aim was to raise the growth of Gross Domestic Product (GDP) by 5 per cent a year, which was even higher than the 4 per cent aim of the National Plan in 1964 (ibid.). In addition, the government reversed its decision to loosen state support for industry. The first steps towards a more interventionist industrial policy had come with the nationalisation of Rolls Royce and the decision to provide subsidies to the Upper Clyde Shipbuilders. Moreover, an Industrial Development Executive was created to aid industrial investment, and an Industry Act was passed to increase incentives for regional development and provide grants to industry in exchange for state shareholdings (Gamble 1994: 245; Dutton 1991: 69). These expansionist measures were consolidated by the 1972 budget when the Chancellor Anthony Barber made significant tax cuts and planned increases in public expenditure.

Finally, in reaction to a subsequent run on sterling, the government allowed the pound temporarily to 'float' in foreign exchange markets so that the expansion would not be halted by balance-of-payments difficulties.

To a large extent, these measures flew in the face of the pattern of economic management that had dominated the postwar political scene. For the first time, a government had 'showed that it was quite prepared to risk inflation in order to boost growth. Public spending was greatly increased and the money supply was allowed to soar so as to raise the level of demand in the economy' (Gamble 1994: 125). As a result, the economic policies initiated by Heath after 1972, and indeed, carried on until 1976, were truly Keynesian in the sense that they were used actively to stimulate demand by increasing public spending during an economic downturn, as opposed merely to stifling it to prevent the economy from overheating, as most prior postwar governments had been inclined to do. Moreover, by coupling demand management with a more active (though albeit limited) industrial policy, the Heath government had, to some extent, broken with the erstwhile liberal variant of Keynesian principles which saw government intervention as being limited to only moderate adjustments to budgetary policy. The immediate effect of these measures was a short-term expansion in the economy of over 5 per cent (Britton 1991: 14; Coopey and Woodward 1996: 11). Unemployment peaked in the first quarter of 1972 and fell by 200,000 in the next year. However, the longer-term consequence of what was later to be called the 'Heath-Barber boom' was an overheated economy, with rising inflation fuelling bitter tensions between government and unions as the latter demanded higher wage levels and the former attempted to impose an incomes policy.

The need to secure union cooperation over wage restraint proved to be an intractable problem for the Heath government, as it had been for the Wilson administration during the latter half of Labour's term in office. Like Wilson, Heath had initially attempted to respond by imposing legislation to reform industrial relations; however, with this policy virtually boycotted by all the major actors, the government now used incomes policy as the main thrust of its counter-inflationary strategy. After tripartite negotiations within the NEDC between government, the CBI and the TUC had broken down, the government announced a statutory wage 'freeze' in November 1972. This was to be followed by a three-stage incomes policy that eventually limited wage increases to 11 per cent. However, the policy proved yet another startling failure. Fuelled in part by a dramatic fourfold increase in the price of oil during 1973, the miners embarked upon a campaign of industrial action that not only killed off the government's incomes policy, but also the government itself. The basis of the miners' action was a demand for a 40 per cent wage settlement, which negotiations between Heath and the National Union of Miners (NUM) had failed to modify. This was backed by an overtime ban that began shortly after the government announced stage three of its incomes policy. As a result, by the end of the year coal stocks were running dangerously low and the government, faced with an energy crisis, was forced to declare a state of emergency and a three-day working week to take effect from 1 January 1974. Despite two attempted 'peace' initiatives from the TUC and the Pay Board respectively, negotiations between the government and the NUM broke down and the miners strengthened their action by voting four to one in favour of a strike. The response of the government was to seek a mandate of support from the electorate by calling a General Election in February on the basis of 'Who Governs'. The election result confirmed the electorate's loss of faith in the Heath administration, which had appeared incompetent and unable to deal effectively with the crises it faced. However, it also reflected a growing lack of confidence in the Labour Party who won by only four seats. The Liberal Party, along with the Welsh and Scottish Nationalists, appeared to be the only real beneficiaries of the result.

In many ways this is hardly surprising, given that since 1966 both the main parties had succeeded in throwing the policy package upon which they had been elected into reverse. Neither had seemed able to commit themselves to a definite strategy and stick with it, and both appeared to have little firm idea of how to deal with Britain's growing economic and political crisis. All in all, it appeared that government strategy, rather than being settled and agreed upon, was actually in a state of constant flux. In many ways then, the electorate had reacted to the failure of both parties to resolve the fundamental conflicts that lay at the heart of policy-making. As Cronin explains:

> the voters in effect rendered a negative verdict on a decade of policy failure. That failure had been rooted in the ambiguities and contradictions of the politics of growth, to which both parties had been, and still remained, committed. The emphasis on growth had, of course, developed out of the failure of earlier policy devices to sustain the commitments embedded in the postwar settlement. But the consensus on growth had not extended to an agreement on how to engineer it, and so policy vacillated between a focus on structural reforms designed to make government or industry more efficient and a concentration upon policies to curb inflation by controlling the growth of wages.
>
> (Cronin 1991: 237)

In the event, Labour called a further election for October, in which it only managed a majority of three seats.

Although the Conservatives' term in office had ended in humiliation for the party, the final two years of the Heath government had demonstrated an interesting form of strategic adaptation. For the first time, Keynesian demand management had been applied in a more positive vein: as a policy instrument designed to achieve the purpose which it had been adapted for, namely, to steer an expansion in the economy during a period of economic downturn. Moreover, this attempt at demand stimulus had been accompanied by positive, albeit limited, measures to intervene in industry. As a result then, this period had seen a partial break with the more limited, liberal, variant of Keynesianism applied throughout most of the postwar period. In the past, this policy instrument had proved a major obstacle to any attempts at industrial intervention, since it focused attention upon the management of short-term economic instability rather than long-term growth. Consequently, we can say that the latter half of the Heath years was, to some extent, exceptional in the evolution of postwar British politics. This having been said, though, of course, the incoming Labour government took up the Heath government's strategy of Keynesian-corporatist expansion with a renewed vigour.

Labour's 'Alternative Economic Strategy'

The events of the late 1960s and early 1970s had contributed to major changes in the ideological balance within both the major parties. Within the Conservative Party, the New Right, inspired by the economic liberalism of Hayek and Friedman, had gained a gradual ascendancy. This had previously been reflected in the Party's adoption of its Selsdon strategy in the run-up to the 1970 election; however, it was now given a further impetus by Heath's apparent 'betrayal' of the cause in 1972, and the subsequent humiliating blow dealt to the government by the miners. Meanwhile, within the Labour Party, the left, led primarily by Tony Benn, had taken control of the NEC, and had succeeded in dealing the more moderate leadership a series of damaging defeats at Party Conferences. The swing to the left had begun in the late 1960s, with the Wilson government's abandonment of its modernisation strategy and its subsequent attack on trade union activity. Initially, this had caused a major rift between the party and its trade union affiliates; however, the relationship had been cemented again by the Heath government's Industrial Relations Act and its ongoing conflict with the unions over incomes policy. The result was that – in the run-up to the 1974 elections – a strong alliance developed between the unions and the Labour Party leadership, while the left had seized control of party policy. According to Coates (1980: 2): 'the shift to the left in language and programme after 1970 was on a scale last seen in the Labour Party as long ago as 1931'.

Thus, when the Labour Party entered office, they did so with 'a series of clear policy commitments more radical in tone and in aspiration than any that the Party had endorsed since 1945' (Coates 1980: 2). These were enshrined in the Party's manifesto *Labour's Programme 1973*. According to Gamble:

> its proposals which were based on the earlier 'social contract' between the trade unions and the Labour Party included new legal safeguards for trade unions; price controls; a radical housing policy; the strengthening

of public transport; a major redistribution of wealth; an end to prescription charges; an increase in pensions; industrial democracy; and the expansion of investment through the creation of a National Enterprise Board, controls on capital movements, and planning agreements.

(Gamble 1994: 172)

Labelled as the Party's 'Alternative Economic Strategy', these proposals would, if implemented, have taken Britain towards the type of social-democratic state settlement that the Attlee government had failed to create. The ethos behind the strategy was that socialist advance could be made by strengthening the power of trade unions, increasing the level of state control over the economy, and extending social rights and democratic participation in all social institutions in order to redress the balance between capital and labour. Demand in the economy would be stimulated through increases in public spending on investment and welfare, while these Keynesian measures would be supplemented by an expansion of state intervention in industry. This would include the creation of a National Enterprise Board to raise the level of industrial investment, as well as the nationalisation of twenty-five of the country's top manufacturing firms and the banking system. In addition, the largest private sector firms would be forced to sign planning agreements, and a permanent incomes policy would be set in place in order to curtail the rise in wages.

Upon entering office, the party's first imperative was to pacify the militancy of the trade unions. This was to be achieved through the so-called 'Social Contract', an agreement between the new government and the unions which had emerged out of a series of meetings of the Labour Party-TUC Liaison Committee while in opposition. The Social Contract enshrined a commitment by the unions towards voluntary wage restraint in return for a number of redistributive measures and the repeal of the Industrial Relations Act. Moreover, the NUM's wage demands were quickly met and the miners resumed normal working hours. In addition, throughout 1974 wage settlements were raised in order to catch up with the rise in prices; in the second half of the year these averaged 27 per cent, which was 10 per cent higher than inflation (Cronin 1991: 239). The next step in the government's strategy was the creation of the National Enterprise Board and the passing of a new Industry Act in 1975. Although the aims of the NEB had been watered down by the leadership in the publication of the White Paper *The Regeneration of British Industry*, the Industry Act did provide it with 'unprecedented scope for economic intervention' which the new Secretary of State for Industry, Tony Benn, intended to exploit (Ceadel 1991: 276). When, shortly afterwards, the government announced its 'new industrial strategy', moves were made towards tripartite 'corporatist' planning procedures on a voluntary basis. In addition, the government also began extending the rights of trade unions and, through the NEB, attempted 'to integrate government money directly into the circuit of productive capital' (Overbeek 1990: 167).

As a result, the Labour government began in a mood of confident optimism and, for a short time, it looked as if its manifesto pledges were being effectively put into practice (ibid.). The government's economic strategy was highly Keynesian, and, coupled with the emphasis upon industrial intervention, this was a period in which Keynesian-corporatist solutions were finally being put firmly into practice. Unfortunately however, no subsequent transformation in the character of the state was to take place, for the appearances were to prove strikingly deceptive. The major reason for this was the fact that the apparent conversion to radicalism by the leadership had proved to be 'visibly only skin deep' (Coates 1980: 3). As Overbeek remarks:

> no truly revolutionary measures were to be expected anyway: the leadership of the Labour Party which came to power in 1974 was hardly different from the leadership which had led party and government in the years 1967–9 and which in that period had been responsible for attempts to curb union rights and to abolish full employment as the foremost policy imperative.
>
> (Overbeek 1990: 167)

Putting aside the assumption that the pursuit of full employment had ever constituted the 'foremost policy imperative', the point here is that this was the same leadership whose strategy of achieving 'governmental competence' (Ceadel 1991: 272) had led the party to abandon its erstwhile attempts at industrial intervention in favour of short-term orthodox economic expediency. This time was to be no different, for the desire to resort to expediency over radicalism was never far from the surface (Coates 1980: 3). As Morgan (1992: 361) explains: 'the main strategy of the Wilson government, domestically, was clearly directed towards self-preservation rather than innovation'.

Wilson's first main act of political expediency was to remove Tony Benn from the Department of Industry. This was shrewdly done by using the issue of Britain's continued involvement in the EC as a means of undermining the left and securing a rightward shift in the party. The European issue arose out of the renegotiations over the conditions for Britain's involvement in the Common Market. At the time, the left had deeply opposed continued membership of the EC because of the perception that it represented nothing more than a 'capitalist club', which would undermine the domestic sovereignty of the government and its attempts to impose an alternative economic strategy (Dorey 1995: 131). With the Cabinet split over the issue, Wilson, motivated by the desire to use the debate as a tool for party management, called a referendum which produced a vote of two to one in favour of continued membership (ibid.:

130–3). As well as serving as a suitable distraction from Labour's promises to implement its election agenda, the referendum provided the leadership with the chance to move Benn from Industry to the Department of Energy. With Benn no longer in charge of industrial strategy, the government was subsequently to renege on the majority of its commitments towards industrial rejuvenation. By this point, the plans to take control of investment in the country's top twenty-five firms had already been dropped. Meanwhile, the idea that private sector firms should be forced to sign planning agreements was abandoned, and the 'new industrial strategy' effectively distanced the government from any future powers to enforce subsequent agreements by leaving the initiative up to the voluntary co-operation of producer groups (Hall 1986: 90). As a result then, Labour's industrial strategy collapsed into the usual formula of simply providing subsidies for 'lame ducks', such as Chrysler, British Leyland and Ferranti.

Overall, the Labour leadership had effectively abandoned its strategy almost from the very outset. This was to be confirmed throughout 1975 when the government refused to honour its commitment to the Social Contract by cutting public expenditure while simultaneously implementing a formal, though voluntary, incomes policy. Wage restraint had become the centrepiece of the contract, while the majority of the reforms that had been promised in return did not materialise. Although the government had initially reacted to its growing economic problems by attempting, for the first time in postwar history, to run a Keynesian budget deficit, it was stopped in its tracks by the usual Treasury pressure to balance the books and deflate. As Overbeek (1990: 169; see also Radice 1984: 126) explains: 'when deficit financing was finally tried for the first time in Britain in 1975, it was almost immediately blocked by the reactions of the City and the Treasury demanding the return to financial orthodoxy'. This again highlights the near hegemonic dominance which the control of inflation and the need for monetary vigilance – even in the face of rising unemployment – had over policy; however, it also emphasises the Labour government's historic eagerness to pacify dominant interests by reversing its strategy in order to assume an air of governing competence and political expediency. The result was indeed a return to economic orthodoxy.

In effect, these were the final death throes of the largely rhetorical commitment to Keynesianism and social democracy. According to Morgan (1990: 378): 'the spectre of supply-side monetarism was abroad in the land'. The year 1975 had been a crucial turning point in Labour's expansionist strategy (Overbeek 1990: 168), but the final nail in its coffin was the economic crisis of 1976. Throughout its term in office the Party had been besieged by economic difficulties. Inflation had spiralled upwards, reaching crisis levels in 1975. Moreover, the balance of payments gradually worsened and, eventually, major pressure was placed upon sterling. As had happened so often in the past, it was the crisis of sterling, and the government's efforts to deal with it, which brought a final halt to the government's strategy. With the pound falling against the dollar in 1976, the government appealed to the International Monetary Fund for credit. At the time, monetarism had gained a virtual ascendancy, both within Britain's financial institutions and abroad (Overbeek 1990: 170–1). Thus, when Britain applied for assistance to the IMF, the chance was seized upon by interests both outside and inside the government to force Labour into tight controls on wages, spending and the overall money supply. At that year's Labour Party Conference, Callaghan, who had by now taken over from Wilson, made a historic speech which acknowledged the government's final abandonment of Keynesianism.

Thus, the period of Keynesian-corporatist expansion suffered the same fate as earlier attempts at increasing the capacities of the state. Effectively of course, the government had abandoned its left-wing programme by 1975, but the year 1976 and the intervention of the International Monetary Fund were perhaps more symbolic of the death of this final attempt at state expansionism (Overbeek 1990: 172). Again, the events of the period highlight the overall lack of real attempts to transform the fundamental nature of the state. As Coates observed soon after the government eventually left office:

> the NEB was a pale shadow of the institution designed in opposition. Planning agreements had simply not materialised. A significant degree of industrial democracy had not been achieved. And the degree of poverty and social inequality remaining in 1979 stood in stark contrast to the Labour Party's claim in opposition that it could achieve a 'fundamental and irreversible shift in the balance of power and wealth in favour of working people and their families'.
>
> (Coates 1980: 148)

Of course, it is true to say that the government did face a hefty number of constraints. Yet nevertheless, the commitment of the leadership to the radical objectives of the left had been weak, and their overall commitment to a strategy of governing competence had been as strong as that of past Labour governments. Thus, although the essential character of Keynesian policy-making had changed to a limited extent in the period 1972–6, the effects of this change were to be short-lived. The strategy had ultimately been damaged by the failure of past governments to: institutionalise a social-democratic ethos into the fabric of the state; disrupt the dominance that the Treasury and financial institutions exercised over policy; remove the short-term fixation with inflation and the value of sterling in favour of a focus upon long-term economic growth; and provide the appropriate mechanisms to make industrial strategy work. Labour had failed to learn from past mistakes; indeed, it had hardly seemed to notice that any mistakes had been made at all.

1945–7
Liberal welfare
expansion

Implementation of wartime plans for welfare provision along with nationalisation of core industries and utilities.

1947–62
Liberal Keynesian
retreat

Austerity measures and 'bonfire of controls' begin state withdrawal and long period of minimal government.

1962–6
Liberal corporatist
expansion

Recognition of decline provokes moves towards quasi-corporatist expansion and limited state intervention.

1966–72
Retreat from liberal
corporatism

Devaluation and Labour 'U-turn'. Retreat from quasi-corporatism and attacks on trade unions.

1972–6
Keynesian corporatist
expansion

Heath 'U-turn'. Moves back to quasi-expansion. 'Social contract and alternative economic strategy'.

Figure 5.1 Strategic adaptation from 1945 to 1976

Conclusion

The year 1976 is often regarded as the key conjunctural moment when Keynesianism and corporate-liberalism were finally laid to rest and replaced by monetarism. According to Riddell (1983: 58–9) the main ingredients of Thatcherism were 'contained in the Letter of Intent sent by Denis Healey as Chancellor of the Exchequer to the International Monetary Fund in December 1976'. In the words of Dutton (1991: 74): 'the control of inflation had overtaken the maintenance of full employment in the hierarchy of economic objectives'.

As we have seen however, this assumption is only partially credible. Certainly, the rhetorical commitments to corporatist expansion, Keynesian demand management, the pursuit of full employment over inflation and a close working partnership between government and unions, were all effectively put to rest. However, it is entirely misleading to suggest that these aims had ever constituted the main ingredients of government policy throughout the postwar era. The development of British politics in the period 1945–76 can only be characterised as following an evolutionary path which was, at best, fitful. It was fitful in the sense that government policy had alternated dramatically between a series of attempts to expand the state using different combinations of measures, and subsequent periods of state retrenchment dominated by a return to economic orthodoxy. In the former periods, objectives such as the maintenance of full employment, greater cooperation between government and producer groups, and the need to extend the role of the state, were afforded priority; however, in the latter cases it was issues such as inflation, reductions in public expenditure, control over sterling and attacks upon the trade unions that had dominated policy, most often at the expense of full employment, industrial intervention and social democracy.

As a result then, evolution in the early postwar period reflected a fundamental 'struggle for survival' between different and often contradictory conceptions of what the main content of policy should be. At no point did full employment ever succeed in overtaking the control of inflation 'in the hierarchy of economic objectives'. Rather, the twin commitments to maintaining full employment and a low rate of inflation co-existed in an uneasy relationship, while ultimately, when it came to a choice between one or the other, it was invariably full employment that had to give way to Treasury demands to deflate. At various points, governments were forced to abandon their domestic commitments in favour of sound monetary policies. Thus, the Labour government's conversion to monetarism in 1976 was only the latest in a long series of attempts to implement policies that showed a broad continuity with what was to be later known as 'Thatcherism'.

What this should tell us, then, is that key elements of 'Thatcherite' philosophy were already present in many of the policies implemented throughout the early postwar period. The evolution of policy before 1976 had been dominated by a continual struggle between progressive and classical liberal ideas and, by the end of that period, the latter had gained an absolute victory in the ascendancy of the New Right.

6 Struggling for survival

The conflictual nature of early postwar British politics

We drag along, knowing and caring little about the world we live in, falling farther and farther behind most other advanced countries, and yet still supposing
that others share our view of our own importance. It is a pathetic spectacle.

(Magee 1962: 184)

Introduction

In the previous chapter, we saw that the evolution of policy in the early
postwar period is best characterised as 'fitful'. In particular, I identified a
continual and evolving struggle for survival between competing and conflicting conceptions of government strategy. In this chapter, the aim is to
develop this empirical observation theoretically by interrogating the main
evolutionary mechanisms which contributed to the lack of continuity in
public policy. Building upon the evolutionary schema outlined in Chapter
Four, I will look at: the major environmental pressures that were brought to
bear upon the implementation of policy; the subjective responses to these by
the main actors of the period; and the processes of political learning that
stemmed from such factors. Overall, I will argue that the overwhelming conflictual pressures placed upon governments in the postwar period created
an environment in which two distinct evolutionary trajectories emerged: a
progressive tendency towards state expansion, and an accompanying, but
no less visible, tendency towards retrenchment. The outcome of these distinct policy evolutions, as we have seen, was a continual oscillation in
government strategy between Keynesian expansion and liberal retreat, an
oscillation which seriously hampered the ability of successive governments
to learn how to deal effectively with Britain's accelerating economic decline.

Environmental conditioning and selection in the early postwar period

Here, it is worth repeating that in order to gain a holistic understanding of the
evolution of political action and state transformation, we need to examine the

dynamic and dialectical relationship between the strategies formulated by governmental actors and the strategically selective environments in which these are played out. As Overbeek (1990: 82) explains: 'the task of the political scientist is to analyse the precise manner in which structural forces and consciously pursued strategic action of social forces become intertwined'. So far, I have considered the main types of strategic adaptation that were employed by politicians during the postwar era. Towards the end of this chapter I will consider how these policy adaptations were shaped and constrained both by agents' selection of their strategic objectives and by strategic learning over time. In the meantime, however, it is important to examine the environmental selection pressures that affected the evolution of strategy. Here, we must consider not only the interaction between agents and their environments, but also the relationship between the external, domestic and discursive environments themselves.

The international environment

One of the main factors which contributed to the struggle over ideas about policy-making in the early postwar period was the contradictory commitments made by politicians towards an external policy of economic liberalism, and a domestic policy based, at times, around largely corporate-liberal ideas. These contradictory commitments had their roots in the deliberate strategic choices made by the main political actors; however, they were also firmly conditioned by selective pressures within the international political and economic environment that emerged out of the war. Here, we can consider two main factors in the international environment which helped to shape the evolution of British domestic policy: first, the growth of the world economy in the immediate aftermath of war followed by the period of stagnation and recession of the 1970s; and, second, the dominance of the United States within the new economic and interstate system. These factors are, of course, all closely intertwined; nevertheless, here we need to separate out as much as possible the relative impact that each had upon the selection of strategy in Britain.

Boom and bust in the international economy

The first factor to consider then is the cyclical trend of postwar economic development that resulted in the 'boom' in world markets directly after the war, followed by the stagnation and recession that developed after the oil crisis in 1973. To long-wave theorists of economic evolution, there is an inherent tendency for capitalism to develop through successive phases of relative growth and stagnation (see for example Freeman 1982; Wallerstein 1983; Taylor 1989; Mandel 1995; Hopkins and Wallerstein *et al.* 1996). Commonly referred to as 'Kondratieff waves' these cycles are normally assumed to span about fifty to sixty years or so, reflecting changes in technology and the balance of power within the world economic and state system. The development of the world economy throughout the postwar period is often assumed to have mirrored the onset of a twenty-five to thirty year Kondratieff A-phase (period of growth) followed by a B-phase (of stagnation) from the early 1970s.

The 'boom' phase began almost directly after the war and was aided by factors such as positive American intervention in postwar reconstruction, a rapid expansion in world trade following the dismantling of restrictions, and a backlog in worldwide demand caused by the war. At the time however, the massive growth in the world economy came as something of a surprise to policy-makers. This is due to the experience of the inter-war years, when the question of how to avoid economic stagnation, recession and crisis had become the dominant issue in economic thinking. According to Cronin (1996: 64): 'the notion that steady growth could become the norm in capitalist economies was foreign to the thinking of the generation of economists and policy-makers who came to maturity when the world economy was trapped in a prolonged crisis'.

Although the postwar boom had begun during the period of reconstruction immediately after the war, it was given a major impetus with the increased military spending that resulted from the Korean War in 1950. This helped to consolidate the general growth in manufacturing and trade, and marked the beginning of what has subsequently been termed a 'golden age', lasting from the early 1950s to around the first oil shock in 1973. Between 1953 and 1963 world income increased by 3.7 per cent per year and world trade at 6.5 per cent (Cairncross 1994: 35). In the ten years after that, the cycle of growth increased with world income expanding at 5.2 per cent per year and world trade by 8.9 per cent (ibid.). All in all, this remarkable phase of growth represented 'the most massive expansion the world-economy has experienced in the whole of the 500 year existence of the modern world-system' (Hopkins and Wallerstein *et al.* 1996: 1).

In order to explain the expansion of the state in the early postwar period then, we need to place this political development within the context of the unprecedented expansion in economic growth and the selective pressures which this placed upon domestic policy-makers. This is the point made by long-wave theorists, who assert that the integration and competitiveness of global markets forces pressures upon all states to accommodate themselves to the wider evolutionary trajectory of the world economy. To date though, the most comprehensive explanations of the relationship between global economic trends in the postwar period and the adaptation to these by domestic political actors have come from regulation theorists (see for example Aglietta 1979; Lipietz 1987; Boyer 1990; Jessop 1990b). The central thrust of regulation theory is that any fundamental reorganization of the production process in order to stimulate economic growth must be supplemented by state regulation to ensure that the new production methods are able to achieve the greatest amount of efficiency. Specifically, each major growth stage in the evolution of capitalism is made up of at least 'three legs of a tripod' (Lipietz 1992: 1). These three basic elements are: a model or 'paradigm' governing the labour process ; a regime of accumulation ; and, an accompanying mode of regulation.[1] This complementary package constitutes what is commonly referred to as a 'development model' (ibid.). The development model which accompanied the postwar boom in world markets has invariably been identified as 'Fordism'.[2] Fordism consisted of both a way of organizing the production process and a mode of regulating the social environment in which production takes place.

Specifically, Fordism can be broken down into its three constitutive elements. As a labour process model it involved: 'mass production based on moving assembly line techniques operated with the semi-skilled labour of the mass worker' (Jessop 1992: 18–19). As a regime of accumulation it involved a 'virtuous circle' based on: increases in productivity gained from economies of scale; accompanying increases in workers incomes in line with greater productivity; increased demand and consumption power due to rising standards of living; increased profits due to mass consumption; and increased investment in mass production equipment. Third, as a mode of regulation, Fordism involved among other things: the provision of social welfare to guarantee a minimum standard of living and consumption power; union recognition and collective wage bargaining; wages indexed to productivity and retail price inflation; and monetary and credit policies to maintain effective aggregate demand. Consequently, the success of Fordism at the level of production depended upon a 'grand compromise' which allowed greater power to trade unions and increased spending power to consumers (Lipietz 1992: 5). In this respect, it was recognised that mass production could only work as long as the level of demand in the economy was raised sufficiently to allow mass consumption. Thus, a significant degree of state intervention was required in order to stimulate demand and raise the overall standard of living.

The literature on Fordism alerts us to the fact that changes in the level of production throughout the 1920s and 1930s exerted pressures upon all governments in the advanced economies to select policies that would complement the evolutionary trajectory of global capitalism. By the end of the war, due largely to the intervention of influential spokesmen such as Keynes and Beveridge, it was being widely recognised that the state would have to adapt itself in order to meet the demands of the changed economic environment. Throughout the 1930s the maladaptation of government policies and economic practices had been clearly demonstrated by the 'gigantic crisis of overproduction' which had resulted in the Great Depression (Lipietz 1992: 5). This does not mean, however, that these pressures can be considered to have (*over*)-determined the direction of state policy. Some smaller economies, such as Denmark, Sweden and Austria, achieved mass consumption levels by filling non-Fordist niches within the global economy, while the majority of the major economies opted to compete within the main Fordist production sectors (Jessop 1992: 20). The important point though is that, in order to gain the benefits of growth, each nation would have to adapt in some way or another to the overall dominant Fordist logic. This meant that pressure was placed upon all advanced nation states to develop policies that would actively help to modernise production, and stimulate demand through extending welfare provision and maintaining a high level of employment.

Thus, when we come to explain the development of a commitment to welfare reform, high levels of employment, and corporate-liberal strategies to modernise industry, we need to examine the way in which this had evolved alongside the growing realisation that government policy had been previously maladapted to meet the needs of production. This is a point which is too rarely acknowledged within the literature on postwar British politics, where the emphasis is invariably placed upon the driving force of ideas such as those introduced by Keynes and Beveridge and personalities such as Attlee and Bevan as if either of these factors existed within a vacuum. Both the ideas which dominated the early postwar period, and the personalities who implemented them, were operating with a global environment which was strategically selective; those nations that adapted most successfully to meet the needs of the production process would gain a clear competitive advantage over those countries that had failed to adapt.

We may well ask ourselves then, why Britain, with its commitment to meeting the Fordist compromise failed to achieve such a competitive advantage. The answer to this lies in the fact that Britain's commitment to Fordism was relatively weak. Britain's struggle for survival within the competitive global market was hampered by the internal struggle for survival of ideas about domestic policy within the UK itself. There was an overall lack of consensus over how Britain should adapt itself to meet the changing needs of the new economic environment. While some argued for industrial modernisation and extensive structural reform, others were clinging firmly to the defence of the status quo and the priority of securing the role of sterling as an international currency. Consequently, Britain's adaptation to Fordism remained incomplete (Jessop 1992: 20).

The failure of British policy-makers and indeed, industrialists, to modernise the production process and forge an effective partnership between employers and unions meant that Britain's returns from mass production techniques were poorer than most of her competitors. As a result, demand in Britain became increasingly met through imported rather than domestically manufactured goods. These factors, coupled with the position of the City within the global market, and the tendency for British industry to cling to former imperial markets rather than the dynamic Fordist economies, contributed to Britain's relatively poor performance within the international hierarchy. According to Jessop therefore:

Britain's mode of growth can be described as 'flawed Fordist'. It
involved a limited expansion of mass production, relatively poor
productivity growth, union strength producing wage increases from
1960s onwards not justified by productivity growth, a precocious
commitment to social welfare and jobs for all, growing import pene-
tration from the 1960s to satisfy the mass consumer market and, from
the mid-1970s, to meet demand for capital goods.

(Jessop 1992: 21)

Even so, Britain's system of 'flawed Fordism' did initially produce enough
growth to satisfy postwar politicians and to stifle any initiatives to
modernise the production process. However, as the relative decline of the
British economy became more apparent through the late 1950s and early
1960s the need to adapt was eventually recognised, and resulted in the
move towards liberal-corporatist expansion under Macmillan and Wilson.
However, these moves were severely constrained by: the former decision to
restore the City's international position; institutional constraints on the
domestic front; and the overall schizophrenic nature of the commitments
endorsed by postwar politicians. As a result, Britain's system of 'flawed
Fordism' remained intact, with the result that, by the late 1960s and early
1970s when economic growth had began to dissipate and global Fordism
entered a period of crisis, Britain's economic decline became even sharper
(Jessop 1992: 21).

The first signs of a crisis in the postwar global economic order came in
1966–7 with a recession which touched most of the advanced capitalist
economies (Overbeek 1990: 144). This marked the beginning of a gradual
downturn in economic growth and the exhaustion of Fordism as the
dominant development model. Underlying the crisis was a fall in profits
reflecting a slowing down in the growth of labour productivity from the
1960s. Moreover, as Wallerstein (1996: 211–12) explains: 'whereas in the
1950s the leading sectors had been relatively monopolised by a small
group of enterprises on the world level, the number of competitors had
grown considerably in the 1960s; the field had become crowded'. This
trend, although evident from the late 1960s, was sealed by the oil crisis of
1973 which dramatically plunged the world economy into recession.

To long-wave analysts this represented the onset of Kondratieff B-phase
in the world economy, while to regulation theorists it marked a crisis in
global Fordism. In either case, the result was a global (though spatially
uneven) increase in inflation and unemployment, leading eventually to a
'fiscal crisis of the state' as governments continued to pour increasing
amounts of resources into supporting the extra burden placed upon welfare provision (O'Connor 1973; Overbeek 1990: 144–5; Pelizzon and
Casparis 1996: 132–5; Wallerstein 1996: 212). Throughout the western
world the change in the economic environment shattered confidence in
Keynesian and corporatist solutions. Centrist and reformist politics

became increasingly challenged as sharp divisions emerged between the left and right. These divisions, although relatively muted in Britain, were reflected in the growth of left-wing militancy in the labour movement towards the end of the 1960s, and the gradual ascendancy of the New Right within the Conservative Party. Overall, the growing crisis in the world economy, mirrored in the fiscal crisis within national state structures, was forcing pressures upon all nation states to select appropriate strategies to deal with the impasse. In Britain and the US these pressures were particularly acute and led to:

> a rapid, schizophrenic succession of policies to reverse our national decline. Sometimes the government stressed liberal market solutions, sometimes it preferred corporatist strategies and sometimes (in despair at market failures and the weakness of its supposed social partners) it resorted to dirigiste solutions.
>
> (Jessop 1992: 22)

Ultimately however, the outcome of this struggle between competing conceptions of state strategy was heavily conditioned by the overall crisis in the international economic environment. As the fiscal crisis of the state heightened, the voice of the New Right grew louder in international circles, particularly in both the US and Britain where the postwar commitment to statism had been relatively weak. As Overbeek explains:

> it was only towards the end of the 1960s that structural transformations in the world economy and a realignment of political forces within Britain transformed the neo-liberal set of ideas into a realistic (that is feasible) political programme, into a concept of control and eventually into the dominating concept of the 1980s.
>
> (Overbeek 1990: 28)

Monetarism as an economic ideology had begun to penetrate leading international financial institutions and, with the growing integration of the world economy, there were increasing pressures upon most advanced national governments to select measures to deal with their fiscal crises by alleviating the burden of welfare expenditure through cuts in public spending (Pelizzon and Casparis 1996: 135). In some cases, these environmental pressures were indirect and channelled through the persistent calls from leading economists and journalists for governments to respond to the crisis through the selection *of* interventions which helped to curb inflation; however, in other cases the pressure was much more direct and channelled through the positive intervention of financial institutions that could use their considerable influence to force governments to select *for* monetarist strategies.[3] The latter was most directly manifested in Britain when in 1976 the IMF was able to impose loan conditions on the Labour government which effectively selected for a monetarist strategy based around the control of inflation and the money-supply.

The important point here, and one which is too rarely acknowledged within the literature, is that the evolution of policy in postwar Britain was heavily conditioned by selective pressures imposed by changes in the global economic environment. At the beginning of the period these had forced all governments in the advanced sectors of the world economy to adopt policies which would stimulate demand through welfare provision and compromises between capital and labour. Towards the end of the period however, these pressures had become inverted amid growing inflation, unemployment and general recession so that the emphasis was placed upon the adaptation of strategy in order to curb public expenditures and reduce the burden of welfare provision. As we shall see however, these global economic conditions combined with other environmental selection pressures, both external and internal. On the international front, these included the onset of US hegemony within the global interstate system, along with Britain's changing status in world affairs.

Britain's changing world role in the period of US hegemony

The boom in world markets and the spread of global Fordism directly after the Second World War did not occur within a political vacuum; rather, it owed much to the environmental conditions created by the United States (Ikeda 1996: 63). The dominant position of the US within the international economic and interstate system had been taking shape since as early as the 1870s (Arrighi 1994: 58; Wallerstein 1996: 215). At that time, the former period of British hegemony was beginning to enter a B-phase and the USA and Germany had emerged as the main challengers to Britain's dominant international status. As Arrighi (1994: 59) explains: 'the German and US challenges to British world power strengthened one another, compromised the ability of Britain to govern the inter-state system, and eventually led to a new struggle for world supremacy of unprecedented violence and viciousness'. Two main factors helped to determine the outcome of this struggle. The first was the fact that Britain had decided fiercely to resist German hopes of world dominance while conceding relatively tamely to the hegemonic aspirations of the United States (Gamble 1994: 59).

The second factor which allowed the US to emerge as the dominant power after the war was the fact that, unlike most of its competitors, its productive base had been left relatively intact. As a result then: 'it was able quickly to transform this economic advantage into a political, military and even cultural advantage that continued and grew in the immediate postwar period' (Wallerstein 1996: 215). In contrast, Britain's own productive base had been severely damaged by the war, while its international economic position had not fared any better (see Overbeek 1990: 90). With its international hegemony relatively unchallenged, the United

States emerged from the war able to forge an economic and political environment which would be selective towards its own interests, while Britain was left to select a strategy that would enable it to adapt to its changed global status.

On the part of the US, measures were quickly taken to ensure that appropriate selection mechanisms were put in place to guarantee its continued dominance. The first of these was the creation of the Bretton Woods system which forged institutions such as the International Monetary Fund and the World Bank. The purpose of such action was to secure the dollar as the leading world currency, and to create the conditions for 'the liberalisation of the movement of goods, services and capital' (Ikeda 1996: 64). This, in turn, facilitated the ability of the US to utilise its relative productive efficiency and flood foreign markets with American mass-produced goods. According to Arrighi (1994: 68), these institutions, together with the newly established United Nations: 'either became supplementary instruments wielded by the US government in the exercise of its world hegemonic functions or, if they could not be used in this way, were impeded in the exercise of their own institutional functions'.

The next major step taken by the Americans to ensure their status as hegemon was the withdrawal of the system of Lend-Lease that had provided financial assistance to Britain's war effort.[4] This had the effect of undermining Britain's attempts at reconstruction and eventually forced the British government to seek a formal loan laden with US conditions. The terms of the Washington Loan – that Britain should not discriminate against American goods in its imperial markets and that sterling should be made convertible within a year – 'spelled out fairly clearly the new balance between Britain and America' (Gamble 1994: 107). All in all, throughout the negotiations over the loan, the British had been 'unable to resist a series of dreary capitulations' which were to ultimately deprive them of much of their autonomy over both their foreign and domestic policy (Brett 1985: 139).

The third major step in the process by which the US strengthened its international position was the introduction of a substantial package of assistance to the major European economies in order to aid postwar reconstruction. This was achieved through Marshall Aid which, by 1951, had redistributed twelve billion dollars to Western Europe to assist economic recovery (Dorey 1995: 32). The Marshall Aid programme had two aims. First, it was designed to counter the growing spread of communism in Eastern Europe by strengthening the capitalist economies in the West. Second and perhaps more important, the programme acted as a: 'precondition for the transatlantic expansion of Fordism' (Overbeek 1990: 91). In this sense, it was designed to improve living conditions in Western Europe in order to facilitate the consumption of American exported goods. Overall, the effect of the Marshall Plan was to consolidate the development of the liberalisation of the world economy, enable national governments to stimulate domestic demand (which in turn could be met with an increasing share of US imports) and lay the foundations for the international political and military settlement that would later result in the Cold War.

Yet there was one final step in the process by which the US dictated the international environment in which postwar evolution took place. This came in 1950 in the wake of the Korean War. Shortly before the war, the US Secretary of State, Dean Acheson, had advocated a massive rearmament programme in order to influence the balance of power in Europe, and simultaneously aid the 'dollar gap' problem in the balance of payments (Reifer and Sudler 1996: 18). Initially, Congress opposed such a policy; however, the outbreak of war in Korea proved the catalyst for guaranteed Congressional approval (ibid.). As a result, the US increased its military expenditures by more than three-fold, providing the final conditions for the long period of 'postwar boom'. Moreover, the rearmament programme also set the final seal on the Cold War by significantly increasing US military presence in Western Europe while 'enmeshing US allies into a US-dominated security structure' (ibid.: 19).

In the new international environment Britain selected a strategy which enabled it to adapt to American leadership; however, its search for a new role was heavily shaped both by its former imperial hegemony and the environmental conditions set by the US. Somewhat surprisingly, the initial position of the British economy in the immediate postwar years was relatively favourable. Several factors outwith the sphere of American control had helped to ensure a rapid recovery for Britain's exports: high global demand; a lack of worldwide competition; protection from American competition in imperial markets; the inconvertibility of sterling; and the dollar shortage (Overbeek 1990: 90). However, as early as 1947 two of these factors – the protection from US competition and the inconvertibility of sterling – were removed by the terms of the Washington Loan agreement. During the negotiations over the Loan, Britain's international strategic aims had been set out by its representative in Washington, John Maynard Keynes. According to Keynes, the primary objective was to restore 'for London its ancient prestige and its hegemony' while avoiding being 'hopelessly at the mercy of the United States' (ibid.; also Brett 1985: 137–8). However, as Overbeek explains: 'Britain succeeded in the first objective precisely by accepting the second, undesirable but unavoidable, consequence' (ibid.).

This remained the story as far as British foreign policy was concerned throughout the postwar period; repeated attempts were made to salvage the last vestiges of Britain's international status, but only at the expense of a complete capitulation to the US. This policy was underpinned by Britain's decision to play the role of 'hegemonic mate' to the Americans (Taylor 1989: 27–8). In return for retaining a significant degree of prestige on the world stage, the British agreed to act as a 'willing American client' (Brett 1985: 141). In this sense, Britain's role was to aid US economic and military expansion by safeguarding the liberalisation of the world economy and standing at the forefront of the fight against communism. However, as I shall go on discuss, the result of this strategy was an increasing tension between domestic and foreign policy as Britain struggled futilely to maintain both. Ultimately, this tension became one of the major factors responsible for Britain's fitful evolution and its eventual 'decline into economic and political mediocrity' (ibid.).

It is often claimed that the basis for Britain's capitulation to the international environment created by the Americans lay in five main events: the 1945 Washington Loan agreement; the crisis of convertibility in 1947; Marshall Aid; the devaluation of sterling in 1949; and the rearmament programme following the Korean War (Burnham 1990: 5). Each case, albeit to different degrees, emphasised a growing loss of autonomy to the United States. This loss of autonomy is most often referred to as the 'special relationship': an alliance between Britain and America which was 'more special for the British than for the Americans, because it was the means by which the British world role was preserved – by being transferred to the Americans' (Gamble 1994: 105). Specifically, the US allowed Britain to retain its international status in two main ways. First, in response to intense pressure from the British, the City of London was restored as a global financial centre, with sterling retained as an international medium of exchange. Second, Britain was allowed to retain extensive military commitments in particular parts of the globe, including Greece, the Middle East, Singapore and Malaysia (ibid.: 106). As regards the first of these concessions, the US had responded to Britain's insistence that sterling should remain 'world money' (Ingham 1984: 203). This was to be achieved in the short term by the Americans underwriting sterling via the Washington Loan, and in the long term by continued support from the US when required.[5] Overall, this decision had two main consequences for the evolution of postwar British politics. First, it formed the basis of the restoration of the City as a major commercial and banking centre. The consequence was the strengthening of the position of financial capital on the domestic front. Second, as Ingham (1984: 205) argues: 'once sterling had secured its international status, it was almost inevitable that the Bank of England and the Treasury would regain their prewar powers in the field of economic management'. Overall, the preservation of sterling, along with the accompanying revival of the City–Bank–Treasury nexus, exerted important selection pressures on the development of domestic policy. In particular, it proved a major factor in deflecting postwar governments from implementing planned growth and ensuring the maintenance of a stable level of full employment.

The retention of extensive military ambitions imposed additional selection pressures. Britain's willingness to extend its military commitments, and therefore ensure the security of the liberal capitalist system against the spread of communism, was one of the key factors that had persuaded the US to humour Britain's ambition to retain its international status. However, as

Gamble (1994: 109) explains: 'Britain emerged as one of the two states bearing the costs of maintaining an international economic and political order, yet it no longer had the industrial base to support such costs'. Military spending in the postwar period, particularly overseas military spending, was higher than any other American ally; indeed, it was even higher in real terms than it had been at the height of the Empire (ibid.: 110). Ultimately, the cost of maintaining this commitment was to prove incompatible, not only with Britain's domestic political responsibilities, but also with its foreign policy of retaining an international world role.

Here in effect then, was an important basis for the struggle of survival over ideas which had dominated the evolution of postwar British politics. The machismo foreign policy of attempting to stand alongside the United States, which brought with it the undue preservation of sterling, the strong commitment to a liberalised international economy and the burden of extensive military commitments that it could not afford, conflicted strongly with the domestic aim of modernising British industry and maintaining a comprehensive system of welfare provision. Overall, 'a sometimes slavish and faintly ludicrous' British support for US ambitions (Brett 1985: 140), combined with British pretension on the international level, forced selective pressures for the abandonment of either its domestic or its foreign policy commitments. As we have previously seen, the major casualty was the implementation of much of the former. Despite the subsequent loss of Empire and the eventual contraction of its overseas commitments, the selective pressures that British policy-makers faced from the global economic and political environment ultimately resulted in Britain attempting futilely to maintain its international status while consistently reversing the policies needed to secure Fordist restructuring.

The domestic environment

We cannot of course assume that such global environmental pressures were (*over*)-determining in their effects on government strategy. It is equally important to examine the ways in which the main conflicts of the postwar era, and ultimately Britain's fitful evolution into decline, were conditioned by domestic selection pressures. This means that we must examine the evolving dialectical interaction between external and internal selection mechanisms. As Jessop (1980: 30) explains: 'if the international decline was largely due to irresistible external forces, it was aggravated by internal forces that delayed and distorted British adaptation to the changed conditions'.

Here I will focus upon two main related internal factors which heavily conditioned the selection of policy: the institutionalised strength of financial capital; and the relatively weak position of politicians and producer groups. Overall, the combination of these factors ensured that the struggle for survival between competing conceptions of government strategy was played out within a domestic institutional context, which favoured the selection of policies geared towards the priority of maintaining Britain's overseas commitments.

The dominant role of financial capital

As we have already noted, the international orientation of the British economy has both strengthened the position of the City of London and, indeed, enabled it to prosper even through Britain's postwar descent into economic and political decline. A major factor in this has been the gradual postwar growth in financial and banking services. In Britain, from 1961 to 1983 annual real growth in banking, finance, insurance and business services was 4.3 per cent: more than twice the rate of growth for all UK industries and four times the growth in manufacturing (Johnson 1985: 34–7). Moreover, this growth was accompanied by a significant expansion in the share of employment; in the same period employment in financial services showed an annual growth rate of 3.7 per cent compared with an average fall of 1.3 per cent a year in manufacturing employment. As a result then, the postwar period saw an almost parallel development between the decline in manufacturing sectors and the growth in financial services. Yet, this development does not explain the dominant position of financial capital in Britain; rather, it represents both an extension and a reflection of its historical and institutionalised strength.

Throughout the period of *Pax Britannica* the City of London was able to establish itself as the foremost international financial centre because of a combination of factors: British domination in global production and trade; the leading role of sterling within the international monetary system; and the political stability associated with Britain's imperial and hegemonic position (Jessop 1980: 30). The global dominance of the City was consolidated by 1870 and reached its peak at the beginning of the twentieth century. It was founded upon a specialisation in servicing international commerce and foreign capital markets. Given that Britain was at this point the 'workshop of the world' for both capital and consumer goods, the City's international focus presented no real problem for the interests of industrial capital. As Overbeek (1990: 107) explains: 'on the contrary, the expansion of industrial capital went hand in hand with, even depended on, the successful operation of the City of London as the dominant international centre of commerce and finance'. Overall then, this 'initial community of interest' helped to consolidate 'the political and ideological hegemony of financial capital in the British Establishment' (Jessop 1980: 30). Since then, the internal hegemony of financial capital has endured and, indeed, has been strengthened by the relative decline of industrial capital, while its effects can be seen in the conduct of government strategy throughout the postwar period.

The overwhelming influence of the City over government policy resides partly on the 'exceptionalism' which it has enjoyed from government inter-ference (Grant 1993: 74). This has enabled a situation to develop in which 'issues which might be awkward to it have not appeared on the political agenda' (ibid.). In addition, the City also has 'a number of sanctions at its disposal', including the ability to conduct 'gilt-strikes', a coordinated refusal to buy government stock (ibid.: 75). However, the main factor that has determined its influence has been the support which it has received from outwith the financial sector. This has come mainly from the other two central institutions at the heart of the machinery of government, the Treasury and the Bank of England. This central 'nexus' has contributed significantly to providing the views of financial capital with a powerful and largely uncontested political legitimacy.

Yet the position of the financial sector was less than favourable in the immediate aftermath of the war. As Ingham (1984: 202) points out: 'the war and the long term development of the economy had produced a gloomy outlook for Britain, and one in which there was little justification for a claim to resume the mantle of the capitalist world's commercial and banking centre'. In addition, given wartime planning, financial capital's powerful ally, the Treasury, had been temporarily subordinated within the machinery of government. Nevertheless, even in the face of such powerful factors mil-itating against the restoration of the City, it did not take long before its erstwhile status was re-established. The key factor in this was the decision by British (and American) policy-makers to restore sterling as an international reserve currency. This decision had a double-edged impact on policy since, in helping to elevate the position of the City, the financial sector, in turn, ensured that the defence of sterling remained a priority throughout the remainder of the postwar period (Nairn 1986: 240). Moreover, the City's prominence was further consolidated after 1951, when the Conservatives re-established the traditional relationship between the City, the Bank of England and the Treasury. As Overbeek (1990: 108) explains:

> under the Conservative governments of the 1950s, relations between the City, the Bank of England and the Treasury were restored to their earlier self-evident normality, owing to the force of habit, the social background of the members of the government, and the newly recon-firmed hegemony of the City over the economy.
>
> (Overbeek 1990: 108)

With the City's position fully restored and sterling's role in the international currency markets at least temporarily secured, the domestic environment was now constituted in such as way as to give rise to, and indeed heavily con-dition the outcome of, the conflicts which were to characterise the remainder of the postwar period. The main conflict, as we have seen, was between the priority of maintaining Britain's overseas commitments and the need to restructure the productive base in order to adapt to the increased competitiveness in the international environment. The close relationship between the City, the Bank and the Treasury ensured that, whenever this conflict arose, appropriate pressure was placed upon the government to select policies which favoured the former objective. Together, these three institutions combined to create what Blank (1978: 120–1) has referred to as an 'overseas' or 'sterling' lobby which: 'shared the belief that Britain's international position and responsibilities constituted the primary policy objectives and that the international role of sterling was vital to this position' (ibid.). The most direct result of the selection pressures imposed by the 'sterling lobby' was Britain's infamous 'stop-go' cycle. Each time the British economy entered an expansionary period, disruption ensued in the balance of payments, due largely to Britain's propensity to import, its extensive overseas military expenditure and its substantial capital exports. This in turn placed pressure upon sterling and, as a result, the financial sector would press for a deflationary package to protect the pound as opposed to the alternative option of devaluation. As we have seen, it is this pattern of economic policy which has repeatedly conflicted with the efforts of policy-makers to expand the state and, in particular, to conduct a planned, coordinated industrial strategy. Thus, according to Blank:

> for much of the postwar period, domestic and international economic policy was dominated by and subordinated to the goals of foreign policy; goals which Britain was incapable of realising. Yet, the attempt to achieve these goals led successive governments to sacrifice the domestic economy again and again. . . . Efforts to create new policies and institutions whose purpose was to confront the problems of the domestic economy and to improve domestic economic performance foundered on the willingness of political leaders to abandon the most cherished symbol of Britain's international position by devaluing the pound.
>
> (Blank 1986: 207)

Moreover, as well as conflicting with attempts at state expansion, the sterling lobby's strict adherence to the policy of maintaining the priority of Britain's overseas commitments also conflicted with the general interests of industrial capital. As Jessop explains:

> the policies intended to maintain the position of sterling discouraged and distorted industrial investment through high interest rates to attract foreign funds and prevent the flight of 'hot money', restrictions on investment outside the sterling area, and recurrent bouts of deflation to restrain home demand and 'free' resources for export production.
>
> (Jessop 1980: 32)

In addition, the massive increases in 'unproductive' military spending in order to defend the sterling area also contributed to stifling industrial growth (ibid.). As a result then, the continued pursuit of the City's interests created an environment which was highly selective against the concerns of domestic industry.

We have already noted that, throughout the era of British hegemony, the international orientation of the City was highly compatible with the overseas expansion of domestic goods; however, in the context of increased competition from American and European markets throughout the postwar period, the interests of industrial and financial capital had significantly diverged. This divergence of interest became obvious by the late 1950s when those who spoke for the industrial sector began to press government to abandon the short-term obsession with sterling's role, and concentrate instead upon a planned, coordinated effort to modernise the industrial base. As we have seen, this resulted in the Macmillan government's move towards tripartite consultation and indicative planning, and ended abruptly when Wilson's own modernisation initiative collapsed amidst City pressure to deflate in order to prevent devaluation.

Throughout the postwar period then, the financial sector, in coordination with its allies within the state, has consistently operated as an important constraint on Britain's ability to adapt to the changed economic climate. The dominance of the City has created an environment that has been highly selective towards the strategic interests of the financial sector, at the expense of the domestic economy and the general interests of industrial capital. Without this dominance many of the conflicts which constrained the evolution of policy in the postwar period might have been avoided. Certainly the damaging effects of the 'stop-go' cycle would have been muted, and without the constant pressure to defend the value of sterling British policy-makers could have focused their attention more squarely on developing policies that were better suited to the need for Fordist restructuring. Having said this however, it is important not to overstate the point as the strength of the financial sector, and the priority given to defending sterling, was as much a product (as a cause) of the decision by successive governments to maintain Britain's international prestige. Moreover, the lack of any coherent strategy of economic modernisation also reflected both the relative inability of either industrial capital or organized labour to coordinate and articulate their interests and, as well, a lack of consensus among politicians as to whether or not increased state involvement was a desirable policy objective. Thus, the enormous influence of the City over policy represented only one of a number of internal factors that prohibited postwar evolution. These other factors deserve our attention in the following sections.

The weak capacity of the state, industry and labour

In order fully to comprehend the significant impact which financial capital has had upon British policy-making, it is equally important to examine the relative weakness of Britain's other two main producer groups, industrial capital and the trade union movement, as well as the weak capacity of the state to implement policies geared towards industrial intervention. British industry has instead suffered greatly from: the negative power and lack of coordination between and within the labour movement and industrial capital; the lack of close involvement by these parties in the formulation of policy; and the lack of any effective capacity (or indeed willingness) for the state to formulate any type of active industrial strategy. The combination of these factors has contributed to the environment in which financial capital has been effective in steering governments away from domestic concerns and dirigiste measures, and towards selecting an overall arm's length approach to economic management in order to satisfy Britain's foreign policy commitments.

The weakness of industrial capital and the labour movement relative to financial capital has its roots in the early process of industrialisation. The fact that Britain was one of the first leading industrialised nations meant that its industrial sector evolved and expanded rapidly into a fragmented and largely uncoordinated productive base: 'with a large range of products, a complex mixture of technologies, a correspondingly elaborate system of occupational groups, skill levels, and work tasks' (Jessop 1980: 34). The result of this rapid and uncontrolled evolution was: 'an initially low level of concentration and centralisation of industrial capital' (ibid.). Moreover, this fragmented system was also reflected in the composition of the labour movement. This, in turn, has: 'inhibited the development of a centralised collective bargaining system and also encouraged strong union organization at plant and company level' (ibid.). This relative lack of coordination within each has endured, and has constrained the ability of both the labour movement and productive capital clearly to express their respective strategic interests. In addition, on the rare occasions when a relative degree of coordination has been achieved by either fraction, neither has been able to impose enough sustained selective pressure upon government to break the historical and institutionalised hegemony of the financial sector.

As far as industry is concerned, the early lead in the process of industrialisation had at least two other, perhaps even more profound, long-term effects. First, it bequeathed to British industry technologies, productive techniques and organizational arrangements that would soon become outmoded and uncompetitive. As Coates explains:

> the organization of industrial production in Britain emerged as too small in scale, too defensive in orientation and too anchored in old industries, methods of production and markets, to be able to withstand easily the growing scale, intensity and quality of foreign competition.
>
> (Coates 1986: 269)

The second long-term effect which Britain's early lead in manufacturing produced was an overall separation between industrial and financial capital. Initially, the monopoly position enjoyed by British industrialists, as well as the vast opportunities available for them to exploit overseas, meant that they were less reliant upon bank capital than their international competitors were to become.

On the part of finance capital, the relative autonomy of the industrial sector and the opening up of imperial markets encouraged the City and the banks to look abroad for their profits. As we have already noted, this international orientation was initially beneficial to both sectors; however, once the monopoly position of British industry began to crumble amid stiff overseas competition, the interests of both fractions began to diverge. According to Coates:

> nationally-based industrialists found themselves locked into increasingly outmoded industries and production methods, while at the same time being both disadvantaged in their access to long-term credit relative to their competitors, and subject to a political class in which financial interests had a disproportionately strong voice.
>
> (Coates 1986: 269)

Moreover, due to its low levels of concentration and centralisation, industrial capital did not possess the capacity to rectify its relative backwardness (Jessop 1980: 34). Rather, its response was to turn increasingly towards the protection afforded by Britain's imperial markets. The long term effect was to reinforce the hegemony of the financial sector which was able to provide enough revenue to finance the growing trade deficit: 'thus British capital tended to neglect its domestic industrial base in favour of industrial and portfolio investment overseas and acting as a middleman in international transactions' (Coates 1986: 269). Since then, the story for industrial capital has been one of continually living in the shadow of its rival fraction: struggling with decline, unable to restructure itself, devoid of any coherent strategic vision and faced with an unsympathetic political elite that has always looked overseas towards the concerns of the financial sector.

These factors combined when, from the early to mid-1960s, British industrialists finally moved towards a more concerted attempt to alter the environmental constraints under which they operated. Faced with increasing decline and no longer afforded the luxury of resorting to imperial markets, industry responded in two main ways. First, significant moves were taken towards increased concentration and centralisation through increased mergers. Second, as we have already noted, the Federation of British Industries (FBI) engaged in a more direct political challenge to the financial sector's hegemony by urging the Macmillan government to look beyond its short-term preoccupation with high exchange rates and the value of sterling in order to concentrate on longer-term planned growth. However, both of these offensives were too late in coming. Indeed, the merger movement was more of a defensive than an offensive move (ibid.: 275).

The second offensive, which did lead to real government moves towards modernisation, and which was followed in 1965 by the creation of the CBI to allow industrialists more coherent political representation, failed in the midst of the financial sector's re-assertion of its influence over policy. These events, perhaps more so than any other, demonstrate the overall political weakness of industrial capital, as the response of the government, which initially looked favourable, was to prove only skin-deep. Not only did industry's representatives fail to exert enough selective pressure to persuade either the Conservative or the subsequent Labour government to postpone the priority given to sterling, they also failed to coordinate their relations with the state sufficiently to produce any type of coherent industrial strategy. Subsequently, the CBI has had a limited influence and has generally failed to resist measures to which the government has been clearly committed (Grant and Marsh 1977; Hall 1986: 92).

As for the unions, orthodox opinion has it that, compared to industry, the trade union movement has had considerable influence over policy in the postwar period. However, this is far from being the case, and in fact, whereas the interests of industrial capital have been indirectly compromised by the state, the trade union movement has often found itself subject to intense overt political attack. Indeed, the history of government–union relations throughout this century has been one of recurring tension, in which the unions have invariably been singled out as politically subversive (Hain 1986). As a result, it is possible to concede that the period of relatively peaceful coexistence between government and unions from 1945 to 1966 marked an exceptional era in which governments generally refrained from infringing upon union concerns (Marsh 1992). However, while this did provide a more favourable environment for the unions, it did not mean that they enjoyed any real influence over policy. On the contrary, until the mid- to late 1960s unions restricted their energies to wage bargaining within a laissez-faire framework consistent with the practice of liberal Keynesianism. This model allowed them to preserve their (much sought after) autonomy from government rather than being integrated into any concrete consultative arrangements (Richter 1973; Marsh 1992). Thus, throughout the postwar period, the ambitions of the bulk of Britain's labour force have largely been limited to sectional concerns over unfettered collective bargaining and general improvements in pay and conditions. Indeed, owing to their policy of abstentionism, the unions have, in fact, generally resisted direct involvement in the political sphere (Crouch 1979). This resistance was evident when, in 1962, the TUC were reluctant to enter into tripartite consultations on the basis that the move would be used by government as a means of securing wage restraint (which indeed proved to be the case). Moreover, it is important not to lose sight of the fact that, even in the period after 1962 when the TUC finally agreed to enter into consultative arrangements with government, union power still remained 'overwhelmingly negative' (Dorfman 1979: 6).

As with industrial capital, throughout the whole of the postwar period the TUC 'consistently failed to convince governments of either party to adopt alternative policies which it favoured' (ibid.). Several factors can be cited to explain why this has been the case (Wolinetz 1988). First, the ties between the unions and the Labour Party (which is most often cited as a major factor in determining union power) have frequently been strained. On occasions where the relationship between both has been at its strongest – usually in opposition – the links have normally been used, once Labour is in power: 'to persuade trade union leaders to endorse government policies' (ibid.: 322). Second, the nature of the tripartite arrangements implemented in Britain has limited the ability of the TUC to make any significant impact on policy. Planning arrangements have invariably been indicative and therefore not binding; as a result, the majority of the decisions reached within tripartite bodies such as the NEDC were never implemented. Third, as with industrial capital (but perhaps to a greater degree) the decentralised nature of British trade unionism has presented major problems for the unions in articulating a clear and unified strategic vision. The TUC has little effective control over its affiliates and, thus, there have always been major divisions between the unions representative body and large sections of the rank and file. Moreover, these divisions have been heightened by the rivalries which exist between major unions (ibid.: 324). Overall, these factors have combined to create an environment in which the unions have had little or no direct impact upon policy. As Wolinetz (1986: 325) explains: 'British trade unions are not equipped to do much more than react to events and proposals'.

After 1966 and the failure of Wilson's liberal corporatist strategy, the unions' reactions to events became increasingly stronger as they came under sustained attack from successive governments. Certainly it is true to say that this had the effect of persuading them to adopt a more active political role. However, this role was largely defensive and was the result of government rather than union activity (Marsh 1992: 56; also Marsh and Locksley 1983: 55–7; Coates 1989: 37–68). Thus, the politicisation of trade unions occurred primarily as a consequence of the political elite's search to find a quasi-corporatist solution to the country's economic decline. Government concern to gain both cooperation and acquiescence from the unions directly threatened the 'voluntarist' tradition in industrial relations which the TUC has historically fought to preserve. Thus, subsequent union offensives against the Wilson and Heath governments were merely counter-attacks in defence of a voluntarist tradition. While *In Place of Strife* and the Industrial Relations Act both served as challenges to the 'laissez-faire' framework that the labour movement aspired to, incomes policies threatened their other sacred preserve, free collective bargaining. As Coates

(1989: 50) explains: 'with the arrival of incomes policy, industrial relations were, so to speak, politicised at a stroke'. However, even throughout this period of politicisation, the unions still only enjoyed a limited degree of sanction and negative influence over government policy. Even in comparison to industrial capital their position was always weak, since the veto power of business did at least provide industrialists with enough sanction at their disposal to prevent any direct political interference.

Ultimately then, these factors allow us to assert that, in addition to the range of constraints within the international environment, 'the hesitant and ineffectual character of government policy since the war is the outcome of a particular balance of class forces in Britain' (Rowthorn 1986: 63–8). While financial capital maintained a dominant influence over policy, industrial capital remained relatively weak and the labour movement weaker still. Yet this does not exhaust the range of factors within the domestic environment which ultimately (*under*)-determined the selection of policy, since another important link in the chain of circumstances which led to Britain's fitful evolution was the nature of the state itself. As Rowthorn (ibid.) again explains: 'the British state has displayed an extraordinary passivity and incapacity in the face of growing economic difficulties'. As we noted earlier, the moves towards liberal corporatism in the 1960s were guided by the growing idea amongst the political elite and the representatives of industry that, in order to reverse Britain's economic decline, the state would need to play a more active role in stimulating growth. This idea was again prevalent between 1972 and 1976 when first the Heath government and then the subsequent Labour government initiated a series of moves towards expanding the state's role. However, the major problem throughout both of these periods was that, despite an increased willingness for statist measures on the part of policy-makers, the British state did not possess the capacity to implement these moves. Historically, the major obstacle to state expansion has been the system of 'Treasury control' within the machinery of government. As Cronin (1991: 5) explains, the Treasury, since the nineteenth century, has: 'enshrined as its guiding principle a fundamentally negative view of the state's role in society and subsequently adopted a more or less "permanent posture of menace and rejection" towards attempts to augment the state'.[6] This principle then has produced 'a powerful inertial logic' which has meant that: 'the creation of the fiscal and administrative capacity necessary for social reform has been, in fact, much more difficult than the creation of a political consensus on the virtues of reform' (ibid.). Thus, any attempt to implement a policy of state expansion has represented a major threat to the system of Treasury control, and, therefore, has traditionally been met with resistance. As a result, any successful attempt would need to involve administrative reform and the effective disruption of the Treasury's dominant status.

The problem for policy-makers has been the historically close association between all three of Britain's central institutions: the Treasury, the

Bank of England and the City of London. The links between these have their origins in the pre-industrial era and 'were based upon the Bank's management of the state's debts by means of loans raised in the City, the interest on which the Treasury levied through the protectionist customs duties and tariffs' (Ingham 1984: 128). Ironically, the strengthening of this relationship in the nineteenth century sprung from an attempt by the state to provide the Treasury with greater independence from the City, by allowing the Treasury to pursue a 'general strategy of rigorous parsimony and balanced budgets' (ibid.: 130). However, through time, as the City expanded its overseas interests and laid the foundations for the international gold-sterling standard, the Treasury's fiscal prudence became an important cornerstone for guaranteeing the stability of the sterling area. As Ingham explains:

> in this way, one of the basic conditions for the City's international activities was actually embodied in the practices of the state – in the Treasury 'view' and Treasury 'control'. . . . Later in the nineteenth century these connections were explicitly recognised, and the increasing demands of the new and expanding state agencies were rejected on the grounds that the sterling's parity with gold and free trade might be threatened by increased state expenditure.
>
> (Ingham 1984: 131)

Thus, by the late nineteenth century the relationship between the Treasury, the City and the Bank had been built around an 'integrated system of interdependencies' (ibid.). The foundation of this system was a general antipathy towards increases in state expenditure and a consensus on the need to secure sterling's world role. As a result, this system of interdependency, and the Treasury' central position within it, provided an environment which has imposed substantial selective pressures upon all governments to withdraw from implementing measures which would place too great a burden upon the state's finances. Yet, as Cronin (1991: 11) suggests: 'the influence of the Treasury on the state has been based only partly on structural features. It has also been based to a considerable extent on the willingness of politicians to submit to the workings of these structures'. Through a combination of these factors, Britain has developed over the years a state and party system which is inherently conservative and generally hostile to dirigiste measures.

Of course, the rapid expansion of the state in the immediate postwar period would appear to contradict this statement (Hall 1986: 91). However, this had been precipitated by a radically altered domestic environment. In particular, the war opened a space for the articulation of an overall critique of the way in which government operated during the interwar years. This crisis narrative was not only aimed at the government's inability to respond to economic failure, but was also directed towards the system of bureaucratic control at the heart of the machinery of government. In particular, the Foreign Office and the Treasury were targeted as having failed to respond to the need to increase public expenditure on defence.

These criticisms were to spark a general rethink of the administrative structure and the potential for reform; in the meantime, however, this issue was to become irrelevant since the mobilisation for war necessarily dictated an end to bureaucratic parsimony and the by-passing of the system of Treasury control. This enabled planning for the war effort to take place outside the supervision of the Treasury; the Chancellor was excluded from the War Cabinet and plans were drawn up by means of the Manpower Budget. After the war, the Treasury's demotion within the administrative structure continued for at least two years as planning was carried out between the Economic Section of the Cabinet office and the Central Economic Planning Staff. This by-passing of Treasury control both during and immediately after the war, combined with the general disaffection with the role of the state, enabled an environment to develop in which detailed plans could evolve, and ultimately be carried through, for an extensive expansion in the state's activities. However, by 1947 this environment had been altered again as the Treasury resumed its normal position as the vigilant guardian of the state's expenses. Moreover, by the early 1950s the City had regained its erstwhile dominance, and the relationship between the Treasury, the City and the Bank of England, and the selective pressures which these brought to bear upon government policy, had become firmly re-established.

In the early to mid-1960s, and later in the 1970s, when governments attempted to adapt their strategic objectives in order actively to promote economic growth, the domestic institutional environment in which they operated was dominated by the central nexus of Treasury, Bank, City relations. Given the selective pressures towards minimal state intervention which these imposed upon government strategy, any serious attempt at extending the role of the state needed to involve some type of structural reform. In particular, an administrative structure would need to be created which would by-pass the system of strict of Treasury control. However, throughout the postwar period, no such attempt to extend the capacity of the state to intervene in economic affairs was ever fully implemented. As such, the quasi-corporatist institutions and planning apparatuses designed to launch an industrial strategy such as the NEDC, the DEA, MINTECH and the NEB, have all been 'set apart from the central axis' (Jessop 1980: 40). These 'para-state apparatuses' were never been fully incorporated into the central decision-making structure and, as a result:

> the Treasury and the Bank have retained control over the instruments of short-term economic policy and over central government expenditure because of the vulnerability of sterling. This dissociation between state economic apparatuses has thus meant that the Treasury–Bank axis

was able to reassert the priority of the balance of payments and the reserves against the priority of growth (and full employment) entailed in the commitment to planning.

(Jessop 1980: 40)

Thus, the attempts at planning suffered from both the overall lack of capacity within the state for extensive intervention and the very nature of the planning arrangements themselves. These latter reflected the overall culture of arm's length government within the political elite. The attempts at planned growth in the 1960s were in fact essentially indicative, and therefore provided no real means through which compliance with growth targets could be secured (ibid.; also Hall 1986: 88). Whereas Labour's plans for industrial restructuring in the 1970s did entail a greater commitment to direct intervention, these were never actually implemented. As a result then, both the administrative structure of the British state and the general predisposition of the political elite have militated heavily against providing the state with the capacity to carry out an effective strategy of state expansion.

Overall then, we have seen that the domestic environment in the postwar period was composed of several factors which made the selection of effective interventionist measures to aid industrial modernisation extremely difficult. As Overbeek explains:

the organizations of both the industrial working class and the industrial bourgeoisie were weak, decentralised, unaccustomed to dealing with each other constructively, and opposed by a state that was just as weak and just as unaccustomed to intervening in industrial relations and the industrial structure.

(Overbeek 1990: 154)

At various times these factors seriously hampered the ability of successive political actors to implement important elements of their domestic policy, while ensuring that Britain's overseas commitments and the interests of the financial sector remained the main priority of government strategy throughout the postwar period. Yet, it would be wrong to assume that such factors were (*over*)-determining in their effect. For, as we have seen, throughout the postwar period the precise role of the state and the priorities of government policy (as well as the balance between class forces) were open to continual political contestation, and opportunities for change did present themselves at various times (Fine and Harris 1985). This is the evolving contestation which I have previously identified as a struggle for survival between different conceptions of state strategy. While the composition of the domestic environment did not directly determine the outcome of this struggle, it did nevertheless present important selection pressures which ensured that it was never going to be a fair and balanced contest.

Discursive conditioning

So far, I have primarily examined a whole range of constraints upon the evolution of policy to expand the state in the postwar period. We have seen that the commitment to the defence of Britain's international role and the value of sterling placed a great deal of selective pressure upon governments to prioritise foreign policy concerns over domestic strategy. Similarly, I have argued that these pressures were consolidated by the impact of American hegemony, the particular balance of class forces that has emerged historically in Britain, and the institutional weakness of the British state. These factors not only gave rise to the struggle over ideas about policy-making in the postwar period, but also affected the outcome of this conflict by militating heavily against state expansion and the effective implementation of domestic policy. In the light of these constraining mechanisms, one might well ask how any real struggle over policy managed to emerge; in particular, what were the main environmental factors which enabled the various adaptations towards greater state expansion to occur?

Until now, we have considered only one major enabling factor; that is, the gradual change in international productive relations towards a Fordist accumulation strategy. This forced considerable selective pressures for policies to re-regulate capitalist growth through the stimulation of demand and the creation of welfare structures. However, on its own this represents only a vague external variable without any concrete definition on the domestic front, while the implication at this stage is that the need for Fordist restructuring imposed a certain type of functionalist imperative upon national states to adapt their political and economic structures accordingly. Certainly this is not the aim of this book, for the evolutionary account that is being developed here is one which rejects any inherent functionalist or determinist logic. Rather, the aim has been to assert that the 'environment' in which strategies are articulated and implemented is the product of a dialectical relationship between objective and subjective impulses.

We have already seen how this dialectic contributed to Britain's obsession over foreign policy. On the one hand, the decision to restore the position of the City and the role of sterling was a political one governed by ideological conviction about Britain's role in the world. However, once this decision was made, the need to secure Britain's status became almost reified, so that it evolved through time into an objective condition (sustained by subjective motives) shaping Britain's postwar economic decline. Similarly, in this section the aim is to examine the way in which the objectively prescribed need for Fordist restructuring (which provided an impetus for state expansion) coincided with the subjective realisation by Britain's political elite that major reform was required in order to avoid the economic conditions of the interwar years. This recognition, which gained ascendancy throughout the course of the war, helped to create a discursive environment which masked the constraints upon state expansion and generated a rhetorical commitment to greater equality, full employment and economic growth.

The major catalyst for the change in the discursive environment was the war. The massive popular mobilisation for the war effort had thrown into stark relief the deep divisions in society that had characterised the interwar years. These had been years of entrenched poverty, recession and unemployment, reflecting as we have already noted, the maladaptation of the British economy to changes that were taking place in capitalist accumulation. Whereas solutions to this crisis had been proposed during the 1930s by progressive liberals such as Keynes, it was the onset of total war that had provided the environment in which these ideas would begin to penetrate the outlook of the political elite. Specifically, it was generally agreed that preparations would need to be made, not just for the war itself, but also for the process of reconstruction which would inevitably follow.

A major factor in ensuring that the plans for reconstruction would take on a reformist discourse was the incorporation of the labour movement into the war effort. This had the effect of 'legitimating aspirations for a "fairer" society' (Hay 1996: 33). During the war these aspirations were realised principally in the form of the Beveridge Report. William Beveridge's recommendations for a universal national insurance scheme that would provide benefits and pensions for the sick, the unemployed and the elderly was met with a popular fervour which 'reflected a deep societal appetite for wide-scale social reform' (ibid.: 29). According to Cronin (1991: 29; emphasis added): 'it was not a particularly profound document, it articulated no new philosophy of the state and no grand vision of the relationship between citizenship and welfare, but it was sufficient to capture and channel the popular desire for change and to *reshape the wartime discourse of social policy*'. As well as receiving widespread popular support, the recommendations forwarded by Beveridge were backed within the establishment, by the gradual development of a Keynesian discourse.

I have noted at various points throughout this book that it is important not to overstate the impact of Keynesian thinking on the actual implementation of policy. Nevertheless, the impact of a Keynesian discourse (however tenuous this might have been in practice) did have the effect of providing a counterweight to the factors that constrained state expansion. Its immediate impact was to help to legitimise the recommendations of the Beveridge Report. As Hay (1996: 32) explains: 'it was the discursive dominance . . . of Keynesianism and of Keynesian assumptions (whether they would ever be put into practice or not) that made Beveridge's commitment to full employment appear realistic, attainable and hence a legitimate expectation of any postwar administration'.

The longer-term impact of Keynesian discourse was its ability to: 'redefine dramatically the boundaries of the politically possible' (ibid.: 31). In this sense, Keynesianism can be characterised as a discursive paradigm which not only opened up a limited space for new types of strategic adaptation, but also helped to shape the expectations of both the electorate and the political elite (Hall 1986, 1993; Hay 1997, 1998). When combined with the powerfully reformist discourse of the Beveridge Report and the general mood for change within the country at large, Keynesianism provided a discursive environment which, in turn, provided a major thrust for progressive liberal expansion. Yet here it is important not to overstate the point, as most authors have been inclined to do. For the problem throughout the literature is that Keynesianism has often been regarded as a doctrine that implied some form of commitment among the political elite to collectivist reform. In this sense, the meaning of Keynesianism has most often been distorted to evoke the idea that it represented a 'middle way' between free market liberalism and pseudo-socialism. This is misguided, since the extent of state intervention implied by Keynesianism was, at best, minimal, particularly in the case of Britain where the liberal variant of Keynesian ideas was restricted almost exclusively to minor adjustments in budgetary policy.

Overall, Keynesianism was very much rooted in classical liberal economics and, as such, represented only a minor corrective to the dogmatic laissez-faire principles which underpinned this school of thinking. Nevertheless, it is true to say that the discourse that surrounded government policy after the introduction of Keynesianism was much more 'collectivist', and indeed 'statist', in tone than the policies and general sets of ideas that underpinned it. Of course, this had much to do with the fact that it was first used to legitimate the policies of a Labour government whose rhetoric was much more collectivist in tone than the policies which followed. Nevertheless, the effect of such discourse was to open up the space for further moves towards statist intervention. This is reflected in the later attempts to extend the definition of Keynesian economic management to include quasi-corporatist ideas, and also in the fact that Keynesian discourse made it legitimate for even Conservative governments to debate the virtues of economic planning.

Generally speaking, therefore, although we must avoid exaggerating both the commitment to Keynesianism and the extent to which it was ever used as the main priority of economic management, it is still important to acknowledge the effect that Keynsian discourse had upon shaping perceptions of the politically possible. The discursive commitment to Keynesianism, full employment and the principles of the Beveridge Report provided an environment for a generally statist discourse built around the promise of 'New Jerusalem'. In turn, this provided a basis for the legitimacy, not only of the war effort itself, but also of later postwar administrations. What Keynesian discourse did, in effect, was to provide an environment that produced selective pressures upon all governments to use the machinery of the state in order to improve economic conditions and maintain the structures of the welfare state. This provided an important counterweight to the enormous pressures to minimalise state intervention. All in all, it provided a stimulus for strategic adaptations towards quasi-corporatist planning and ensured that the subsequent pressures to withdraw the state would not lead to a serious reversal of the commitment to welfare provision and full employment. Its effect was to heighten the fundamental conflicts over policy and delay the final victory for the forces of classical liberalism.

Agents' interpretations of their strategic objectives

So far, we have examined both the environmental conditions which exerted selective pressures upon government strategy, and the strategic adaptations taken by postwar governments in order to negotiate those pressures. This has enabled us to consider the evolving dialectical interactions between agents in the postwar period and the various types of selective environment in which they operated. However, in order fully to understand the connections between these distinct evolving variables, we still need to examine another important link in the explanatory chain, namely, the differentiated strategic positions of the major relevant actors. In order to do this, we need briefly to review the different interpretations of strategy that each brought to bear upon the evolving postwar political scene. As we discussed at some length in Chapter Five, the idea that variables need to adapt in response to changing environmental conditions is central to any evolutionary schema, whether in the natural or social sciences. In social science, however, unlike biology, social and political theories of evolutionary change need to reassert the centrality in this process of human subjectivity. It is important to emphasise that the way in which adaptations are made in the social and political world depends to a very large extent upon the precise interpretations of the environment that subjectively motivated agents bring to bear upon the selection of strategy. Agents must be viewed as being continually involved in the process of extrapolating meaning from their environment (through their own narrow ideological heuristics), and interpolating their own intentionality into their strategic responses. Thus, actors are never passive creatures in the formulation of strategy; rather, they continually furnish their strategic objectives with their own ideologically prescribed meanings and interpretations.

Taking this into account, we need briefly to examine the distinct strategic positions of the main groups of actors in the postwar domestic scene. Clearly, there is a whole host of potential groups that we might look at. These include: the different spectrums of the leading parties; senior civil servants; various interest groups; trade unions; business associations; and perhaps even the electorate. Such a venture would, of course, be an immense but useful task; in particular it might prove fruitful in dispelling the myth of an enduring national consensus. However, for the purpose of making my own task manageable, this section will build upon the work of Bob Jessop (1992) and Colin Hay (1996), who have examined the differentiated position in the postwar period of three main groups of actors: politicians, producer groups and financiers. As these authors have emphasised, the interaction between the diverse strategic objectives of politicians, producer groups and financiers provided a central dynamic to the evolution of policy in the postwar period; in particular, it cemented the contradictory pressures and conflicts that would result in the oscillation of government strategy between attempts at state expansion and subsequent periods of retrenchment.

Jessop's (1992) analysis derives from his attempt to dissect the nature of the 'postwar welfare-state settlement' (hereafter PWS). The author identifies two major contradictory commitments within the PWS: a commitment by politicians (actually more broadly defined as voters, parties and (shadow) cabinet members) to redistributive measures and full employment via Keynesian demand management; and a commitment by producer groups (including business, unions and state economic institutions) towards planned modernisation. These ambiguous strategic objectives, 'expressing different modes of calculation, images of social justice, goals and means of delivery' (Hay 1996: 61), combined to produce a 'twin settlement' which was essentially contradictory in character.

Unfortunately, Jessop's analysis of the 'twin settlements' thesis remains largely undeveloped, but it has been taken up and extended by Hay (1996: 61–3; 113–15). Hay advises us that – in assessing the strategic interests of these two groups – we should not be led into overstating the commitment to either redistribution or indeed, corporatist modernisation. Nevertheless, he does generally conclude that the twin settlements thesis provides us with a useful framework for analysing the inherent conflicts of the postwar period, provided that we add a third dimension, the interests of the financial sector. It is surprising that Jessop neglects to include the distinctive position of the financiers in his twin settlements thesis, given that their strategic interests remain central to the rest of his highly perceptive work on the postwar period. In his account, the financiers are treated as part of the producers' settlement. Nevertheless, it is doubtful that he would find any real objection to Hay's thesis that there were in fact three conflicting (and distinctive) postwar settlements. This was because the financial sector's interests lay primarily in defending the value of sterling and thus limiting the state's attempts at industrial modernisation.

Hay's analysis of Britain's three postwar settlements, like Jessop's, is left largely undeveloped. Perhaps the major reason for this lies in the fact that the idea of two or three distinct settlements rests uneasily with the theoretical basis of both authors' work. At the heart of both accounts lies a determination to stress the essential accord/compromise/agreement (if not consensus) between capital, labour and the state throughout the postwar period. Thus, both authors make great use of the term 'postwar settlement' in order to emphasise the relative level of assent over the general direction of policy. However, as soon as we begin to acknowledge the existence of two or perhaps even three distinct and contradictory settlements, then it becomes difficult to sustain the idea that there was any real settlement at all. This is the point that is central to this book, for the reality is that the so-called contradictions of the postwar settlement (and the fluctuations in policy that resulted from them) merely highlight the overall lack of settlement (and of course consensus). Clearly, the work of Jessop and Hay highlights the conflicts at the heart of policy; yet the idea of conflicting twin settlements is merely a contradiction in terms. As such then, we need to reject the idea of two or three distinct postwar settlements and choose instead to view the postwar period as an era in which the fundamental aims of policy had never been settled, given the constant and evolving struggle for survival between very different conceptions and interpretations of state strategy.

As such, we need to take this as a starting point for examining the selective pressures that distinctive and conflicting interpretations of strategy among the main political actors placed upon the outcome of policy. These interpretations were never fixed due to the evolving nature of the environment in which they were fought out; yet, it is still possible to generalise at a high level of abstraction. As we have seen, the strategic position of the financial sector was perhaps the most coherent throughout the course of the postwar period. The maintenance of high exchange rates and a strong value for sterling remained central to their interpretations of not only where their strategic interests lay, but also of what the role of government strategy should be. To the financiers, the state's commitment to full employment and high levels of public expenditure on welfare provision were of secondary importance and, indeed, merely provided a distraction from the overall need to ensure financial stability. Thus, there emerged Britain's continual 'stop-go' cycle, as the City continually fought to impose the primacy of its own strategic interests, most often at the expense of industrial capital and the commitment by politicians to the maintenance of Keynesianism and the welfare state.

It would of course be misleading merely to accuse financial capital of having 'failed' the domestic economy in this respect (Harris 1985: 19). For, as I have already noted, the dislocation of interests between financial and industrial capital has its roots in the historical formation of capital in Britain. Given the relative autonomy of industrial capital during the process of imperial expansion, the City was forced to look abroad for investment. Thus, when those in the financial sector came to survey the postwar environment, their extensive overseas commitments and their relative lack of investment in domestic industry made it inevitable that they should attach an international perspective to their strategic objectives. As such, the 'blame' for the overall international orientation of policy lies not so much with the City, but in the tameness with which industrial capital opposed the financial sector's dominance and the overall eagerness of politicians to maintain Britain's world role.

The strategic position of Britain's producer groups was a lot less coherent throughout the period. As for industrial capital, the eventual conversion to the idea of industrial planning during the early 1960s was matched by its antipathy towards state intervention in the immediate aftermath of the war. It has been widely acknowledged that the Attlee government's attempts to enhance the role of the state in economic affairs were consistently thwarted by both the business sector and the civil service (see for example Cain and Hopkins 1993: 269–70; Tiratsoo and Tomlinson 1993; Tomlinson 1994: 157–9; Hay 1996: 35). Thus, as Mercer explains:

> Labour was unable to implement even [the] mildest of 'modernisa-tion' strategies because it relied on co-operation from industry which was not forthcoming, and the main peak representatives of British businessmen at the time, the Federation of British Industries . . . adhered rigidly to its hostility to state intervention.
>
> (Mercer 1991: 72–3)

This was largely born out of the historical tendency of British capital to resist direct state involvement in economic affairs. It is hardly surprising that, after more than a century of entrenched laissez-faire politics, produc-tive capital should interpret its interests as being best served through continued opposition to state planning. What perhaps is more surprising is the change of attitude during the middle of the period. This was occasioned by the success of indicative planning in France, the growing realisation of decline, and the realisation that the dominance of financial interests was detrimental to the long-term profitability of industrial capital. Thus, throughout the course of the postwar period, in response to changing envi-ronmental conditions, those in the industrial sector re-interpreted their strategic objectives. After having supported the government's withdrawal from state intervention, they then came to view their interests as being best served by moves towards extending the basis of Keynesianism to include economic modernisation through coordinated planning agreements. Yet this re-interpretation of strategy was never ambitious enough to allow the industrial sector to exert significant selective pressure upon the state to implement an effective industrial strategy, nor would it allow the business community to cooperate with the Labour left's plans for industrial rejuve-nation in 1974. As a result then, the position of the industrial sector was always ambiguous, torn between the growing recognition, on the one hand, that its interests lay in state-led modernisation, and a historical antipathy towards direct state involvement on the other.

The trade unions' position was no less ambiguous. The unions had historically interpreted their strategic interests as being best served by avoiding political involvement, and this had ensured that throughout the postwar period they adhered firmly to the defence of collective bargaining. Yet their close ties with the Labour Party meant that this policy would continually have to be reviewed and, at various times, they voluntarily acquiesced to the need for wage restraint in return for the guarantee of wider concessions in social and industrial relations policy. In addition, the unions, like industrial capital, reluctantly came to concede the need for tripartite planning arrangements, again on the basis that this would bring longer-term gains for the labour movement. Thus, they also eventually embraced a commitment to extending the basis of Keynesianism and the role of the state in the economy. However, as with industrial capital, this commitment remained tempered by the unions' historical distrust of state involvement in industry.

If the interpretations of strategy on the part of Britain's main producer groups appeared ambiguous, constantly changing and often contradictory, then this was as nothing compared to the complete lack of any firm commitment by politicians. The orthodox assumption is that the interpretation of strategy on behalf of the political elite was simple; it involved a strong primary commitment to redistributive measures, the maintenance of full employment, and greater cooperation between government and producer interests. However, when we look at the repeated major oscillations in government strategy, it is a mystery how most authors could have reached this conclusion. At various points the political elite came to re-interpret, and then re-interpret again, the fundamental basis of their strategic objectives. Sometimes the commitment to Keynesianism and the welfare state was strong, sometimes it was weak, and at other times it was almost abandoned altogether. In some instances the government attempted to develop a strong partnership with industry and the unions, while in others it abandoned the protection of industry and directly attacked the position of the unions. Every single period of government, with the exception of the Churchill–Eden administrations, involved either a significant change in government strategy or a complete policy U-turn.

If we were to point to one constant in all of this, it would be the interpretation on the part of all politicians that British interests would be best served by maintaining Britain's world role. This ensured that, no matter how strong or how weak the commitment to Keynesianism and the welfare state, the value of sterling always remained a priority. Whereas the discursive attachment to full employment and welfare provision was often the result of political calculation (particularly on the part of Conservative administrations), the interpretation that sterling needed to be secured was forged by ideological conviction. Thus, as Tomlinson (1994: 266; also Strange 1971) argues: 'the value of the pound became entangled with all sorts of grand issues about Britain's place in the world, rather than being seen as just a question of economic policy'. As a result, the only ideological conviction of the political elite that endured unscathed throughout the postwar period was the idea that Britain's position in the international hierarchy needed to be secured, even if this was at the eventual expense of British industry's ability to compete with foreign competitors.

Overall then, the actual implementation of government strategy was hampered by the various interpretations of their strategic objectives by Britain's main groups of actors. The financial sector remained committed to Britain's overseas position at the expense of domestic industry, the two main producer groups were wedded to industrial strategy through corporatist expansion on the one hand, and to a historical antipathy to state intervention on the other, while Britain's politicians showed an overall lack of ability to commit themselves firmly to any coherent strategy. The result of these evolving interpretations was an ever-growing conflict at the heart of policy-making accompanied by a fitful struggle on the part of politicians to resolve not only the contradictory demands placed upon them, but also the vacuum of ideas within the political elite about how to deal with Britain's accelerating economic decline. As we shall see in the final section, all of this seriously hampered the processes of policy learning that might otherwise have enabled the state to resolve its growing dilemmas.

Adaptive learning

As we saw in Chapter Four, the idea of adaptive learning over time has become central to various evolutionary conceptions of political and economic change. The work of Peter Hall provides us with the most elaborated notion of political (or, in his account 'social') learning. According to Hall:

> learning is conventionally said to occur when individuals assimilate new information, including that based on past experience, and apply it to their subsequent actions. . . . [W]e can define social learning as a deliberate attempt to adjust the goals or techniques of policy in response to past experience and new information. Learning is indicated when policy changes as the result of such a process.
>
> (Hall 1993: 278)

This type of work is particularly relevant here, as, it is used to describe the process through which Keynesianism developed in Britain and was eventually superseded by monetarism. According to Hall, social learning occurs within the confines of dominant policy 'paradigms'. Keynesianism and monetarism represent the two main distinctive paradigms of the postwar period; as such, these provided 'a framework of ideas and standards that specifies not only the goals of policy and the kind of instruments that can be used to attain them, but also the very nature of the problems they are meant to be addressing' (Hall 1993: 279). In this sense, Hall is attempting to assert the centrality of ideas to the process by which political evolution occurs. Specifically, he argues that, in the early postwar period, policymakers responded to past failures in a distinctly Keynesian fashion, continually updating and extending the instruments through which

Keynesianism could be applied more effectively. This then provides an explanation for the development of Keynesianism, from simple demand management to a more corporatist, interventionist, set of measures. Finally, towards the end of the period, as Keynesian solutions became less and less effective in dealing with the growing crisis, Hall argues that monetarism came to replace Keynesianism as the dominant ideational paradigm, thereby providing a new conception of government strategy through which policy could again begin a new evolutionary trajectory.

Hall's main contribution to our understanding of the postwar political scene is that he provides us with a (significantly) more sophisticated and theoretically rigorous assertion of the consensus thesis. In this sense, Hall's policy paradigm approach gives us a new slant on the orthodox idea that policy-making took place within the context of an agreed 'set of governing expectations and assumptions' (see Kavanagh and Morris 1994). What differs in Hall's account however, is the insertion of the idea that this set of expectations and assumptions was continually open to evolution through time as a result of adaptive learning. Thus, the author provides the consensus thesis with a notion of the temporality of political change, a notion which, as we have seen, has otherwise been overlooked within the literature. Yet, Hall's conception of evolutionary change remains essentially appreciative, rather than formal, as it regards policy evolution as being driven primarily by a limited dynamic; specifically speaking, ideas drawn from past experience. As such, the author argues that 'policy responds less directly to social and economic conditions than it does to the consequences of past policy' (Hall 1993: 277). For this reason, Hay (1998) argues that Hall's evolutionary schema has, in turn, a limited utility, since it neglects a proper consideration of the way in which evolution is conditioned by contextual or environmental factors. Here Hay is worth quoting at some length, as his view accords with one of the central themes of this book:

> the evolution of policy cannot be assumed to be so simple. . . . [T]he outcome of policy is highly contingent. It is dependent upon a constantly changing context with which the policy-making process is complexly implicated and upon which it impinges to yield both intended and unintended consequences. It is dependent upon the responses made to it by those whose lives and life chances it impacts . . . were that not enough, it is also dependent upon a complex array of apparently unrelated, independent and unpredictable factors – from the actions of multi-national corporations, international and transnational regulatory bodies, to the development of new technologies, to such parochial and ephemeral factors as the perceived probity of the minister responsible or, indeed, the weather.
>
> (Hay 1998: 23)

With this qualification in mind, Hay proceeds to develop Hall's policy paradigm approach. He reminds us that, even though policy learning occurs within an evolving ideational and discursive paradigm, this paradigm has it roots in an evolving conception and narration of crisis, as well as a co-evolving institutional (and strategically selective) environment.

Certainly, Hay's revised conception of strategic learning does come very much closer to the conception of evolutionary change outlined in Chapter Four. Yet, here we must reject at least part of it. That is, the view that policy learning in the early postwar period occurred solely within the context of a coherent Keynesian paradigm. Keynesianism did provide policy-makers with a coherent discursive environment, and this discursive environment did provide significant selection pressures for the implementation of measures to secure full employment and maintain high levels of welfare provision. However, it would be somewhat superficial to assume that Keynesian discourse provided the only major dynamic in the postwar period. Moreover, it would also be fallacious to assume that the ideas that informed policy were the same as those which were used to legitimate it discursively.

As we have seen in some detail, postwar governments were committed to a number of constantly changing, and often contradictory, strategies, to the extent that it is impossible to detect any overall paradigm informing the actual implementation of policy. Consequently, the process of adaptive learning in the postwar period was far more complex than most authors have hitherto assumed. Specifically, learning occurred over two main evolutionary trajectories. On the one hand, there were repeated attempts to learn better and more effective ways of making Keynesianism work. On the other hand, however, such attempts were accompanied by a learning process that involved finding ways of relieving the state's burden of Keynesian commitments. These contradictory learning processes reflected the fundamental conflict and lack of agreement over the 'set of governing assumptions and expectations' that should inform policy. All in all, the effect of this conflict was that the overall process of learning how to reverse Britain's decline was seriously jeopardised, amid a series of contradictory and mutually incompatible selection pressures. As we shall see, this experience contrasted sharply with the Thatcher years, when the relative lack of conflict over government policy contributed to an environment whereby the Conservatives could learn over time how to put a relatively consistent set of objectives into practice.

Conclusion

This chapter has laid the basis for turning the conventional understanding of postwar British politics on its head. In orthodox accounts, the early postwar period is viewed as a comparatively consensual era dominated by an overall continuity in government politics. In contrast, the Thatcher era is seen as a period characterised by continual conflict and lack of agreement over policy. With regard to the first of these assumptions, we have seen that the so-called period of Keynesianism was by no means a consensual era; rather, it was dominated by fundamental conflicts and resulting changes in government strategy. This 'struggle for survival' between competing conceptions of policy was partly the product of conflicting and contradictory selection pressures from the environment in which policy was played out, and partly the result of a lack of agreed aims on the part of the political elite. As we have seen, the overall result was a fitful evolution, as governments continually adapted their strategic responses in order to deal with the conflicting pressures placed upon them. In contrast, we will see that the Thatcher years represented the final outcome of this struggle between progressive and classical liberal ideas; they reflect a period in which the aims of government strategy were finally resolved in favour of the latter (at least for the time being). In this sense then, Thatcherism emerged out of the conflict of the early postwar years as the first major postwar settlement; an era in which the overall direction of government policy was agreed upon at the very heart of the policy-making apparatus. This is not to suggest that Thatcherism was an era of consensus politics in the sense in which the term is normally applied. Clearly, the implementation of Conservative strategy did provoke deep-rooted conflicts. However, within the actual decision-making structure, these conflicts were relatively muted; there was no fundamental struggle between the government and the Treasury–Bank–City nexus or, indeed, between foreign and domestic policy. As a result then, this provided the Conservatives with an environment in which they could continually adapt their strategic objectives along a single evolutionary trajectory. It is to an analysis and a periodisation of Thatcherism that we must now turn.

7   Struggling for definition
The evolution of Thatcherism, 1976–97

Introduction

So far, I have set out in some detail the context within which Thatcherism was to emerge. Early postwar British politics had been dominated by an evolving struggle for survival between competing and contradictory conceptions of government strategy. A coherent discursive commitment to Keynesianism and liberal-corporatism had served to disguise the fact that government strategy throughout the period had oscillated between two distinct evolutionary trajectories: a tendency towards state expansion and an accompanying tendency towards liberal retreat. This evolving conflict between progressive and classical liberal ideas had been played out within the context of a strategically selective environment which consistently favoured the success of the latter; as a result, British policy-makers were prevented (and indeed through their own actions, prevented themselves) from creating any type of firm and distinctive postwar settlement. Thus, when Britain entered the 1970s amid a heightening of the fundamental conflicts surrounding policy-making, there was a growing feeling that the internal struggle within the country would need to be resolved through some form of settlement. Heath had initially attempted to throw the balance in favour of classical liberalism by resorting to a market strategy which would later be seen as proto-Thatcherite. With the failure of this strategy, the initiative again rested with the forces of progressive liberalism and, indeed, after the election of the Labour Party in 1974, it even seemed that social democracy had gained an ascendancy for the first time. Yet, as we have seen, the latter strategy failed to get off the ground and, in the end, amid a growing political and economic crisis, the International Monetary Fund imposed its own settlement on Britain's long-term postwar conflict.

Thus Thatcherism emerged from the ashes of Labour's failed strategy as an era in which the battle over ideas had finally been settled in favour of a classical/neo-liberal conception of the state. Certainly, the Conservative governments would continue to provoke deep-rooted conflict at the heart of British society: they would be opposed by a myriad of forces demanding a return to an expansionary direction. As a result, it would be wrong to claim that the Thatcherite era reflected a period of 'consensus politics' in the traditional sense of the term. Yet, after the experience of the late 1970s, classical/neo-liberalism had won a decisive victory that seriously damaged the efficacy of the opposition to Thatcherism. This meant that, in relative terms, the Conservatives would not be faced with the fundamental conflicts at the heart of policy-making which successive postwar governments had to endure. Overall, the discursive commitment to Keynesianism had been stripped away and in this context the Conservative strategy fitted more favourably with the institutional apparatus of the British state. Unlike previously, there would now be no fundamental ideological conflict between government and the Treasury–Bank–City nexus, nor would there be a decisive struggle between the priorities of domestic and foreign policy. Faced with this relative lack of conflict, the Conservative strategy, though conceptually weak to begin with, would have more space to evolve along a single evolutionary trajectory and, as we shall see, become increasingly radical as the Conservatives continually learned through time how both to define and to implement their strategic objectives.

Labour's monetarist retreat and Thatcherite ascendancy 1976–9

The year 1976, and the intervention of the International Monetary Fund, had signalled the end of Britain's fitful evolution in the early postwar period.[1] From this point on, the struggle for survival between the discursive commitment to Keynesian expansionism and the historical commitment to arm's length, limited government was essentially over. Of course, there were still factions throughout the Conservatives' term in office that continued to advocate a movement back towards state expansion; these voices, however, had little impact, and there would certainly be no future policy adaptations in their favour. In the meantime, though, Thatcherism had not yet fully arrived. Certainly many of the essential ingredients of Thatcherite economic policy were present after 1976, but in the areas of social policy and political strategy, the Conservatives still had decisively to win the hearts and minds of the electorate. However, there was a significant move in that direction during the final months of Labour's term in office, amidst an enormous wave of industrial unrest after the breakdown of the Social Contract. As we shall see, the years 1976–9 marked the final victory for neo-liberalism as Labour stumbled on from crisis to crisis. Both parties emerged from the ruins of Labour's strategy with their fortunes radically transformed: Labour lost its legitimacy amongst the electorate for over a decade and a half, and the Conservatives re-staked their claim to be the natural party of government.

The forward march of Labour halted

As we saw in Chapter Five, Labour's erstwhile strategy of expansionism had ended abruptly when the IMF intervened in favour of an essentially monetarist and deflationary package of economic measures. The main conditions of the $3.5 billion loan from the IMF were: large cuts in public expenditure; the maintenance of high interest rates; tight levels of wage restraint; and the sale of £500 million of government shares in British Petroleum (Overbeek 1990: 172; Brett 1985: 164). Although the Labour government's strategy in this period was essentially monetarist, their subsequent conduct of policy still reflected the fundamental conflicts at the heart of the party's overall strategic objectives. On the one hand, the government disengaged itself from high levels of public spending and moderate levels of state intervention in order to control inflation and the money supply, but on the other hand, it was also attempting to combine this with very limited attempts at fiscal expansion and industrial strategy (Coopey and Woodward 1996: 13). The ultimate aim of policy was to bring down inflation without causing a dramatic increase in unemployment. This was combined initially with an attempt to lower interest rates in order to protect the competitive position achieved after the earlier sterling crisis, along with a moderate expansion in fiscal policy. Eventually, however, these limited measures had to be abandoned and policy became overwhelmingly deflationary (ibid.). Nevertheless, the main thrust of Labour's strategic adaptation was their resort to incomes policy.

A major plank of the Labour government's former strategy had been the Social Contract – an agreement between the Party and the trade unions worked out in opposition – which, it was said, would replace any formal policy of imposed wage restraint.[2] Yet, as early as 1975, with the onset of crisis, this strategy was reversed and the Social Contract was broken before it had been given any real time to take effect. The first steps towards wage restraint involved a total pay freeze for those earning over £8,500 per year, and a maximum increase of £6 per week for those below that (Dorey 1995: 150). This had been accepted by the TUC, partly because it invoked a flat-rate rather than a percentage limit which, in effect, would be more beneficial to the low paid (ibid.).

In the following year 'stage two' of the incomes policy was announced under the premiership of Callaghan. This was to involve a 4.5 per cent norm for the next twelve months. This time however, the TUC accepted on the understanding that there would be no further enforced wage restraint the following year. Nevertheless, the bargain was broken when, in the face of an ever-growing crisis of mounting inflation, rising unemployment and the need to meet the conditions of the IMF loan, the government announced 'stage three', involving a limit of 10 per cent. Overall, the 10 per cent limit imposed by stage three proved highly effective due to a combination of falling inflation, tacit TUC consent and the willingness of the government to use sanctions against any unions that defied the limit; as a result, twelve million workers settled for pay claims within the government's guidelines within the first thirty six weeks of the policy (Coates 1980: 76).

Despite the large degree of union compliance, stage three had tested the relationship between the government and the unions (particularly the rank and file members) to the full. As a result: 'the gap between government aspiration and working-class response which had begun to emerge under stage three came fully into the open in the fourth year of the Labour government's incomes policy' (ibid.: 77). In a White Paper, *Winning the Battle Against Inflation* published in 1978, the government had announced its intention to impose a 'fourth stage'; moreover, it had indicated that this would provide the stepping stone for 'a transition to . . . longer term arrangements' (quoted in Coates 1980: 77). All in all, the government had toughened its stance towards incomes policy, with the announcement of a new 5 per cent pay norm and its intention to make way for a more permanent policy (ibid.). The outcome was a flare-up of tension between the government and unions, with the latter demanding a return to the Social Contract at their annual conference. However, the government remained resolute and the result was a major conflict which left both sides permanently bruised.

The subsequent 'Winter of Discontent' had been presaged by a breach of the government's incomes policy by Ford workers, who had gained a settlement of 17 per cent in November 1978 following a nine-week strike (Cronin 1991: 240). This significantly undermined the government's 5 per cent target and made it highly unlikely that other unions would fall into line with official government policy. The result was a series of strikes throughout the winter for settlements above 5 per cent. These reached a peak shortly after the New Year when widespread and disruptive action was pursued by large numbers of public sector workers. In addition, strikes by over one million local authority manual workers caused further disruption as refuse began to pile up and roads remained ungritted and unsalted. Accordingly, as Dorey (1995: 153) explains: 'with roads treacherous, train services disrupted, and lorry drivers on strike, Britain was literally coming to a standstill'. This impression of virtual anomie was richly exploited (and indeed created) by the media who were hungry for images and exaggerated accounts of those hit hardest by the industrial action. As Hay (1996) explains, these media constructions (and indeed, distortions) of Britain in 'crisis' played a crucial role in simultaneously de-legitimising the actions of the labour movement and granting legitimacy to the rhetorical machinations of the New Right. In particular, they provided an environment in which the Conservatives were able to portray the 'Winter of Discontent' as a crisis of an 'overloaded' state 'held to ransom' by the unions (Hay 1996: 120).

In actual fact, the reality was quite the opposite; for as Hay (ibid.: 118) explains, the 'Winter of Discontent' emerged out of a situation in which 'the trade unions were effectively being held to ransom by the government'. Often overlooked within the literature is the fact that the Winter of Discontent had been preceded by a long Summer of Comparative Content which had lasted almost four years (ibid.; also Coates 1980: 260). During this period, the unions had engaged in a highly disciplined round of wage restraint.[3] This had been exercised on the premise that the main conditions of the Social Contract would still apply. Yet, by 1978 this strategy was both dead and buried in spite of the unprecedented levels of union discipline.

As a result, the unions were faced with a government which was announcing its intent to impose a permanent and unconditional system of statutory wage restraint that would further erode workers living standards, and an opposition determined to implement a major assault on the unions, and hungry to exploit any divisions which might appear between the Labour government and the union movement (Hay 1996: 119). The response of the government was to take advantage of the weak position of the unions, by attempting to limit wage increases to only 5 per cent. Meanwhile, the response of the TUC was to try to limit the extent of confrontation between the government and the unions. This left TUC leaders vulnerable to the charge, from rank and file members, that they were playing the role of co-conspirators in the government's betrayal of the union movement. Consequently, the 'Winter of Discontent' reflected the reaction of the rank and file movement, rather than the TUC in general, to the 'hostage situation' in which they found themselves (Gourevitch *et al.* 1984: 374–7). Discouraged by the relative passivity of the TUC leadership, and by the overall absence of any reward for their earlier co-operation with government strategy, the rank and file began to enact a series of 'local rebellions' against the imposition of the 5 per cent target from above (Hay 1996; 119).

Overall then, the conflict had resulted not from the strength of the unions' position but from a relative weakness (Dorfman 1983: 59–60; Marsh 1992: 62; Hay 1996: 120). Unable to prevent themselves from being backed into a corner by the Labour government, the unions had also suffered from their historical fragmentation which had prevented them from implementing a coordinated and coherent response to the significant losses in real wages within a very short period of time. Ironically, the overall result was that, having been forced by their relative lack of power into a bitter and damaging conflict with the government, they had now opened up room for a political strategy that would rob them of the very limited power which they had left.

Thatcherite ascendancy

Labour's strategy from 1976–9 has been variously described as modified Keynesianism (Coopey and Woodward 1996: 13), unbelieving monetarism (Keegan and Pennant-Rae 1979; Brittan 1977) and proto-Thatcherite (Riddell 1983: 58–9). All of these labels are essentially accurate to different degrees, though none are quite adequate to tell the full story. The first fails to illuminate the fact that that Keynesianism had been modified, adapted and even abandoned at several points throughout the postwar period, while the second implies that somehow a retreat back into financial orthodoxy represented an affront to the Labour Party's deepest principles. That view, however, neglects the fact that this was the third consecutive postwar Labour government to have abandoned expansionism in favour of deflation and retrenchment. Moreover, this was virtually the same leadership that had turned so spectacularly against the unions a decade earlier. Finally, it would also be wrong to view Labour's strategy as essentially Thatcherite; this would be again to neglect the fact that the policy of retreat had become a (if not *the*) dominant feature of postwar British politics. What is more, it also ignores the important fact that Thatcherism eventually emerged as a state strategy which was somewhat larger in scope than the narrow content of its economic policy. As Overbeek explains:

> monetarism was used by Labour as if it were indeed a class-neutral, objective policy, and it was not recognised that for monetarism to 'work' it would necessarily have to be embedded in a wider *political* strategy, in a truly global concept of control.
>
> (Overbeek 1990: 174–5)

While the 'Winter of Discontent' was rapidly pulling the carpet out from under the feet of the labour movement, the political strategy designed to put monetarism into effect was being slowly pieced together within the Conservative Party.

Thatcherism had gained its ascendancy within the Conservative Party following widespread internal disillusionment over the failure of Edward Heath's strategy and the victory of Mrs Thatcher in the subsequent leadership contest. Yet, as Overbeek (1990: 176) explains, Thatcherism 'did not drop out of a clear blue sky'. As we saw in the previous two chapters, many of the essential ingredients of what was to become Thatcherism were not just present (and continually evolving) throughout the postwar period within the Conservative Party; they were also institutionalised within central state structures such as the Treasury and the Bank of England. Thus, in many respects, the Thatcher project emerged as a final evolutionary stage in the development of forces which had continually raged against efforts to expand the state in the postwar period. A whole stream of different factors had combined to enable these forces to gain an ascendancy in Britain. These included:

- the structural selectivity of the British postwar political and economic environment against state expansion and social democracy, thereby rendering attempts at state expansion ineffective

- the failure of successive postwar political actors to alter their environment and thereby create a space for a firm and coherent settlement over the direction of government strategy
- the continuing global crisis of capitalist accumulation and the accompanying fiscal crisis of the state
- the failure of the corporate-liberal and social-democratic strategies of the Conservative and Labour governments in the mid-1970s to halt these crises
- the growing disillusionment of the electorate in the face of the growing crisis
- the success of the New Right in being able to narrate a particular conception of the crisis which pinned the blame on excessive union power and state intervention.

Where Thatcherism did differ most from earlier experience was the way in which it combined traditional liberal beliefs (this time stripped of any 'one nation' pretensions) with a pervasive social and moral conservatism (Hall 1979; King 1987; Gamble 1988).[4] This combination of values tilted the 'liberalism' of the Thatcher governments further towards the right of the political spectrum than most of their predecessors and helped to ensure that, during its early years, Thatcherism encountered significant opposition from the remaining corporate-liberal elements within the Conservative Party. Yet, it would be wrong to place too much emphasis upon the ideological content of Thatcherism since, as we have seen, ideological commitment at a discursive level can often be used to disguise a much more pragmatic, or even cynical, approach to policy-making. Moreover, a determined ideological vision does not automatically provide policy-makers with a clear indication of the type of specific policy adaptations that are necessary to achieve their overall ideological aims. A consideration of these points is necessary for a proper understanding of the evolution of Thatcherism. For, although the Thatcherite strategy was underpinned by a relatively clear (though often contradictory) ideological vision, it would be some time before the Conservatives discovered for themselves what the actual application of their strategic objectives entailed.

Monetarist experimentation 1979–83

The 'radicalism' of the Thatcher governments had been proclaimed even before the Conservatives had entered office in 1979. While the Conservatives had of their own accord been busily elevating themselves to the status of radical pioneers in a new type of governmental strategy, academics and journalists were endorsing these claims amid a flurry of articles pronouncing that Thatcherism involved a fundamental change in the direction of postwar British politics. The authors of *Marxism Today* asserted that the Conservatives intended to achieve a new type of hegemonic control. As such, the term 'Thatcherism' (more commonly referred to then as 'authoritarian populism') was coined even before there was a 'Thatcherism' in any material sense. These proclamations of the radicalism of the Thatcher project had a subsequent effect upon our interpretations of not only the Conservative governments, but also of the early postwar period. At this stage of the so-called Thatcher project, however, there were no real institutional reforms or policy successes upon which to judge the radicalism of the Thatcherites.

A few moments of sober reflection amidst the hysteria and hype surrounding the ascendancy of the New Right may have curtailed the exaggeration of Thatcherism's radicalism. On the one hand, we could have reminded ourselves that the Thatcherite philosophy contained many elements that were already familiar in postwar British politics, while, on the other, we may also have observed the fact that the Conservatives had entered office with what amounted to only a limited set of policy prescriptions for change (Marsh and Rhodes 1992). In order to satisfy their highly abstract strategic objective of rolling back the state, the Thatcherites would have to engage in a protracted process of policy experimentation and adaptation over a substantial number of years before the precise contours of their strategy would become clear, even to the Conservatives themselves.

It is precisely this process of experimentation which became the dominant feature of the Thatcher governments' first phase in power. Throughout this period, the Conservatives proceeded slowly, concentrating almost exclusively upon a narrow monetarist economic strategy which they eventually abandoned in favour of significant strategic adaptations. The result was that they would meet with little success and significant opposition and, in the end, be bailed out of their dilemmas by a war that would serve as a distraction from the fact that they had few real policy initiatives at their disposal.

The first Thatcher government

When the Conservatives entered office in 1979, they did so with a relatively clear parliamentary majority of forty-three seats. This gave them an important amount of breathing space, compared to the heavy parliamentary constraints suffered by the previous Labour government. Above all, it meant that the new government did not need to get bogged down in a protracted bargaining process with other parties or groups of actors to secure the passage of its legislation. However, the Thatcherites within the party did not have a ringing endorsement for the implementation of their strictly monetarist objectives, either from the electorate or, indeed, from the party itself. At this stage, 'Thatcherism', although largely in the ascendancy, still had to consolidate its power base and establish its overall legitimacy (Jessop *et al.* 1988: 62–3).

The first Cabinet of the new government was balanced between Thatcherite supporters and more traditional 'one nation' Tory 'Wets', most notably James Prior. Overall, this ensured that on many issues, but on the application of a strict monetarist philosophy in particular, the Cabinet – for the next few years at least – remained deeply divided. This proved a major restraint upon the ability of the Thatcherites to pursue their strategic objectives as forcefully as they would otherwise have wished. Nevertheless, the strategic agenda of the first Thatcher government was limited to implementing an overall monetarist economic doctrine. According to Butler and Kavanagh (1980: 154; also Krieger 1986: 72), the Conservatives manifesto: 'took the "highground" and presented the party's style and philosophy rather than a shopping list of proposals'. In part this reflected the tenuous balance of power held by the Thatcherites, but it was also perhaps more a reflection of the narrow content of the Conservatives strategy.

In opposition the Thatcherites had expounded their strategic objectives at a high level of abstraction, concentrating more on the direction in which they did *not* want to go. Overall, they had pledged to end some (though in their eyes most) of the policies implemented by previous postwar governments, such as: corporatism; Keynesian budgetary policy; the priority of maintaining full employment; the consolidation and incorporation of key producer interests; and direct state intervention. Of course, they omitted to mention that their own strategy would consist of other goals which had been dominant in the earlier postwar period such as: the priority of controlling inflation; an assault on trade union power; tight controls on public expenditure; and a liberal policy of arm's length government. Overall, in their first term the Conservatives were involved in the process not so much of creating a new direction as of ending the previous constant fluctuations in government strategy. They were stripping away the conflicts and contradictions at the heart of policy and forging an identity which was negatively defined by the types of direction that were to be rejected. In this sense then, as McAnulla (1997; 1999) perceptively notes, the Thatcherites were initially involved in 'symbolic politics'; their overall strategy was conceptually weak and, as a result, they had to rely upon distancing themselves from a whole series of symbolic 'others'.

In place of the strategies that the Thatcherites were rejecting there was an overwhelming emphasis upon the abstract promise to reduce the role of the state. Yet, at this stage, this seemingly grand vision remained devoid of many substantive ideas on how this would be achieved. Instead, the Conservatives put the vast bulk of their first-term energies into the control of inflation through the application of monetarist discipline. As we have already seen, prioritising inflation was by no means a radical aim for a postwar government, yet the economic philosophy of monetarism did represent a new means of achieving this goal. Monetarism had already become

popular amongst a number of economists, journalists and economic institutions throughout the western world. It was premised essentially upon the
idea that inflationary spirals were a direct result of fluctuations in the supply
of money, and thus any attempt at controlling inflation needed to involve
concomitant restrictions upon monetary targets. However, for the
Thatcherites, monetarism was interpreted, during their first phase of power,
in a very narrow and dogmatic sense. As Britton explains:

> the proposition that 'money matters' was by this time common ground
> for most commentators, for the Treasury, the Bank and backbench
> MPs. But for the first twelve or fifteen months of the new government,
> economic policy was governed by the far stronger proposition that
> 'only money matters'.
>
> (Britton 1991: 45)

The Thatcherites' first two budgets signalled their monetarist intent, as
well as their determination to achieve a secondary policy objective, that of
providing tax incentives for the Conservatives' own electoral constituency.
As Gamble (1988: 98–9) explains, the first budget, introduced a month
after the election: 'had two principal objectives – lowering the rate of
inflation through a severe monetary and fiscal squeeze and beginning a
major restructuring of the burden of taxation'. The first of these objectives
was to be achieved primarily through the announcement of restrictions on
the Public Sector Borrowing Requirement, a cut of £1.5 billion in public
expenditure and a tightening of cash limits which would reduce spending
by a further £1 billion (ibid.). Moreover, the government also set about
raising interest rates from 12 to 14 per cent: they later reached as high as
17 per cent. The aim to restructure the tax system was signalled by an
increase in the rate of value added tax (VAT) from 8 to 15 per cent and an
accompanying reduction in income tax from 33 to 30 per cent. Moreover,
the budget also announced a rise in personal tax allowances while the top
rate of income tax was reduced from 83 per cent to 60 per cent (ibid.). The
government's second budget in March 1980 saw an extension in the
commitment to a monetarist economic approach. This time, a medium
term financial strategy (MTFS) was announced to set targets for the growth
of the money supply, defined as £M3, over a four year period. Moreover,
the PSBR would be reduced gradually through cuts in public expenditure.
In addition, the government quickly abolished exchange controls. The
environment for this move had been set by the relative strength of sterling
as well as the lesson, drawn from the experience of 1976, that exchange
control did not necessarily prevent a run on sterling.

At this stage however, the government's reliance upon a narrow and
strict application of monetarist philosophy did provoke significant opposition from different quarters. This was mainly due to the rapid
deterioration in the economic environment. As Gamble explains:

during 1980 the recession deepened rapidly. High interest rates and soaring oil prices combined to push up sterling by 12 per cent. The competitiveness of British companies declined by 35 to 45 per cent. Both profits and liquidity were severely squeezed. A mounting wave of bankruptcies, plant closures, and lay-offs was the result. Unemployment rose rapidly month by month. By the end of the year it had reached 2.13 million, an increase of 836,000. Inflation was soaring too, peaking at 21.9 per cent in May 1980.

(Gamble 1988: 101)

The worsening economic situation placed mounting pressure upon the government to change its course. This dissent became worse after the 1981 budget took the monetarist onslaught a stage further by announcing drastic austerity measures in the midst of industrial crisis and accelerating unemployment. According to Jessop *et al.*:

the industrial crisis intensified under the impact of the 1981 budget and the de-industrialisation process and unemployment accelerated. The crisis of government authority also deteriorated and the opposition to Thatcherism mounted. By mid-1981 it was threatened on all fronts: the Cabinet, the Conservative party in Parliament and the country, the Lords, most sectors of commerce and industry, the City, the newly formed Social-Democratic Party, the electorate, the streets.

(Jessop *et al.* 1988: 63)

While popular opposition could be expected, the weight of dissent within the Establishment and central institutions such as the Bank and the City reflected the final residues of the conflicts of the postwar era. The forces arguing for Keynesianism and a commitment to state expansion may have been defeated in 1976, but they had never been truly killed off. As we saw in the previous chapter, the strong discursive commitment to these elements of postwar policy had provided an environment which created selective pressures that made it difficult for classical/neo-liberal forces to gain an absolute ascendancy. By the beginning of the 1980s, the effect of this prior discursive terrain was still strongly felt by the Thatcherites, whose control over the discursive environment was by no means complete. However, in time these would prove to be the last vestiges of the fundamental conflicts that had dominated the heart of postwar policy-making.

Overall, the government pressed ahead – and indeed, made a virtue out of pressing ahead in the face of opposition – with its strategic direction in spite of the growing dissent and the failure of their monetarist experiment to control the money supply. During their first eighteen months in office, the Thatcherites dismantled fifty-seven quangos, most notably among these the Price Commission (Gamble 1988: 102). Moreover, reforms were made in industrial relations with the introduction of the Employment Acts of 1980 and 1982 which imposed restrictions on closed shops and secondary picketing. These measures had been relatively moderate, however, compared to the government's crusading rhetoric and the exaggerated accounts of most commentators. Few significant structural changes had taken place, or were even proposed at this stage of the Conservatives' strategy. Virtual sole reliance had been placed upon the control of the money supply and, in the face of a failure to achieve this objective, the Conservatives had shown a relative dearth of ideas. Eventually, after 1982, even this objective was modified and then abandoned. Thus, by the end of the Conservatives' first term in office, there were few achievements and precious few radical initiatives or structural reforms for the Thatcherites to point to. Nevertheless, three things did act significantly in their favour: the Falklands War; their retreat from monetarism as an economic doctrine; and eventual signs of economic recovery. These all provided an important breathing space and a strong basis on which Thatcherism was able to consolidate its power. As Jessop *et al.* explain:

> in combination these enabled Thatcher to establish her control over the Cabinet, the Party, the Establishment and the country. The wets were finally defeated in the Cabinet and the Party and the main axis of conflict became consolidation vs radicalism; the Establishment was pleased to see the retreat from monetarism; and the electorate was pacified through the Falklands war, the reflationary budget in 1982, and the cyclical upswing after the 1980–1 recession. Thus the stage was set for the second election victory.
>
> (Jessop *et al.* 1988: 64)

More importantly, the stage was now set for a final settlement of Britain's long period of postwar political and ideological conflict.

Consolidating Thatcherism, 1983–7

With talk of economic recovery having replaced that of recession, and the Conservatives back in power in 1983 with a massive 144-seat majority, the Thatcherites were now in a position to consolidate their power base and proceed relatively unopposed to define the contours of their strategy. Yet, at this point, there were still few indications as to what the precise contours of the Conservatives' strategy would entail. Although the Thatcherites claimed that economic recovery had been brought about by monetarism, it was clear to most commentators, and increasingly to the Thatcherites themselves, that this was not the case. In fact, the recovery had been experienced throughout the capitalist world and was due largely to increased global demand and a reflation in the US economy (Gamble 1988: 111). In Britain, there was a widespread belief that monetarism, rather than having contributed to the upswing in the economy, had merely added to the country's difficulties by heightening the long-term industrial crisis and causing social and economic turmoil. These latter problems did not deter the Thatcherites from their overall strategic direction, but the acknowledgment that monetarism was not working did persuade them to search for new solutions to the problem of controlling public expenditure and inflation. As we shall see, it was this search for a strategy which dominated much of the Conservatives' second phase of power, along with successive attempts to consolidate the position of Thatcherism. The immediate solution to both problems was the 'privatisation' of Britain's most profitable industries. This programme allowed the Conservatives to extend their electoral constituency by providing incentives to middle-class and even working-class voters; however, perhaps more importantly, it also served as an effective smokescreen for the fact that, at an institutional and policy level, the Thatcherites were still lacking any substantive strategic direction.

The shock-waves of Thatcherism

In many ways, the period from 1983 to 1987 was the most overtly shocking episode of the Thatcherite strategy. Boosted by their sweeping electoral victory, the control of the Cabinet and the victory in the Falklands War, the Thatcherites utilised their ascendancy in order to impose an aggressive onslaught on the last vestiges of institutionalised progressive liberalism and social democracy. This attempt to kill off any remaining conflict and opposition saw the government engage in a protracted, brutal and sometimes violent struggle with a whole series of so-called 'enemies within'. Foremost among these were the miners. The government had from the outset openly espoused its intention of reforming the trade unions; in their first term, however, their radical rhetoric had been accompanied, as in most areas of policy, by limited institutional reform. In part, this was due to the fact that the Conservatives had been sidetracked by economic difficulties, while Mrs Thatcher herself had been persuaded by colleagues that the time was not right for an open confrontation with the unions. Nevertheless, the experience of the Heath years had left its scar, and the government's determination to take on the unions had never receded (Marsh 1992). In 1984, the Trade Union Act was passed to erode further trade union rights and limit the potential for strike action. It built upon the two previous pieces of union legislation which, when combined, appeared to reveal an evolving and incremental strategy of industrial relations reform. This impression, however, belied the reality that the government's policy had been developed in a pragmatic and ad hoc manner, usually in response to external circumstances rather than ideological conviction (Marsh 1992; Dorey 1993). Again, this served to underline the fact that in general, the Conservatives overall strategy was evolving and adapting over time as the Thatcherites continually worked out and developed the contours of their strategic objectives through experience.

In place of structural reform, the Conservatives' strategy at this stage was largely composed of a series of 'symbolic' (though by no means insignif-icant) acts (McAnulla 1997; 1999). The assault against the miners during 1984–5 was one of the most potent and highly shocking of these. Rather than initially take on the union movement as a whole, the Conservatives had chosen to demoralise the trade unions by confronting and defeating the strongest union, the National Union of Mineworkers. This was of significant symbolic importance, for it was the miners who it was alleged (albeit wrongly) had brought down the Heath administration in 1974. By contrast with most other areas of policy, the strategy for dealing with the miners had been worked out in opposition, by the then shadow energy minister Nicholas Ridley. The 'Ridley Report' (which had been leaked to *The Economist* in 1978) had laid down a series of recommendations about the steps that a future Conservative government should take in order to confront the miners. As Dorey explains:

> the recommended measures included: building up coal reserves by encouraging overtime and productivity bonuses to miners; making contingency plans to import coal; recruiting non-union lorry drivers through road haulage companies, to guarantee the movement of coal during a strike; reducing social security payments to strikers; and ensuring that the police were well-organised and resourced, in order to tackle mass picketing.
>
> (Dorey 1995: 189)

These measures had been taken and, by the time the miners' strike was called following the announcement by the Coal Board, under the tough chairmanship of the newly appointed Ian MacGregor, that Cortonwood Colliery in South Yorkshire would be closed, the Conservatives were ready for a bitter confrontation. The strike lasted eleven months and in that period the government showed an overwhelming ruthlessness in its deter-mination to defeat the miners, deploying the police in a manner more akin to that of a military conflict. Eventually success was achieved, due largely to the overall fragmentation and demoralisation of the left following Labour's two election defeats, and to the Thatcher government's ability to divide working-class interests through tax incentives, council house sales and the extension of share ownership.

On other fronts, the Thatcherites were no less brutal in their attempts to subordinate any remnants of opposition. In local government, they abolished the Greater London Council and the six metropolitan authori-ties in the face of determined and bitter opposition. The period was also dominated by a protracted struggle between the government and Labour-controlled local authorities over imposed control of local government spending. Unions were banned from Government Communications Headquarters (GCHQ) while the print unions were faced down in bitter confrontations at Warrington and Wapping, and even the BBC was subjected to attack.

Behind these overt manifestations of Thatcherite radicalism, however, Thatcherism had still made little impression at a policy and institutional level. In essence, the Conservatives' strategy was displaying a great deal of drift (Jessop *et al.* 1988: 64–5). Thus, a significant gap had appeared between the public face of Thatcherism and the less public 'piecemeal measures' that characterised the implementation of Thatcherite policy (ibid.: 65). As Jessop *et al.* (ibid.) explain: 'the basic strategy was to consolidate past gains, press ahead cautiously on a broad front, launch more radical attacks on selected targets and move carefully beyond legal and monetary restraint towards a broader-based neo-liberal strategy'. The problem for the Thatcherites was that there was little core to their neo-liberal strategy following the retreat from monetarism.

In the medium term, this vacuum was temporarily filled by an emphasis upon 'privatisation'. Again, the government's privatisation programme reflected the essentially ad hoc nature of the evolution of Thatcherite strategy during this period (Marsh 1991). In opposition, the government had placed little emphasis upon tackling the nationalised industries, and during their first term had taken few steps to institute any major reforms. Nevertheless, some initial steps had been taken between 1979 and 1982 with the relatively moderate sale of shares in firms such as British Petroleum, British Aerospace, Cable and Wireless and the National Freight Company. Learning from this experience, and from the success of the government's sales of council houses, the Conservatives began, during their second term, to place privatisation at the centre of their strategy. As a result, moves were taken to sell off significant shares in the most profitable nationalised industries such as telecommunications, gas and electricity.

Much has been made within the literature of the radicalism of these measures. To the Conservatives and most commentators, the privatisation programme appeared as the most tangible evidence of the Thatcher 'revolution', since it accorded favourably with their free-market rhetoric and the newly emerging discourse of creating a 'share-owning democracy'. Yet, this rhetoric disguised two important facts. First, the denationalisations were in many respects a convenient way of hiding the fact that the government were largely bereft of a coherent and effective strategy for meeting their overall strategic objectives. At this point, the strategy amounted to nothing more than a series of experiments with supply-side measures, and a host of arbitrary controls on government spending (Gamble 1988: 114; Jessop *et al.* 1988: 65). Second, the process of selling off shares did not, in itself, represent any type of strategy to replace monetarism; rather, it represented a supreme example of short-term political expediency. This was reflected in the fact that the revenues gained from the privatisation programme were cynically used to manipulate the figures for the amount the government was spending. Moreover, the programme was also used to bolster the Thatcherites' principal objective during this period: that of consolidating their power base and electoral constituency.

Overall, the privatisation programme did little to achieve broader economic objectives (Marsh 1992). While it failed on the whole to extend competition and efficiency, it was also accompanied by a significant increase in government regulation. Thus, the series of denationalisations during this phase represented an appropriate distraction from the overall lack of government strategy, while enabling the Conservatives to maintain their hold on power and appear to be making significant institutional reforms broadly in line with their New Right, free-market rhetoric. Once again, this was an exemplary lesson in symbolic politics.

Generally speaking however, throughout the 1983–7 period the Thatcherites had taken the gloves off and unleashed a series of major assaults upon the last vestiges of progressive liberalism and social democracy. These incidents, along with the Conservatives' dogmatic market rhetoric, and cynical 'two-nations' strategy, were particularly shocking to most right-minded observers. Yet, the aggressiveness of the Thatcher governments during this period disguised the fact that, in strategic terms, they were running short of ideas about how to meet their overall objectives. Privatisation provided their strategy with apparent coherence; it worked well for the Thatcherites for it could be justified in ideological terms as an extension of their belief in market forces and the creation of private property. However, the selling off of government shares represented a cynical strategic adaptation designed to provide the Conservatives with a stopgap to replace the failure of monetarism, and enough breathing space to calculate their next moves. Other than privatisation, the period was dominated by a series of ad hoc experimentations with ways of relieving the burden of public expenditure. Few of these were successful and, as a result, it would take the Conservatives until their third term before they finally hit upon a coherent and decisive strategic adaptation which could evolve over time into an ever more radical series of structural changes.

Reinvented Thatcherism, 1987–90

In the run-up to the 1987 election, the view that the Thatcherite strategy was starting to drift began to dominate Conservative thinking. As a result, at their 1986 party conference the Conservatives announced their intention to enter the general election with a firm commitment to radical structural reform. In effect, the Thatcherite mix of traditional liberal beliefs and strong moral conservatism had thus far displayed very little liberalism and a great deal of institutional conservatism. Throughout their first two terms, the Thatcherites had been engaged in a long process of ad hoc interventions and experimentation. This reflects the struggle which they had to develop the broad contours of their own strategy. What had initially begun as an abstract commitment to pushing back the state had in effect revealed itself short of any fundamental ideas about how this was to be achieved. By 1987 however, several strands of the Conservatives' ad hoc strategy began to evolve into a more coherent body of thought. As we will see, this period represented an important conjunctural moment for the Thatcherites (in more senses than one, given that it saw the end of Mrs Thatcher's term in office) since it represented the point at which the broad contours of their strategy began to fall into place and gain a radical momentum for the first time since their election in 1979.

Radical Thatcherism

Mrs Thatcher had called the 1987 general election without invoking any real risk of being defeated (Garnett 1996: 83). At the time 'the economic omens were still cheerful', while the opposition to the Conservatives was badly faltering (Morgan 1992). Thus, the Conservatives were quietly optimistic and could promise a series of more radical reforms. The tone for the Thatcherites' heightened reformist zeal had been set by the 1986 party conference, which had responded to a growing recognition that the Thatcher project was showing signs of having run out of ideas. In the approach to the election, their manifesto reflected the Conservatives' ambitions with pledges to: cut the basic rate of income tax to 25 per cent; impose further industrial relations reforms; introduce a national curriculum in the area of education; and introduce a Community Charge, or 'Poll Tax' to replace the existing system of domestic rates (Garnett 1996: 83). In fact, by the end of their third term these proposals would appear relatively tame in comparison to the series of institutional changes that the Conservatives eventually introduced. One of the factors which had a profound effect upon the Thatcherites' strategy in their third period had occurred during the election campaign itself, when the issue arose of what should be done with the increasing expenditure in the National Health Service. A growing sense of crisis in the NHS had been developing before the election and, given that Labour had turned the issue into a central part of its campaign strategy, the Conservatives were forced to respond by promising to review their policy. In the end, the reform of the health service became a major plank of the Conservatives' strategy, and this experience, combined with their growing interest in tackling the public sector in general, resulted in a series of radical institutional changes thus far unprecedented in the evolution of the Thatcher project.

Of course, one factor which would have an important effect upon the Conservatives' ability to heighten their radicalism in their third term was the relative lack of effective opposition. In parliamentary terms, they had won the general election with a majority similar to that gained in 1983, picking up a 43 per cent share of the vote (376 seats), compared to

Labour's 30.8 per cent (229 seats) and the Alliance's 22.6 per cent (22 seats). However, the lack of fundamental conflict was more profound than this, for by this stage the Conservatives had effectively nullified most pockets of effective resistance by either overt assault or dividing the opposition using financial incentives such as council house sales and the sale of shares. As Garnett (1996: 84) explains: 'after the 1987 election, the absence of dangerous enemies outside the Conservative Party meant that the government was able to focus on consolidating its[self] by re-designing the institutions of the welfare state'.

It is, of course, true to say that the changes that were to come were not entirely unprecedented. Throughout their first two terms the Thatcher governments had experimented with several ways of reforming both the public sector and the welfare state. These included: the 1980 Education Act; the Financial Management Initiative; the Griffiths Report into the National Health Service; and the Fowler Review of social security. These, though, had mainly led to only minor and certainly ad hoc changes; they reflected disparate types of ideas, underpinned by a coherent discourse but by no means part of a coherent and consistent strategy. In the third term however, some of these former initiatives were combined with previous measures such as contracting-out and privatisation, and with ideas which had been tried in other countries, in order to create a more determined and effective strategic mutation that took shape and evolved throughout this phase of 'radical Thatcherism'.

The resulting process, which appeared as something of an international trend towards 'reinventing government' (Osborne and Gaebler 1990), or 'hollowing out the state' (Rhodes 1994), manifested itself in a wholesale reform of the basic system of welfare provision and the public sector in general, following publication of the *Next Steps* report. Building upon the previous Social Security Act (1986), the Conservatives introduced the Education Reform Act (1988), the Housing Act (1988), the National Health and Community Care Act (1990), and a wider reform of the NHS following the publication of the 1989 White Paper, *Working for Patients* (Pierson 1996: 206).

As regards welfare, the most radical policies were those implemented in the areas of education and health. In education, the main measures included: the introduction of a new national curriculum; a policy of open enrolment that would enable parents to choose which schools their children would attend; the transference of the management of schools from Local Education Authorities to the schools' own governing bodies; the option for schools to 'opt-out' of local authority control and become grant-maintained; and new funding and planning arrangements for universities and polytechnics (ibid.: 207). In health, the reforms were based around the creation of an 'internal market' entailing a basic split between those responsible for purchasing health services and those responsible for health provision. These included measures for: delegating decision-making to district, hospital or general practitioner (GP) levels; allowing hospitals and other health service providers to opt-out of local authority control and establish trust status; allowing health authorities to have the freedom to buy services from a variety of different providers; allowing GPs to hold their own budgets; and encouraging managerialism within the health service based upon private sector methods (ibid.: 210).

Meanwhile, the implementation of the main recommendations of the Ibbs Report – *The Next Steps* – into the functions of government departments, heralded similar wholesale changes to the structure of the public sector in general. In particular, the 'Next Steps' process involved the creation of: 'a division in departments between those who are policy advisers and makers at the core of a department, and those concerned with service delivery' (Smith 1996: 153). The central plank of the policy was the hiving off of the parts of departments responsible for service delivery into management agencies which would have greater freedom to determine the delivery of services, control budgets and staffing levels. Overall: 'this proposal would effectively dismantle the apparently monolithic and unified civil service established in the nineteenth century' (ibid.: 153). In its place would be a 'loose federation of many smaller agencies, units and core predominates' (Kemp 1993: 8; quoted in Smith 1996: 153).

However, while these reforms marked the most energetic and radical period of the Thatcher project thus far, they were accompanied by a whole series of problems which led to the eventual downfall of Mrs Thatcher herself. The first of these was the implementation of the Community Charge, or Poll Tax, designed to replace the existing system of domestic rates. This policy, of replacing a progressive system of taxation with a profoundly regressive one, clearly aimed at satisfying the Conservatives' own electoral constituency, had been widely associated with Mrs Thatcher herself. Overall, the implementation of the Poll Tax proved to be one of the most important political blunders of the entire postwar era (Dorey 1995: 210). It provoked widespread, and (given the overall lack of popular mobilisation against Thatcherism) unprecedented levels of opposition which the government met with characteristic aggression, yet even this could not dampen the deep-seated hostility to the policy. Even within the Conservative Party, Mrs Thatcher faced fundamental conflict over the decision to implement the Community Charge.

Meanwhile, on an economic front, Mrs Thatcher experienced other major difficulties when Nigel Lawson's 1988 budget, which had been unnecessarily expansionary at a time of economic growth, caused the economy to overheat because of a massive increase in demand and levels of consumer credit. In response to rising inflation, the Chancellor pushed interest rates up. This measure had three major effects (Dorey 1995: 217). First, it caused an increase in unemployment and, for the first time since the beginning of the Thatcher project, this affected large sections of middle-class workers, particularly in the South of England. As Dorey (ibid.)

cynically notes: 'many of those who had been used to clasping a Pimms suddenly found themselves clutching a P45'. Second, Mrs Thatcher's natural electoral constituency was further hit by falling house-prices, thereby introducing the concept of negative equity into popular discourse. Third, the financial hardship for the middle classes was worsened by the overall rise in mortgage values instigated by the rises in interest rates.

As a result, the economy was plunged back into recession, thereby provoking a new round of criticism of Mrs Thatcher. These criticisms became even more widespread following Mrs Thatcher's toughening stance towards Europe and her treatment of those ministers closest to her, particularly Geoffrey Howe and Nigel Lawson. Such factors, along with the unpopularity of the Poll Tax and the general state of the economy combined to increase the opposition to Thatcher to an extent that made her position ultimately untenable. However, it is important here to emphasise that, although large pockets of resistance had begun to appear, these were not primarily aimed at the Thatcherite project. Perhaps the best evidence for this lay in the fact that, as the Conservatives' strategy rolled on, it was now being given further legitimation by the Labour Party whose policy review had endorsed many of the reforms which were taking place. Rather, opposition was aimed at Mrs Thatcher herself, who was increasingly viewed as having become detached from political reality and despotic in her approach.

Thus, when, on 22 November 1990, Mrs Thatcher was finally forced to resign by her Cabinet colleagues, the scene was set for a continuation and, indeed, a major extension of the Thatcher project without Mrs Thatcher at the helm. Overall, the 1987–91 period represented a key conjunctural moment in the evolution of the Conservatives' strategy. In effect, Thatcherism had reinvented itself and, as we shall see, subsequently was able to begin the process of reinventing large parts of the public sector.

Thatcherism's Major offensive, 1990–7

Mrs Thatcher's departure from office reflected a growing conflict over Thatcherism, within both the Conservative Party and the general public. It is important, however, to place this conflict in perspective. As Jessop *et al.* (1988: 64–5) explain, from around the end of Mrs Thatcher's first term the major conflict had been between those who wished to consolidate Thatcherism and those who wanted to press on with more radical reform. By the end of the Conservatives' second phase of power, this conflict was temporarily resolved in favour of further radicalism; by 1990 however, as the Conservatives prepared to enter the new decade, the balance appeared to have swung back towards the consolidators again.

What is important to emphasise though, is that at the heart of policy-making these conflicts did not fundamentally threaten the Thatcher project of state retrenchment in such a way as successfully to threaten attempts at state expansion in the postwar period. There were no serious and effective calls for a reversal of the Thatcherite strategy, especially not from the Labour Party who, in their long-running policy review, appeared to be running to catch up with Conservative philosophy (Hay 1999). Instead, the opposition was to the excesses of Thatcherism rather than to the direction in which the Conservatives were travelling. Thus, although most people appeared outraged at the divisiveness of the Thatcherite project and its increasing authoritarianism, the basic underlying Thatcherite philosophy remained the dominant mode of 'common sense' (Hall 1991). As such, Thatcherism still represented something of an uncontested policy paradigm. By 1990 a demand had appeared, not for an end to Thatcherism, but for Thatcherism with a more human face.

The candidate considered most likely to satisfy this demand was John Major, a willing supporter of Thatcherism (who was indeed, supported by Mrs Thatcher herself), yet popularly acclaimed as possessing a conciliatory air that would allow him to adopt a more consensual approach than his predecessor. Major's outward appearance of traditional 'one-nation' Toryism, combined with his inner belief in Thatcherite philosophy, provoked questions as to whether he would emerge as a consolidator who would aim merely to clear up the debris caused by his predecessor, or whether he would press on with radical reform.

Unfortunately, as we saw in Chapter Two, these questions have not been seriously examined by political scientists, who appeared either disinterested in analysing Major's impact on policy, or content merely to judge his achievements at face value. At face value, 'Majorism' appeared to give no real value-added. The grey image that surrounded Conservative policy-making at this time convinced most commentators that this was a rather banal period of the Conservatives' strategy. Major was portrayed as a 'ditherer', an incompetent who merely reacted to circumstances, rather than as an instigator of radical reform (Kerr, McAnulla and Marsh 1997; McAnulla 1997, 1999). In part, this is because many of the same commentators had been proclaiming Mrs Thatcher's radicalism for a number of years. Thus, the Thatcher 'revolution', it seemed, had already taken place and all that was left to do was to summarise its long list of achievements. However, as we have already seen, until the Conservatives' third term in office, these achievements lay largely at a symbolic rather than an institutional level.

Mrs Thatcher's early years had been dominated by attempts to smash the main icons of progressive liberalism and social democracy. At the policy-making level, the impact of Thatcherism was sketchy, and dominated by a seeming lack of substantive ideas about what the precise contours of the Conservative strategy should entail. By 1990, these contours had begun to take shape; the Thatcher project was in the process of beginning to carve up and hive off the central structures of the public sector and the welfare state. Yet this process was only starting to get off the ground and the main test of Major's radicalism as such would be whether or not he would choose to take up the initiative left by his predecessor and see the process of public sector and welfare reform through to its logical conclusion. As we shall see, this is precisely what the Major government strove to do, with an aggressiveness that belied the outward appearance of incompetence. Under Major, the Thatcherite project reached a crescendo and gained a level of radical momentum which Mrs Thatcher had certainly started but had been unable to follow through.

Late-Thatcherism

Throughout his term in office, John Major suffered from a whole series of constraints and environmental difficulties. His government inherited a complex and tenuous environment which had to be negotiated cautiously and which made it consistently difficult for Major to appear to stick to any firm and consistent direction. Here, it is worth reviewing in some detail the political, economic and ideological contexts in which Major found himself, since these help us to explain the gap between the appearance and the reality of the Conservatives' strategy that appeared during the Major years (Kerr, McAnulla and Marsh 1997).

Politically, by the time Major took over as leader of the Conservatives, Mrs Thatcher had already alienated much of the electoral and party support that had enabled the party to coast relatively easily through the 1980s. Thus Major inherited a legacy of discontent which, in turn, led to a whole range of political and electoral constraints. Major's main problem was the government's dwindling Parliamentary majority. The majority of twenty-one gained in 1992 was considerably smaller than anything in the 1980s. Thus, from the outset, Major had to cope with a significant and obvious loss of electoral confidence. This support declined still further after the election; consecutive by-election defeats and high-profile defections from the party eventually reduced the government's majority to one. As a result, Major had to strike a delicate balance between the demands of an electorate showing greater enthusiasm for a change of government, and those of a section of his parliamentary colleagues who remained solidly committed to the Thatcherite agenda. These factors significantly hampered Major's ability to show decisive and authoritative leadership.

However, the situation was made infinitely worse by the persistent splits within the Parliamentary Party. As Ludlam (1996: 98) points out: 'long before John Major could celebrate five years as Conservative Party leader, the party had fallen prey to the worst bout of in-fighting since the war, and arguably in this century'. Backbench rebellions plagued the Major administration to an unprecedented degree, and were sparked by a wide range of issues, including the decision to place VAT on fuel bills and the announcement of further pit closures. However, the central focus of intra-party division remained the issue of Europe. In 1993 the decision to ratify the Maastricht Treaty resulted in 'the most serious defeat sustained in Parliament by any Conservative government in the twentieth century' (ibid.: 101). More than a year later the fissure caused by the European issue led Major to take the unprecedented step of withdrawing the party whip from eight Euro-rebels, while in 1995 the split persuaded Major to resign in order to hold a premature leadership contest aimed at resolving the discontent.

However, perhaps the most disconcerting aspect of the post-Thatcher political inheritance for John Major was the resurgence of support for – and indeed, the public re-imaging of – the Labour Party. During his premiership Major faced an increasingly confident opposition from New Labour, which underwent further transformation following the Policy Review of the 1980s sparked by Neil Kinnock. In many ways the re-casting of the Labour Party, including its accommodation to many key aspects of the Thatcherite agenda, meant that it provided an unfamiliar style of opposition. Moreover, it attempted to steal the rhetorical ground from beneath the government on issues such as law and order and family values, long considered to be the Conservatives' own property. Overall then, Major was never afforded the luxury, which his predecessor had enjoyed, of being able to define a single, resolute, *rhetorical* direction for his government. Instead, party splits and electoral problems caused him to walk a very precarious tightrope between a whole set of often contradictory political demands.

On an economic front, the position for Major was no less tenuous. One of the main reasons for Mrs Thatcher's electoral success had been the fact that, throughout the 1980s, the Conservative Party exuded an image of economic competence. They were able successfully to present Labour as a party which would cause calamitous economic difficulties if they were elected. However, the Labour Party's accommodation to key elements of the Conservative Party's economic rhetoric meant that, under Major, the Conservatives started to become judged on their own economic record, rather than on the erstwhile appeal to the electorate's perceived fear of socialism. This had detrimental consequences for Major's own electoral fortunes, given the dire economic context in which he operated.

As Dorey (1995: 242–8) explains, three main factors had a damaging effect upon the Conservatives' economic strategy under Major. First, and foremost, was the protracted economic recession largely inherited from the Thatcher years. Although the Party successfully convinced voters during the 1992 election campaign that 'green shoots of recovery' were visible, these had failed to bring economic growth. This resulted in economic hardship which, again, not only affected areas previously hit during the earlier Thatcher years, but also damaged the Conservatives' own electoral constituency. As a result, Major, unlike his predecessor, found himself unable to provide economic benefits to potential Conservative voters.

A second key factor determining Major's economic difficulties was the size of the Public Sector Borrowing Requirement. By 1993 this had reached £50 billion, with little evidence of recovery taking place (Thompson 1996: 180). This severely compromised both the Conservatives' claims to economic rectitude and, most importantly, Major's commitment to cutting income tax. It also led directly to an unpopular budget in which the Chancellor, Kenneth Clarke, was forced to raise levels of indirect taxation and announce cuts in public spending of £10 billion over three years, adding further disaffection amongst the Conservatives' electoral constituency (Dorey 1995: 245). Further cuts were made into traditional areas of middle-class concern, such as mortgage tax relief and student grants. In this way, Major found himself robbed of a tool that was crucial to his predecessor: the ability to grant economic sweeteners to middle-class voters. The effects of a growing number of problems such as unemployment, mortgage arrears and negative equity among the middle class, meant that Major was unable to stick as rigidly to the confident commitment to New Right, free-market rhetoric as his predecessor.

The most pressing economic problem for Major, however, was the debacle over the government's membership of the Exchange Rate Mechanism (ERM), which resulted in the collapse of the Conservatives' economic strategy in September 1992. Major was personally implicated by his decision as Chancellor to take Britain into the ERM in 1990, against the advice of both Mrs Thatcher and her economic adviser Sir Alan Walters. Following a gradual depreciation in the pound over the two years after Britain entered, and a wave of financial uncertainty in September 1992, pressure on sterling grew and forced the government to spend up to £10 billion in order to try and rescue the UK's membership. On 16 September 1992, now known as 'Black Wednesday', the government's efforts to save sterling, and hence their economic strategy, failed in the face of an effective devaluation of 13 per cent (Dorey 1995: 244). The result was a massive blow to the image of economic competence which the Conservatives had previously relied upon. Overall then, the experience of 'Black Wednesday', combined with the increasingly damaging effects of a protracted recession and high borrowing figures, contributed to an economic context within which Major had to move from crisis to crisis. As Jay (1994: 176) explains: 'the inheritance which John Major thus received was, in macro-economic management terms, about as poisoned as it could be'. Consequently, Major was left without any solid ground upon which to build a successful, coherent economic discourse. He was consistently made to look incompetent and weak and was thus unable to enjoy the electoral benefits that the Conservatives' economic strategy had given his predecessor.

Major's problems were exacerbated by the tenuous ideological environment in which he found himself. Right-wingers, such as Michael Portillo, insisted that the party should continue its attachment to Thatcherism, retaining the ideological high-ground and regaining its electoral constituency by promoting greater affluence (Evans and Taylor 1996: 253). However, Major also came under mounting pressure from both inside and outside the party to 'soften' the hard-edged drive towards the individualistic ethos characteristic of the 1980s. As a result Major found himself forced into an ideological predicament – namely, the inherent tension in Conservative philosophy between individualism and communitarianism (Gamble 1996) – which, while evident during the Thatcher years, became particularly acute after Mrs Thatcher left office. While Thatcher's stronger electoral standing appeared to protect her from the need to reconcile these divisions, Major's more tenuous position re-emphasised the importance of maintaining a delicate balancing act between the two wings of the party. This severely constrained his ability to commit himself strongly to a coherent discourse that would convey the type of ideological conviction more generally associated with his predecessor. Instead, Major found himself forced to accede to demands for a re-statement of the traditional Conservative concern with social responsibility and cohesion.

The most infamous attempt to recharacterise the contemporary Conservative vision was Major's 'Back-to-Basics' campaign. However, this thinly-veiled search for a rhetorical theme in order to recapture the 'hearts and minds' of the electorate amounted to little more than a negative reaction to the moral ambiguities of Thatcherism (Garnett 1996: 152). The most awkward ideological inheritance for Major, though, was the heightened tension within the party between those who remain committed to closer European integration and the infamous band of Euro-sceptics whose opposition to Europe has become increasingly vociferous since Mrs Thatcher left office. Under John Major, long-standing underlying tensions caused by the European issue became increasingly evident and, at times, threatened to split the party. The main focus of these divisions was on the terms of the Maastricht Treaty. At the heart of the Euro-sceptics' position was the question of national sovereignty, which most felt to be threatened by the prospect of monetary union and the creation of a European Central Bank. The spectre of a federal Europe is one which haunts the majority of the party and, for this reason, Major was involved in intense negotiations to have the dreaded 'f-word' omitted from the terms of the Maastricht Treaty. To most Conservatives, his success in these negotiations, together with his decision to opt out of the Social Chapter, represented a satisfactory position from which to proceed towards monetary and political union. However, for those on the right of the party, the deep ideological antipathy to these developments remained unaffected. Overall then, many of the paradoxes of Mrs Thatcher's ideological legacy begun to unravel under Major. This meant that Major was bequeathed a very complex and difficult environment in which to define his own ideological rhetoric. He was forced into a very difficult balancing act between the interests of the two wings of his party, both on the domestic front and, in particular, over the question of Europe. Thus he

consistently found himself having to make a series of rhetorical commitments which appeared neutral and consolidatory by virtue of their sheer
emptiness.

What is clear, however, is the fact that the absence of coherent rhetoric
was not matched by the same hesitancy at a policy level. Instead, Major,
beneath his image of governmental incompetence, remained steadfastly
committed to a more aggressive strategy of re-structuring the state at a
domestic level and consolidating Britain's integration with the rest of
Europe on the external front. As a result, the lack of coherent rhetoric did
not present significant policy change. This point has been acknowledged
by only a few authors. For example, Garnett (1996: 146) notes that:
'Major's style brought the Conservative Party credit for a rethink that never
took place'. Meanwhile, Barker (1995) has pointed out that, in areas such
as local government, rail, the civil service, prisons, the NHS, education,
quangos and coal, Major pursued a 'trouble-seeking', ideologically aggressive Thatcherite strategy, despite his own 'agreeable greyness'. Moreover,
according to Ludlam and Smith (1996: 278), 'it has been in precisely those
areas (such as rail/coal privatisation, commercialisation of public services
and European opt-outs) where Thatcherism was incomplete that Major has
remained most faithful to the Thatcher project'.

Overall then, despite the misleading appearance of 'dithering' caused
by the environment in which they operated, the Major governments stuck
rigidly and often aggressively to the implementation of the Thatcherite
strategy. Major's main role was to oversee the implementation of the Next
Steps programme and the general movement, initiated by Mrs Thatcher,
toward the creation of an 'enabling state'. As Burch and Wood (1997: 38)
remark: 'it was really only under the Major governments from 1990
onwards, that the new package of measures that constitute this new form
of state began to be implemented'. Indeed, under Major, the process of
reform proceeded apace and was given a new radical impetus with the
introduction of the Citizens Charter and more importantly, 'market
testing' (Smith 1996: 159). Through market testing and contracting-out,
the Major government was able to claim, by 1995, that in the previous two
years it had reviewed £2 billion of government work and transferred more
than £1 billion to the private sector. Moreover, it had cut 26,000 posts from
the public sector, including 10,600 which had been transferred to the private sector and put out over 50 per cent of government work to the private
sector without any competing, in-house, Civil Service bid (Kerr, McAnulla
and Marsh 1997). As Smith (1996: 161; see also Harden 1992) explains,
through market testing Major pushed the state 'much closer to 'contract
government' whereby 'the state no longer provides services but is responsible for drawing up contracts for the development of services'.

Similarly, in welfare and social policy, Pierson argues:

>   Major's government [had] been putting in place, sometimes against

fierce opposition, the most profound institutional changes for half a
century, notably in the process of implementation which is, in many
ways, the decisive state in policy elaboration.

(Pierson 1996: 205)

The measures specifically initiated by the Major government in the area of
welfare provision included the setting up of league tables in schools and
the privatisation of school inspectorates, as well as subsequent moves
towards the introduction of a 'workfare' programme for the unemployed
(see for example, Kerr, McAnulla and Marsh 1997). In economic policy:
'the Major government differed from Mrs Thatcher's only by being less
flexible; it courted electoral defeat through its inactivity when economic
problems were affecting its natural supporters in the south' (Garnett 1996:
146). Part of the Major government's economic strategy was to see through
legislation for the privatisation of rail and coal in the face of stiff opposition. In industrial relations, the government pressed ahead unshakeably
with the direction taken by its predecessors. The 1990 Employment Act
had outlawed the closed shop, while the 1993 Trade Union Reform and
Employment Rights Act offered employers the right to provide financial
incentives to encourage employers to give up their union membership.
Other aspects of the Act included: the abolition of wages councils; the provision that trade union ballots were to give employees seven days notice
(after the result of the ballot) of strike action; the redefinition of the terms
of the Advisory Conciliation and Arbitration Service (ACAS) so that it was
no longer required to promote *collective* bargaining; and the provision that
customers of 'public services' could seek injunctions to prevent or termi-
nate unlawful industrial action within the public service (Dorey 1995: 249).
All in all, this legislation had taken the previous reforms by the Thatcher
governments to a new level of radicalism. As Dorey (ibid.) explains: 'the
Conservatives were concerned not merely to limit the power of the trade
unions through legislation, but also to by-pass them as far as, and whenever
possible'.

Meanwhile, in local government: 'the Major government seemed even
more anxious to replace local government with its unelected and secretive
quangos . . . by 1994 a joint study by Essex University and Charter 88 found
that there were 5,521 of these appointed bodies in the UK' (Garnett 1996:
144). Together, these reforms constituted a degree of change that the
Thatcher governments had never been able to match. Under Major, the
Conservative strategy had evolved into an increasingly coherent and
aggressive project which fundamentally transformed the nature of the
public sector and injected an ever more radical conception of the market
into the provision of public services. This period of 'late-Thatcherism' represented the fruition of Mrs Thatcher's early attempts at experimentation
and her efforts to see off any remaining effective opposition to the overall
direction in which the Conservatives wanted to go.

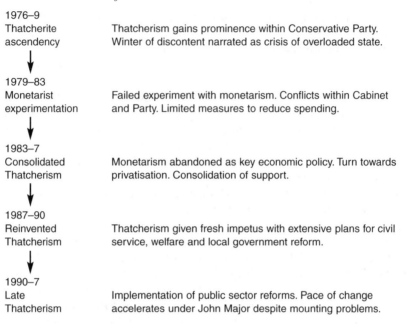

1976–9
Thatcherite
ascendency

Thatcherism gains prominence within Conservative Party.
Winter of discontent narrated as crisis of overloaded state.

1979–83
Monetarist
experimentation

Failed experiment with monetarism. Conflicts within Cabinet
and Party. Limited measures to reduce spending.

1983–7
Consolidated
Thatcherism

Monetarism abandoned as key economic policy. Turn towards
privatisation. Consolidation of support.

1987–90
Reinvented
Thatcherism

Thatcherism given fresh impetus with extensive plans for civil
service, welfare and local government reform.

1990–7
Late
Thatcherism

Implementation of public sector reforms. Pace of change
accelerates under John Major despite mounting problems.

Figure 7.1 The evolution of Thatcherism
Source: adapted and extended from Hay (1996), Jessop *et al.* (1988).

Conclusion

Overall then, the period of 'late-Thatcherism' witnessed the most fundamental institutional reforms of the postwar era. Here, the Conservatives
strategy had assumed an aggressiveness that was unprecedented even
during the bleak days of Mrs Thatcher's mid-term period, when the
unions, local authorities and many other pockets of resistance had been
systematically routed. The offensive this time was aimed at the institutional
structures of the state and, as a result, appeared a lot less visible than previous Thatcherite offensives. As a result, this period represented the most
radical phase of the Thatcherite strategy, even though it was dressed up in
the most banal and ineffectual clothing. Certainly, it is true to say that it
was Thatcher rather than Major who had instituted many of the changes
that had taken place. Thus, in this sense, the Major period was perhaps less
innovative than the third term of the Thatcher governments. Nevertheless,
it is the actual implementation of policy and the desire to drive it through
which determines the institutional impact of an era rather than the
rhetoric which precedes it; otherwise most governments could legitimately
claim to represent a fundamental change in the direction of policy.
Despite the institutional aggressiveness of the Major governments however,
perhaps the most disturbing aspect of this period was the overall neglect of
political scientists to acknowledge the fundamental changes that were

occurring beneath the grey image of John Major. The main reason for this lies in the fact that, to most commentators, the radicalism of the Thatcher project had been proclaimed even before it had properly revealed itself. Thus, to the majority of political scientists, Thatcherism had already exhausted itself. As we have seen, this was far from being the case, and, in actual fact, when Mrs Thatcher left office, there were large sections of the public sector that had escaped the ravages of the Thatcher project. When these finally were exposed to the Conservatives assault,' most political commentators had failed to recognise the changes, let alone criticise them. Consequently, the Conservatives under John Major were given an almost free rein systematically to alter Britain's public institutions one by one; not only did they encounter little resistance, they actually appeared to evoke next to no interest at all.

8　Final settlement
Thatcherism's hollow victory

Introduction

As we have seen, Thatcherism emerged out of the conflicts of the earlier postwar period as an antithesis to the Keynesian-corporatist strategy of 1972–6. Whereas both Heath and the previous Labour government had attempted to extend the evolving trend throughout the postwar period towards increased state expansion, Thatcherism represented an extension of the accompanying tendency towards liberal retrenchment. As a result, the Thatcher project did not simply mark a break with past practices; rather, it signalled a break with *some* of the practices of the postwar period and a continuation of others. Thatcherism therefore came to represent a final settlement – for a period at least – to Britain's postwar political conflict between progressive and classical liberal ideas about the role of the state.

With their firm pledge to reduce the capacities and responsibilities of the state, the Thatcher governments entered office with a resolve to kill off any remaining pockets of resistance to state retrenchment. In order to achieve this it was first necessary for them to interpret the source of the crisis facing the British state in a way that legitimised their strategic ambitions. As such, the Thatcherites narrated the problems of the 1970s as a crisis of an 'over-loaded' state, caused by the general agreement of both parties, throughout the postwar period, to extending the state's role. In this sense, the Thatcherites reinterpreted the experience of the post-1945 era as a single evolutionary trajectory towards expansionism underpinned by a broad social-democratic consensus. However, in their eagerness to assert the rad-icalism of the Thatcher governments the vast majority of political scientists and historians readily acquiesced to this view, thereby implicitly strength-ening the Thatcherite claim that there could be 'no alternative'.

Beyond their attempts to establish hegemony for their discursive narra-tion of the postwar period, the Conservatives still needed to engage in other important battles. Foremost amongst these was the struggle to see off any residues of progressive liberalism and social democracy within the state and society at large. Perhaps the most important battle for the Conservatives, though, was the struggle which they had to engage in to define the contours of their own strategic objectives. Behind the aggression of the Conservatives' first two terms in office lay a fundamental vacuum in government strategy at an institutional and policy level. Having experimented unsuccessfully with monetarism and then with a range of arbitrary supply-side initiatives, the Conservatives, by the beginning of their third term in office, had largely failed to deliver the radical institutional initiatives which they had promised. The policy which had enabled the strategy to appear relatively coherent and consistent by the Thatcher governments' mid-term was privatisation. This did much to disguise the fact that, beneath the zealous reforming rhetoric, the Thatcher project evolved in an ad hoc, pragmatic and often arbitrary manner. Overall, this initial fitful evolution reflected the fact that Thatcherism was a phenomenon which was worked out over time and therefore constantly changing. In order to explain this evolutionary process more fully, we need now to turn to the environmental conditions, strategic interpretations and processes of learning that both enabled and constrained the development of the Conservatives' strategy.

Environmental conditioning and selection of Thatcherism

Given the heavy emphasis upon the ideational component of Thatcherism, it is unsurprising that most authors have insisted that ideology was a primary factor in determining the direction of the Thatcher project. However, while ideology did play a crucial role, it is important not to take the Conservatives' strategy out of its context and treat it as if it existed within a political and economic vacuum. Any satisfactory explanation of the evolution of the Conservatives' strategy must take account of the fact that Thatcherism emerged in response to a whole series of pressures both at home and abroad. In this sense then, Thatcherism was a particular type of national manifestation – shaped by nation-specific environmental forces – of an international phenomenon. In the sections that follow, we will see that New Right ideology, in conjunction with the Conservatives' interpretations of their own narrow political and economic objectives, did play a crucial role in shaping the Thatcherite strategy. However, we will also see that the evolution of New Right ideas about the state were similarly shaped by important selection pressures from within the international, domestic and discursive environments in which they were articulated.

The international environment

We have seen that the development of Keynesian ideas and welfare state systems throughout the major developed capitalist nations in the immediate aftermath of the Second World War had been shaped by important selection pressures emanating from changes in the international productive base. In particular, the earlier international movement towards 'Fordist' mass production techniques had required a range of national responses designed to restructure patterns of domestic demand in order to meet the needs of the new production processes. The economic crisis of the 1930s, which had helped to precipitate the changes, has since been interpreted as evidence of the maladaptation, at that time, of domestic structures to the 'Fordist' changes which had been taking place within capitalism. Similarly, the crisis of the 1970s has since been interpreted by many theorists as a Kondratieff B-phase in the world economy precipitated by both the crisis of 'Fordism' and the maladaptation of Keynesian solutions to new changes taking place within the international system of productive relations. These conditions, along with the accompanying decline of American hegemony, created important selection pressures upon all states within the international capitalist system to develop a coherent response to the crisis of Fordism by introducing new forms of social regulation, and encouraging the development of more flexible processes of capital accumulation. It was within this global environment that Thatcherism emerged as both a response to the international search for solutions to the changed environmental conditions, and a political strategy which played a positive role in shaping the type of solutions that would be selected for.

The transition of the world economy

For most advanced nations, the postwar political and economic order had created a long-term stable social environment reflecting a 'Fordist' compromise between capital and labour, based around mass production and scientific management techniques at the level of production and the stimulation of demand at a societal level. As we have seen, under the heavy influence of American hegemony, the Keynesian policy of stimulating domestic demand and full employment had operated within a liberalised international economic environment underpinned by the Bretton Woods system. According to Gilpin:

> Governments could meet the demands of their domestic constituents and promote full employment through demand-stimulation policies and welfare programmes without sacrificing their commitment to a stable international economy. Harmony between domestic economic autonomy and the norms of a liberal international economic order constituted a major factor in the stability of the international political and economic system.
>
> (Gilpin 1987: 355)

Of course, this harmony did not manifest itself in Britain, where its peculiar adjustment to a former position of hegemony alongside the configuration of its domestic structures and class forces meant a fundamental series of conflicts between domestic and foreign policy. Yet, for most advanced countries the international postwar settlement did provide a stable environment for economic growth and relative consensus. However, by the end of the 1960s this system was beginning to show important signs of decay and maladaptation to changed circumstances.

First, America's brief period of unrivalled hegemony was coming to an end. American leadership in the world economy had played a crucial role in sustaining the stability of the postwar system, but it became increasingly clear that the rate of US productivity was falling behind that of other advanced nations, particularly Japan and West Germany. By 1973, America's economic decline had affected its ability to take a political lead in foreign affairs. With the breakdown of the Bretton Woods system and the transition to flexible rates, the US had lost control over the world monetary system. Similarly, the 1973 oil shock had revealed a similar loss of control over the world energy market (Gilpin 1987: 345). Both these events had been the result of the increased willingness of foreign governments to assert themselves against the United States. The first had stemmed from the unwillingness of West Germany to defend the falling dollar in the light of its decision to assume a monetary leadership in the European Community and the second had been caused by the increased assertiveness of OPEC (Organization of the Petroleum Exporting Countries). Overall, the decline in American hegemony had helped to erode the favourable international political environment which had enabled growth in the early postwar period. Moreover, with the United States in retreat, this left a significant power vacuum within the world economic and inter-state system, given that there were no obvious candidates to take up its former mantle. The result was a deepening trend towards 'increasing protectionism, monetary instability and economic crisis' (ibid.: 351)

Second, and in the context of the growing crisis in the international economic environment throughout the 1970s, most other advanced nations began to suffer a similar fate to the United States. Rates of productivity started to fall dramatically throughout the Fordist economies and the level of demand had become increasingly volatile. In many ways, this crisis stemmed from the peculiar 'compromise' within Fordism between capital and labour (Lipietz 1992: 15). This had involved gains in real wages for labour at the expense of significant losses in worker autonomy from the introduction of Taylorist and assembly-line mass production techniques. All in all, by the end of the 1960s, the 'dehumanisation' aspects of this compromise had led to:

> a worldwide wave of revolts or 'micro-conflicts' in firms and offices, by workers stripped of their initiative and dignity by Taylorism. . . . Ten years later, the revolts had become a general left-wing upsurge, and employers' attempts to 'make workers pay for the crisis' had been met by strikes, often unsuccessful ones.
>
> (Lipietz 1992: 15)

Moreover, the strength of labour had also managed to push up real wages in most countries, without any accompanying increase in productivity. The immediate solution of most firms to falling profitability was to push up prices, leading to increases in the level of inflation. Once inflation rates began to exceed wage rises, this led to an inevitable fall in demand and an increased slow-down of economic activity in most manufacturing sectors. The overall result of the growing crisis in Fordism was the new phenomenon of 'stagflation', a combination of low growth, mass unemployment and high inflation.

Third, the effect of this crisis was made worse by the increased 'internationalisation' of the world economy. As other advanced and developing economies began to catch up with and overtake the United States, a growing trade war had begun throughout the world economy. This had intensified in the wake of the 1973 oil crisis. The result, as Lipietz explains, was that:

> to recover their profitability, multinational companies spread their operations over entire continents, and forged subcontracting links with certain Third World countries. . . . World trade began to grow much more quickly than demand . . . the management of growth became less and less amenable to government control.
>
> (Lipietz 1992: 18)

Due to the increase in foreign suppliers, rises in domestic demand were leading to a flood of imports as national economies became increasingly interdependent. The response by most advanced nations was to attempt to decrease demand in the hope that surplus production would be absorbed by exports to other countries. However, given that most countries were doing the same, the result was an international demand-side crisis to add to the domestic supply-side crisis (ibid.: 19).

By the end of the 1970s the international environment – which had formerly restored stability and growth throughout the domestic economies of the advanced nations – was now in a state of crisis, thereby exerting significant pressures upon all national governments to search for appropriate solutions. Within Britain, this crisis was being felt even more acutely than in most countries. As Overbeek explains:

> the ratio of new investment to output in the period 1968–73 was highest in Britain, and the gap between Britain and the other major capitalist countries increased dramatically after 1973: the differential with the US increased from 0.9 to 7.6; with Germany, from 1.0 to 4.8; and with Japan, from 2.1 to 5.1.
>
> (Overbeek 1990: 145)

Three possible options for dealing with the British crisis had presented themselves from the end of the 1960s (ibid.: 154). The first had been to ride the storm in the hope that conditions would gradually begin to improve. The second, advocated mainly by the Labour left, involved acknowledging the crisis and attempting a dirigiste solution by increasing state involvement in industrial restructuring, while engaging in a relative retreat from the world market. Finally, the third option, put forward by the New Right in the Conservative Party, was to increase the operation of market forces and lower the strength of trade unions. These options were more or less mirrored internationally. The initial response to the crisis, from 1973 to 1979, was distinctly Keynesian, based upon the stimulation of demand (Lipietz 1992: 19). However, this had failed to deal with the supply-side crisis and, as a result, failed to halt the fall in profits or the rise in inflation. Consequently, the legitimacy of Keynesian responses became seriously undermined throughout the globe. This loss of legitimacy had been heightened by the growing realisation that national economies were becoming increasingly 'open', thereby making purely national-focused economic responses more difficult as the internationalisation of the world economy grew apace. As Gilpin explains:

> increasing flows of goods, money and capital made it more and more difficult to isolate the domestic from the international sphere. The increased openness of national economies meant that macroeconomic interdependence became a more important factor and the economic policies of one nation impinged upon others. The combination of increased demands by society on the government, decreased policy autonomy of national governments, and increasing similarity of national economies was undermining the system. Nations were living in an increasingly interdependent world but continued to behave as if they were not.
>
> (Gilpin 1987: 355)

With Keynesianism virtually exhausted as a potential solution to the crisis by the end of the 1970s, the pressure for the selection of supply-side measures to restructure domestic economies and restore capitalist profitability had reached a peak. Here, Britain and America, where the commitment to statism had been weakest and monetarism had been able to achieve an ascendancy, led the way. The response in these countries after 1979 involved prioritising inflation by reducing the cost of labour and maintaining a tight rein on monetary growth. As we have seen, this policy did not represent a profound change in the British experience, where breaks with Keynesian orthodoxy and attempts to cut public expenditure and reduce the power of the trade unions had been commonplace throughout the postwar period. Nevertheless, Thatcherism, and its American equivalent 'Reaganomics', did represent a more direct and sustained attempt to respond to environmental pressures by breaking with Keynesianism and restructuring the productive base.

These strategies reflected an attempt to re-adapt state intervention in order to meet the needs of the changed economic environment. As with the experience of the 1930s and 1940s, the recognition of the maladaptation of the state's role in the regulation of capitalism had lagged behind changes in the pattern of capital formation and accumulation. As Murray explains, throughout the 1960s and 1970s:

> economists and politicians were re-fighting the battles of the last slump. Private capital on the other hand was dealing with the present one. It was using new technology and new production principles to make Fordism flexible, and in doing so stood much of the old culture on its head.
>
> (Murray 1990: 42)

In Britain, the changes in production and consumption patterns had begun in retailing in the 1950s, with the introduction of computers to transform distribution processes (Murray 1990: 42). This had enabled retailers to overcome the problem of forecasting demand, since computers could be used to regulate supply continually in order to meet sudden changes in demand. Since the 1960s, the flexibility of the supply-side and the deliberate manipulation of consumer preferences through advertising has pulled many sectors, including manufacturing, away from Fordist mass production techniques towards a more flexible system of organization and production.

These changes have since provoked much academic interest, and controversies have emerged over whether or not they represent a transition to a 'post-Fordist' accumulation regime, or a mere extension and development of Fordism. Nevertheless, the overall consensus amongst most theorists appears to be that, in many sectors at least, the productive base has been significantly transformed and the beginnings of a post-Fordist economy are clearly visible. At the level of the labour process, 'post-Fordism' has been identified as: 'a flexible production process based on flexible machines or systems and an appropriately flexible workforce. Its crucial hardware is micro-electronics-based information and communications technologies' (Jessop 1994: 19). As a regime of accumulation:

> its virtuous circle would be based on flexible production, growing productivity based on economies of scope and/or process innovations, rising incomes for polyvalent skilled workers and the service class, increased demand for new differentiated goods and services . . . increased profits based on technological and other innovation rents and the full utilisation of flexible capacity, reinvestment in more flexible production equipment and processes and/or new sets of products and/or new organizational forms, and a further boost to productivity due to economies of scope and constant innovation.
>
> (Jessop 1994: 19)

Even if we choose not to regard these changes in the productive base as evidence of 'post-Fordism' there is little doubt that the increased flexibility in capital accumulation has made the Fordist mode of societal regulation obsolete and thereby provided significant environmental pressures for the selection of new regulatory practices. Therefore, the shift towards supply-side economics reflected in the strategies of the Thatcher/Reagan governments, and since then the majority of advanced nation states, represents an adaptive response to the need to re-regulate capitalist profitability.

It is widely accepted that the development, and therefore the regulation, of 'post-Fordism' is still in a transitionary phase. However, the main features of the mode of regulation governing the transition have evolved throughout the 1980s and 1990s in favour of supply-side innovation and greater flexibility in the forms of regulation. As Jessop (1994: 22) explains: 'the transitional regime is Janus-faced and must engage in creatively destructive interventions. It must both "roll back the frontiers" of Fordist state intervention and "roll forward" those for post-Fordist intervention'. The evolution of the Thatcherite project reflected this process of creative destruction, as the Conservatives continually experimented with ways of dismantling old modes of regulation and replacing them with new regulatory mechanisms. Yet the Thatcher governments did not merely passively react to the changed environment, they also significantly contributed to the way in which other nations sought for new solutions. This is particularly so in the case of privatisation and financial deregulation, which represents a policy adaptation that has since been reinforced and emulated in other advanced economies. However, in other areas, such as welfare reform, the Conservatives have drawn lessons from abroad, particularly the United States (Dolowitz 1998).

Overall then, Thatcherism emerged out of an environment at the end of the 1970s that had created considerable pressures for the abandonment of Keynesian responses to the crisis, and the selection of strategies aimed at improving the flexibility of the supply-side to enable the restructuring of capitalist profitability. Throughout the 1980s, after a period of experimentation, these selection pressures became even greater as the advanced nations began to emulate and reinforce favourable responses to the new environment. This process of adaptation has been relatively slow, yet it accelerated considerably within Britain given that the domestic environment for Thatcherism was, in some ways, even more favourable than the international context.

The domestic environment

As we have seen, the configuration of institutional structures and class forces in Britain created selection pressures that favoured the intervention of Thatcherism. However, other factors within the domestic environment have also prevailed to limit the success of the Conservatives' strategic interventions.

The root of this paradoxical situation lies in Britain's peculiar variant of 'flawed Fordism' (Jessop 1992; 1994). As we have seen, unlike many of its competitors, Britain had failed to undergo the type of fundamental restructuring and industrial modernisation required to ensure an effective transition to a Fordist productive base. Moreover, due to the conflicts of interest at the heart of policy-making, the state was also unable to commit itself fully to implementing the necessary social regulatory structures that would enable Fordism to work effectively. As a result, Britain had failed overall to derive the full benefits of the virtuous circle of Fordism enjoyed by many of her key competitors. The incomplete nature of Fordist transformation in Britain, and in particular the conflicts which accompanied it, created a range of selective pressures which would enable Thatcherism both to gain an ascendancy and to evolve more easily. Yet at the same time the domestic environment inherited by the Thatcher governments, coupled with other factors which we shall look at later, also served to militate against the efficacy of Thatcherism as a state project designed to ensure a successful transition to a restructured, modernised industrial base.

The paradoxes of Britain's ungrounded statism

Dunleavy (1988) notes that Britain has enjoyed an unprecedented degree of state intervention despite the fact that many factors in British political development have militated heavily against the introduction of statist measures. Consequently, the development of 'statism' in British politics could be said to be largely 'ungrounded' and to have represented something of a paradox. Clearly, the 'ungrounded' nature of statism in Britain produced paradoxical selective pressures upon the Thatcher project. On the one hand, it enabled an environment to emerge in which Thatcherism's aim to *de*-regulate many of the functions of the state did not meet with any serious political obstacles. Yet, on the other hand, the lack of core state capacities also served to restrict the ability of the Thatcher project effectively to harness the powers of the state in order to *re*-regulate the conditions for economic growth.

The overall effect of the struggle for survival between competing conceptions of state strategy in Britain was that the 'statist' measures initiated during periods of state expansion were never properly institutionalised. As we have seen, the quasi-corporatist structures set up by the Macmillan, Wilson and Heath governments were merely 'para-state' apparatuses that were never fully incorporated into the central decision-making process. Likewise, the major interests that might have supported greater moves towards statism, such as industrial capital and trade unions, remained at the fringes of power and, indeed, were either directly or indirectly undermined by the successive moves back into liberal retreat and state retrenchment. In contrast, the forces dedicated to ensuring that Britain maintained its tradition of minimal government remained deeply entrenched within the institutional structure of the postwar British state. These were largely represented by the central institutions at the heart of policy-making, the Treasury, the City of London and the Bank of England. As a result, a significant array of selective pressures was already present within the domestic environment which favoured the implementation of Thatcherism as a strategic adaptation to the crisis within the international environment.

By the end of the 1970s, Thatcherism had been made easier by the internationalisation of the world economy and the crisis of capitalist accumulation which had effectively eroded both the efficacy and legitimacy of Keynesianism on a global level and, thereby, the potential conflicts between domestic and foreign policy. On the domestic front, however, it was made even easier by the fact that the overall faith in Keynesianism and active government had been previously damaged in Britain by the inherent conflicts in the domestic institutional environment that had largely nullified the efficacy of statist interventions. Thus, in many ways, Thatcherism was more attuned to both the evolutionary trajectory of the international environment and the so-called postwar settlement in Britain than the social-democratic strategy of the previous Labour government had been. Within the Conservative Party itself, the selection of the Thatcherite strategy was facilitated by the strong historical tradition of a commitment to moral authoritarianism and free market liberalism. Even though these elements had been, to some extent, weakened in the postwar period by the ascendancy of corporate-liberal elements, they had never been properly dissipated. Thus, the Thatcher governments' stance on a host of economic and social issues, although in some ways different from the ideological tenor of the Macmillan and Heath governments, accorded favourably with the overall outlook of the Churchill–Eden administrations.

As Bulpitt (1986) has perceptively noted, the arm's length statecraft of the Thatcher governments was very much in line with traditional Conservative Party statecraft dating back to the time of Lord Salisbury. Moreover, as Marsh and Tant (1989; also Tant 1993) have highlighted, this statecraft also accorded favourably with the historical top-down elitist tradition built into the institutional structure of the British polity. These factors, combined with the lack of an effective social-democratic ethos within the British state, enabled key elements of Thatcherite philosophy to reside comfortably within both the Conservative Party throughout the postwar period and the postwar British state's key institutions.

Thus, in many respects, the Conservatives' strategy showed important areas of continuity with the configuration of the domestic environment. The key task for the Conservatives was to kill off any remaining institutional anomalies by attacking certain pockets of resistance to Thatcherism. This involved the Thatcherites in attempts to assault the power of trade unions and to dismantle quasi-corporatist institutions. Yet, due to their overall separation from the central policy-making environment, the ability of such institutions to resist Thatcherism was severely weakened. Moreover, the seeds of Thatcherism's anti-statism were so firmly grounded within both the Establishment and the Conservative Party itself that the initial resistance from both quarters was relatively easily and effectively killed off by as early as 1982. Subsequently, the domestic environment placed very few obstacles in the way of the evolution of the Thatcherite strategy. Whereas anti-statist forces had continually stood in the path of any attempt at state expansion in the early postwar period, there was no fundamental statist opposition blocking Thatcherism's path, and any of its proponents who did remain were relatively easily trampled over. After the 1987 election, and the maturation of the Thatcherite strategy, the strategic selectivity of the state became increasingly anti-statist, thereby frustrating the labour movement by forcing it into virtually complete acquiescence to the general principles of Thatcherism.

Generally speaking, then, Thatcherism was able to bring about a final settlement to the fundamental conflicts over postwar British policy-making largely because the domestic environment provided a favourable climate for its policy of re-establishing a system of arm's length government by de-regulating some former state activities. Yet the system of flawed-Fordism in Britain, and the overall anti-statist culture which predominated, also brought negative selection pressures to bear upon the ability of the Thatcherites to *re*-regulate the conditions for future growth. The Conservative governments proved to be very effective at harnessing state power in order to meet many of their objectives; for example, they created many regulatory bodies and institutions to accompany the process of the 'hollowing out' of the state. It is, however, precisely in the areas necessary for securing the modernisation of the productive base that Thatcherism failed overall to use the capacity of the state in order to bring about a successful post-Fordist transformation (Jessop 1994). In this respect the Conservatives' strategy largely fell into the same pattern of earlier postwar economic management; it similarly failed to meet the needs of producer interests by utilising state mechanisms in order to bring about positive industrial restructuring. In this sense at least, the anti-statist culture inherent within the postwar domestic environment has militated heavily against the successful implementation of Thatcherism. By stripping the British state of its former, limited, capacities for industrial intervention, the Thatcherites ensured that their so-called 'economic miracle' would amount to nothing more than the graceful management of national decline (ibid.: 34).

The discursive environment

So far we have mainly dealt with the impact of Thatcherism at an institutional and policy level. We have seen that, at the policy-making level, the environment in which Thatcherism emerged was one that, in many ways, was conducive to the overall strategic direction that the Conservatives wanted to pursue. As such, given the variety of environmental pressures that existed for the selection of the Thatcherite strategy, the institutional obstacles to Thatcherism were never as great as those encountered by the advocates of state expansion in the earlier postwar period. However, if there was one major obstacle that the Thatcherites had to overcome, it was the strong *discursive* commitment throughout the postwar period to Keynesianism, social democracy and active government. As we saw in our analysis of the early postwar period, the discursive environment in which policy was formulated represented one key area of relative consensus in which the commitment to progressive liberalism and social-democratic ideas remained strong. This played an important role in maintaining a relative balance in the continual oscillation of strategies between expansion and retrenchment. It provided an environment that produced positive selection pressures for policies aimed at protecting the welfare state and the commitment to full employment, as well as maintaining the need for consultative arrangements between government and producer groups. Consequently, when the Conservatives entered office in 1979 the residues of the discourse of social democracy still provided important selection pressures upon the evolution of the Thatcherite project which initially helped to define the limits of the strategy pursued by the Thatcher governments. As we shall see, this important area of constraint was one that the Conservatives needed to act aggressively against in order to create the space for the subsequent evolution of their strategy. This involved them in a continual attempt to uncouple themselves from the selection pressures incurred by the discourse of the earlier postwar period and to impose their own hegemonic 'common-sense' perceptions of what the role and responsibilities of the state should be.

The Great Moving Right Show

Undoubtedly, the most important study of the discursive environment of Thatcherism has been that provided by Stuart Hall (1979, 1983; although see also O'Shea 1984; Fairclough 1989, 1992; Hay 1996; Philips 1996). Hall notes that Thatcherism emerged out of the political and economic crises of the 1970s as an attempt radically to alter the dominant discourse of British politics, and to constitute Thatcherite philosophy as a new form of hegemonic 'common-sense'. The importance of Hall's contribution is that it highlights Thatcherism's need to overcome the constraints of popular conceptions of the role and responsibilities of the postwar British state. Despite the fundamental incoherence of government strategy at a policy level in the early postwar period, the dominant *discursive* commitment to Keynesianism, the maintenance of full employment, the welfare state and the need for active government had remained relatively unaltered. Consequently, the underlying conflicts of the postwar period were rarely

represented at a discursive and popular level. Instead, successive governments found themselves discursively reinforcing their commitments to
these themes, even as their strategies were systematically uncoupling the
very commitments that they were espousing.

The experience of the Heath government's earlier humiliating policy
'U-turn' was critical in shaping the Conservatives' dogged refusal after
1979 to alter their strategic direction. Thus the Thatcher governments
aimed to dismantle any residues of progressive liberal and social-democratic discourse which might incur similar selection pressures for a reversal
of strategy. These attempts to alter the discursive environment were
initiated before the Thatcherites had entered office. They involved the
Conservatives in a particular narration of the crisis of the 1970s which
essentially placed 'statism' and 'collectivism' in the forefront of the reasons
for Britain's decline (Hall 1979). By narrating Britain's crisis as a crisis of
'an over-extended, overloaded and ungovernable state "held to ransom by
the trade unions"', the Thatcherites set about 'distorting and simplifying,
but above all . . . *interpreting and giving meaning to*' the events which had
brought Britain to the brink of crisis (ibid.). Thus, the Thatcherites were
able to mobilise popular perceptions of the crisis into a coherent, anti-
statist, free-market, populist discourse that attributed Britain's long-term
decline to the so-called prevailing consensus over statism. Writing at the
time of these events, Hall explains:

> Thatcherite populism is a particularly rich mix. It combines the
> resonant themes of organic Toryism – nation, family, duty, authority,
> standards, traditionalism – with the aggressive themes of a revived neo-
> liberalism – self-interest, competitive individualism, anti-statism. . . .
> 'Freedom/free market' is once again in the foreground of
> Conservative ideological repertoire. 'Free market – strong state':
> around this contradictory point, where neo-liberal political economy
> fused with organic Toryism, the authentic language of 'Thatcherism'
> has condensed.
>
> (Hall 1983: 29–30)

As we have previously noted, most of these themes were already present in
the early postwar period, even if they were not all represented within the
dominant discourse surrounding policy. Thus, as Hall (1983: 31) explains:
'the process we are looking at here is very similar to that which Gramsci
once described as *transformism*: the neutralisation of some elements in an
ideological formation, their absorption and passive appropriation into a
new political configuration'.

It is precisely this process of neutralising particular aspects of the earlier postwar period and reinforcing others which the Thatcher
governments had set about trying to achieve before and during their
ascendancy to power. Here, they were helped, as Hall (ibid.: 29; also Hay

1996) perceptively notes, by 'the colonisation of the popular press', which had played a crucial role in bolstering the Thatcherites' narration of the crisis. Yet, in acknowledging this point, it appears that Hall and others remained unreflexive about their own role in legitimating the spread of Thatcherite hegemony: Hall's analysis paid too much credence to Thatcherism's attempts to reconstruct the history of the postwar period into an account which emphasised the dominance of social democracy, collectivism and statism at an institutional and policy level. Despite the fact that the analysis put forth by the authors of *Marxism Today* was inherently critical of the Thatcher project, their assessment of the earlier postwar period resulted in a passive acceptance of the Thatcher governments' own historical narrative.

Although Thatcherism had made a concerted attempt during the 'Winter of Discontent' to mobilise popular support against progressive liberal ideas, the residues of the earlier postwar discourse did still provide an element of constraint on the Thatcher governments, particularly during their first term. This is reflected in the Cabinet splits and opposition from within the Establishment that occurred as a result of the government's strict adherence to monetarism despite rising unemployment and economic recession. Clearly, at this stage, the Thatcher governments' attempts to rid themselves of the selection pressures for a reversal of strategy had not entirely succeeded, and important elements of the Keynesian, social-democratic discourse remained. Yet it was not long before these remaining residues of statist discourse were dissipated, and Thatcherism was able to instil its own strategic vision in a manner which, if not entirely hegemonic, certainly created a discursive environment that was strategically selective in favour of the Conservatives' project. Over time this discourse evolved in line with the subsequent strategic adaptations implemented by the Conservatives. Thus, the discursive environment itself evolved from a strict anti-statist, free-market, rhetoric to an emphasis upon the virtues of a 'share-owning democracy'. Eventually, the discourse that emerged out of the radical and late phases of Thatcherism stressed 'choice' and 'consumerism' and even erstwhile 'un-Thatcherite' concepts such as 'community' and 'citizenship' (Philips 1996: 235). As Philips explains: 'the transformed Thatcherite discourse . . . was reproduced through collocations that combined the vocabulary of consumerism, the market vocabulary and the Enlightenment vocabulary of citizenship and rights' (ibid.: 233).

Overall then, the Thatcher governments played an important role in overcoming the conflict in the earlier postwar period between rhetoric and reality. They were able to colonise the discursive environment with the rhetoric of classical liberalism and organic Toryism. Whereas the earliest phase of the evolution of the Conservatives' strategy had been constrained by selection pressures to abandon the direction of policy, the eventual success of the Thatcher governments in overcoming these led to an evolving discursive environment which biased the future selection of Thatcherite strategy. Thus, by the mid-phase of the Conservatives' term in office, Thatcherite ideas had begun to colonise not only the institutional environment, but also the discursive terrain in which policy was both formulated and implemented. This, of course, had a profound effect upon the labour movement which increasingly found its attachment to statism floundering in an overall environment that militated heavily against the selection of expansionist discourse. Thus, by the 1990s Thatcherite discourse had become so widespread that it was even being extensively developed by the Labour Party, who were able to appropriate the key themes of citizenship and community (Philips 1996: 235). As a result, the Conservatives eventually found themselves the victims of their own success, since the dispersion of their own strategic and ideological rhetoric had effectively stripped them of their erstwhile discursive dominance (McAnulla 1999).

Interpretations of strategic objectives

We have already seen that different, and often contradictory, interpretations of strategy between the key actors involved in the formulation of policy had helped to consolidate the conflicts that dominated the earlier postwar era. Producer groups remained torn between their commitment to arm's length government on the one hand, and the need to urge the state directly to involve itself in active industrial restructuring on the other. Meanwhile, the financial sector, with backing from central state institutions such as the Treasury and the Bank of England, retained its historical commitment to limited government and thus provided a serious obstacle to attempts at implementing a coherent industrial strategy. Finally, the strategy adopted by politicians had dramatically alternated throughout the period as they attempted to balance both concerns along with their own sets of confused and contradictory objectives. Overall, the effect of these different interpretations of strategy placed further cross-cutting selection pressures upon successive governments, thereby contributing to Britain's fitful postwar evolution.

With the election of the Conservatives after 1979, however, these conflicting pressures were greatly diminished. A deliberate aim of the Thatcher governments was to distance themselves from key groups of actors such as the trade unions and the CBI in line with the New Right view that the erstwhile involvement of such groups in policy-making had contributed to Britain's supposed 'ungovernability' (Bulpitt 1986; Wolfe 1991). Of course, as we have seen, the extent to which producer groups had been incorporated into the decision-making process in the earlier postwar period was limited. Nevertheless, successive governments had retained at least a discursive commitment to balancing the concerns of different interests and, although this commitment was only adhered to on a fitful basis, it did help to enhance the overall conflicts at the heart of policy-making. As a result, the Thatcher governments entered office with a determined resolve to end these conflicts and to press ahead with their own narrow agenda. As we shall see, this policy, along with the subsequent destruction of British industry and the weakening of the labour movement, helped to remove an important obstacle from the evolution of the Conservatives' strategy.

Nevertheless, although the Conservatives were able to work within an environment that was relatively free from external conflict, their often confused interpretations of their own strategic objectives did throw up an important internal obstacle to the success of their strategy. In particular, the Conservatives faced two main problems resulting from their narrow interpretations of their strategic objectives. First, at an ideological level, the Conservatives had extrapolated information from their external environment through the confines of a neo-liberal paradigm, and this had prevented them from recognising the need to harness state power in order to promote serious 'post-Fordist' industrial restructuring so as to halt Britain's long-term economic decline. Second, despite the Conservatives' commitment to New Right ideology, their overall objective of restructuring relations between state and society in order to deal with Britain's crisis was more often than not sacrificed in order to meet other narrow political and economic objectives.

The dominance of internal rather than external conflicts

Before we examine the Conservatives' interpretations of their objectives, it is important briefly to consider the strategic stance taken by other key actors in the policy-making field. As we have previously noted, during their first term in office, and to a more limited extent into their second phase of power, the Thatcher governments did encounter the last remaining residues of the conflicts that had dominated the earlier postwar period. These came from various sources, including the Conservative Party itself, industrial capital, and the labour movement. Here, I will briefly examine the relative strategic interests of each of these in turn.

Within the Conservative Party itself, the main period of division occurred in the Thatcher government's first term and was primarily concentrated within the Cabinet. As Holmes (1985: 74) notes: 'at no time since the 1940 confidence vote which led to Neville Chamberlain's resignation had the Conservative Party been so divided'. The division between the Thatcherites and the so-called one-nation 'wets' during this period manifested itself in wrangles over trade union reform and the issue of public expenditure cuts (Dorey 1995: 169–70). While the Thatcherites were interpreting Britain's crisis through the confines of a narrow neo-liberal and monetarist paradigm, traditional Conservatives, such as Jim Prior, remained attached to the corporate-liberal ethos characteristic of Macmillan and Heath. The result was a series of bitter feuds over the social

consequences of a strict monetarist approach which led to serious specu-
lation that the government would rescind its strategic position and embark
upon an expansionary course similar to that of the Heath government. As
we have seen, however, by the time of Conservatives' second term and
following the retreat from monetarism and the victory in the Falklands
War, these divisions were successfully dissipated and the Thatcherites established their hegemony over the party. Subsequently those within the Party
who opposed the aggressiveness of the Thatcher project re-oriented their
strategic position to accept the underlying principles of Thatcherism and,
as result, internal party dissent was mainly restricted to concern over the
social consequences of the Thatcher project. Thus, as Jessop *et al.* (1988)
explain, the main area of division was between those who wished merely to
consolidate the gains made by Thatcherism and those committed to
further radical institutional reform. By the end of the 1980s, it appeared
that the consolidators had gained an ascendancy, given the weakening of
Mrs Thatcher's personal position and the eventual promotion of John
Major to the leadership. However, this had failed to prevent the increasingly aggressive onslaught of institutional reform under Major, while the
main source of conflict had centred around issues such as Europe and
economic management rather than the general principles of Thatcherism
itself. As a result, although Thatcherism had always provoked a general
conflict within the Conservative Party, the key opponents to the Thatcher
project had – after the Conservatives' first term – largely interpreted their
main strategic objective as softening the blow of the Thatcher project,
rather than reversing its overall strategic direction.

Second, the conflict between the interests of industrial capital and the
state, which had figured prominently at various points in the earlier
postwar period, did resurface in the wake of the Thatcher project.
Although industrial capital had largely opposed the social-democratic
strategy of the previous Labour administration, large sections of this
fraction of capital were no more greatly enamoured by the strict monetarist approach of the Thatcher governments. Again, much of this
opposition was largely confined to the Conservatives' first term. The main
source of the discontent was the Conservatives' dogged refusal to intervene
in order to prevent the destruction of Britain's ailing manufacturing
sector. The position of the industrial sector was hampered throughout the
postwar period by its historical internal fragmentation, its overall dislocation from financial and commercial capital, and its inability to exert
enough effective pressure upon the state to select appropriate measures
for industrial restructuring. Traditionally, the (con)Federation of British
Industry (FBI, although later the CBI) constituted the main representatives of industrial capital. Although the interests of industry at several
points in the postwar period had conflicted fundamentally with those of
the state, they had nevertheless enjoyed relatively favourable relations with
postwar administrations when compared to Britain's other main producer

interest, the trade union movement (Overbeek 1990: 202; Grant and Marsh 1977). However, as Overbeek explains:

> the advent of the new Tory government in 1979 caused a relatively far-reaching turnabout in these relations. The CBI was increasingly critical of the government's economic policies as the number of bankruptcies skyrocketed. The culmination of the CBI's criticism came with the announcement of a 'bare-knuckle fight' against the monetarist policies of the government by CBI Director-General Beckett.
>
> (Overbeek 1990: 202)

As Jessop (1992: 35) argues, these tensions can perhaps be best explained by the continuing divergence of interests between producers and politicians. As we have already seen, throughout the postwar period, whereas the latter had largely favoured an arm's length approach to industry, the former had intermittently interpreted their own strategic interests in terms of the need for Fordist restructuring. In the context of Thatcherism, these fundamental divisions remained, although somewhat altered. Whereas the main strategic aim of the Thatcher governments was to withdraw almost completely from industrial intervention, producer groups still clung to the belief that government strategy should be oriented to industrial (this time 'post-Fordist') reorganization based around the promotion of enterprise and greater flexibility (ibid.). Unlike in the postwar period, these divergent interpretations of government strategy did not impose the same conflicting pressures upon the Conservatives as they had done on previous governments. One reason for this was the fact that the Thatcher governments remained committed to by-passing any system of functional representation, thereby excluding input by producer groups from the overall process of policy formulation. Perhaps more important however, as Britain's industrial base continued to suffer the ravages of decline, their overall influence over the government withered dramatically. This was reflected in the fact that the CBI was eventually 'elbowed out' of government circles by the Institute of Directors (Overbeek 1990: 202). As Riddell (1983: 54) explains, the IoD was able to curry favour with the Thatcher governments and as a result: 'has become an active lobbyist for private enterprise and against the public sector'. Moreover, as (Overbeek 1990: 203) explains: 'after 1983, the links between the IoD and the Thatcher inner circle were intensified through the appointment of Sir John Hoskins, a personal adviser to Mrs Thatcher during her first years in office, as its new Director-General'. As a result therefore, the Conservatives, although subject to initial opposition, were able, for various reasons, to shrug off these conflicts in order to pursue their own narrowly defined strategic interests.

Third, a similar movement from conflict to relative consensus can be detected in the strategic position adopted by the labour movement. As regards the Labour Party itself, the initial years of the Conservative governments were met with bitter hostility. Relatively undaunted by the failure of its previous strategy, the Party initially moved to the left under Michael Foot. This enabled them to adopt a strict ideological opposition to the Conservatives. Yet, despite this, even at such an early stage, the Party was in a state of crisis that effectively stripped it of its efficacy in opposing the Thatcher governments. At the heart of the crisis was a series of bitter feuds between moderates and the left-wing of the party. While the latter interpreted their strategic objectives in terms of overturning the leadership's erstwhile betrayal of the left, the former were content to interpret Britain's crisis from a more traditional corporate-liberal stance. These divisions were eventually to reach a peak with the defection of the so-called 'gang of four' and the creation of the Social Democratic Party, which, by fragmenting the opposition, effectively damaged any remnants of both parties' electoral hopes. After 1983, and the election of Neil Kinnock to the leadership, Labour retained its bitter confrontation with the government, but this time there was a more definite, if gradual, movement towards the centre.

Meanwhile, throughout this phase of the Conservatives' reign, the trade union movement were no more effective in their opposition. As with industrial capital, the unions were initially content to work within the parameters of a modernisation ethic, yet their strategic position was no less seriously damaged by the destruction of British industry. Moreover, the unions had been further demoralised by the experience of the 'Winter of Discontent' and subsequent accusations from sections of the Labour Party that their actions had been responsible for the government's downfall and the election of the Thatcher governments. The combination of growing unemployment, public dissatisfaction with the union movement, and the subsequent industrial relations reforms, meant that union opposition to Thatcherism remained relatively limited. After Labour's third successive electoral defeat in 1987, the labour movement as a whole began a serious re-interpretation of their strategic objectives. Within the trade union movement, a growing trend towards 'new realism' emerged as the unions began to accommodate themselves to the realities of the Thatcher project. Meanwhile, the Labour Party's long-running Policy Review and restructuring, initiated by Neil Kinnock, extended by John Smith and later consolidated by Tony Blair, resulted in a similar accommodation to the underlying principles of the Thatcher project (Hay 1997). Consequently, although initially opposed by an ideologically hostile labour movement, the Conservatives strategy had succeeded in both demoralising the left and creating the conditions for a fundamental re-interpretation of the labour movement's strategic aims.

As a result, the period since 1979 has witnessed fundamental changes in the interpretations of strategy by most of the key groups at the heart of the policy-making arena. As the Conservatives' strategy evolved, much of the initial opposition to it rapidly dissipated. Yet, while the strategy faced a very limited external opposition, there were internal obstacles to its success because of the Conservatives' own conflictual, and often contradictory, interpretations of their strategic objectives. While both the domestic and external environment within which Thatcherism emerged exerted pressures for the selection of strategies to re-regulate the conditions of future capitalist accumulation, the Thatcher governments compromised many of the strategic innovations necessary to accommodate flexible growth by focusing upon short-term political and economic goals (Jessop 1992). Much of their energy was spent on adapting their strategic interventions in order to pursue a two nations strategy which would provide material gains to key sections of Conservative voters. The most obvious example of this was the Conservatives' de-nationalisation programme (Marsh 1991). Although this appeared as a response to global pressures for deregulation, the Conservatives' programme was adapted to meet short-term political and electoral needs (through its material effects upon key sections of the electorate and its symbolic significance as part of a popular assault upon collectivism) rather then longer-term economic requirements.

The foremost problem however, has been the narrow ideological heuristics which the Conservatives brought to bear upon the selection of their strategic interventions. In particular, they relied upon a dogmatic adherence to a narrow, anti-statist, neo-liberal strategy. As many authors have pointed out, this led them to abandon the active use of state mechanisms in order to ensure the successful re-regulation of Britain's failing economy. Instead, their energies were spent in a succession of attempts to reduce the role of the state in economic regulation, while strengthening the state's power in areas such as law and order. This merely allowed them to deal with the heightened crisis and contradictions that emerged from their failure to halt Britain's ever-growing loss of competitiveness within the global economic environment.

In this sense, the Thatcher governments demonstrate the fact that the bounded rationality of agents, and indeed, the inherent biases and ideological heuristics which they carry, combine to ensure that successful strategic interventions to environmental crises are not inevitable. Rather, they are continually extrapolated through, and interpolated with, governments' own sets of meanings, objectives and discursive articulations. Thus, although the selective pressures imposed by environmental exigencies are crucial to explaining the development of Thatcherism, we must also recognise that the trajectory of Conservative strategy was dependent upon the Conservatives' own narrow ideational and political interventions. We therefore need to focus attention upon the particular ideological and discursive articulation of the environmental crisis and the ways in which the Conservatives inserted their own political aims and objectives into their longer-term strategic responses. This allows us to avoid an explanation which emphasises Thatcherism as a functional response to environmental pressures, since it focuses our attention upon the necessarily contingent and subjective interventions of government actors. It allows us to view the Conservatives' strategy as an often ad hoc process governed and hampered as much by the satisfaction of short-term political goals as by longer-term ideological aims.

Adaptive learning under the Conservatives

As we have seen from our earlier periodisation of the Conservatives' strategy, it is clear that the Conservatives' strategic interventions gained some form of unity, and hence a coherence and, indeed, a radical momentum, through time. Throughout the 1980s, a stream of solutions to the (narrowly perceived) crisis of the state were thrown into the political market place. These included monetarism, denationalisation, contracting-out and management reform. While these initial responses to environmental demands appear to have been relatively inconsistent and random, by the Conservatives' third and fourth terms these strategic adaptations (backed by an increased emphasis upon market-testing and quango-isation) were beginning to display a greater degree of consistency and sophistication. While selective pressures were brought to bear through the evolving environment which they inhabited, and indeed the Conservatives' own extrapolation and interpolation of their strategic objectives, this evolutionary process also reflects the governments' capacity, and indeed willingness, to adapt and respond to previous failures.

Initially formulated around a discursive commitment to reduce the role of the state through monetarist strategies, the Conservatives' strategy was consistently subject to a redefinition of the parameters within which this aim could be met. Early Thatcherite policies reveal an overall lack of strategic direction, even though they were held together by a very coherent, though vague articulation of ideological discourse. It is this ideological discourse, or strategic vision, together with a cleverly constructed electoral strategy which enabled the Conservatives to gain the space to adapt to, and learn from, the environmental pressures that made up their strategic context. This enabled the strategy to become more consistent and develop through the Conservatives' successive terms in office. However, the narrow articulation of a non-regulatory, neo-liberal discourse, together with the narrow satisfaction of short-term political aims, also proved damaging to the Conservatives' ability to formulate successful adaptations which could improve Britain's performance in the overall changing global climate. These problems created longer-term difficulties for the Conservatives which ultimately damaged their electoral fortunes under John Major, and revealed latent contradictions in the state settlement that emerged from the periods of 'radical' and 'late-Thatcherism'.

However, having adapted their strategy to cope with the exigencies imposed by selective environmental pressures, the Conservatives were faced with the problem that – throughout both the Thatcher and Major periods – they were learning the wrong lessons. While crises and contradictions within their environment necessitated the re-regulation of the UK economy to cope with its strategic re-adjustment to changing global political and economic relations, the Conservatives' consistently failed to respond effectively. Therefore Thatcherism, although a dynamic and evolving process, can be considered to have been an essentially flawed evolution. This was because of the narrow conceptions which the Conservatives' brought to bear upon the types of crises that they faced and indeed, the optimal solutions required to resolve these. This consistently resulted from their dogmatic attachment to an anti-statist, neo-liberal ideology which directed their attention away from the need to learn the appropriate means by which state mechanisms could be used in order to generate economic growth and successful accumulation. Instead, the Conservatives were merely content to engage in an almost constant and ongoing process of learning how to satisfy their twin fetishes for welfare retrenchment and the depoliticisation of the very areas that could generate successful adaptation to the environmental crises brought about by the failure of Fordism.

Conclusion

In conclusion then, Thatcherism must be regarded as a period in which Britain finally inherited a certain degree of postwar settlement. By successfully colonising the political debate with the spread of Thatcherite discourse, the Conservatives were able to eliminate any remaining residues of effective opposition from progressive/corporate liberal forces. This relative lack of fundamental conflict over the direction of policy enabled the Thatcherite strategy to evolve over time, through processes of selection, adaptation and learning, into a more radical and coherent attempt to accommodate Britain to the wider evolutionary trajectory of the global economy. Yet despite the Conservatives' attempts to dismantle Britain's flawed Fordism, the application of a strict, narrow neo-liberal ideology, along with an equally narrow two nations electoral strategy, presented internal obstacles to the success of Thatcherism. In any evolutionary schema, some would argue that this type of naked, aggressive neo-liberalism coupled with blatant electoral nepotism could only be characterised as nothing other than neo-lithic.

9 Conclusion

From conflict to consensus – the evolution of postwar British politics

The established narrative as 'common sense'

The major purpose of this book has been to question the established narrative of the postwar period that has so far pervaded the vast bulk of the literature. Here, it is perhaps fruitful briefly to remind ourselves of the content of this narrative. As we saw in the introductory chapter, the established narrative revolves around the issue of *change* versus *continuity* in British politics. Specifically, most authors assert that there have been two main periods of policy *change*. It is suggested that, in the immediate aftermath of the Second World War, the Attlee governments fundamentally altered the direction of British politics through a succession of decisive interventions which changed both the institutional structure and the ideological apparatus surrounding policy-making in favour of a Keynesian, social-democratic, state settlement. Similarly, it has most often been asserted that the Thatcher governments after 1979 set about fundamentally restructuring Britain's postwar settlement by reversing the direction of policy, and dismantling the main pillars of Keynesian social democracy in line with New Right ideology.

Throughout the literature, these two periods of supposed radical change have been consistently contrasted, thereby creating a binary opposition between Thatcherism and its historical 'others'. Thus, to most authors, Thatcherism emerges as the direct antithesis of its postwar historical antecedents. Moreover, it has been overwhelmingly assumed that between these two contrasting eras British politics was dominated by a long period of policy *continuity*, which resulted from a large degree of bi-party agreement over the main priorities of government strategy. In effect, it is argued that the 'postwar consensus', based around a firm commitment to Keynesianism, social democracy, and active government, solidified the postwar settlement and helped to keep it in place, relatively unchallenged, for a period of about thirty years or so, until the decisive intervention of the Thatcher governments.

The above narrative has become so established within the literature that it has remained relatively unchallenged, and largely unscathed, since its construction. This, above all else, should be viewed as a problem, whether we are historians, political scientists or state theorists; for, in a Gramscian sense, the established narrative of the postwar period has become something of a 'common sense' set of assumptions. This is perhaps something of an irony, since the narrative achieved its overall ascendancy within the context of the initial attempts by neo-Gramscian authors to assert the hegemonic purpose of the Thatcher governments. To the authors of *Marxism Today* (whose analyses of the specificities of Thatcherism nevertheless remain among the most insightful and illuminating on offer), the supposed radicalism of the Thatcher project was, in itself, a taken-for-granted assumption. Yet, at the time, Thatcherism had been put into play at one level only; that is, at the discursive level. At this stage, Thatcherism had still largely to reveal itself at a policy – let alone an institutional – level. No one could know what to expect from the Thatcher governments, except by listening to what it was that the Thatcherites themselves were telling us.

Yet this is a dangerous yardstick for measuring government performance, since a central element of the Thatcherites' attempts at achieving hegemony was their assault upon the forces of corporate-liberalism and social democracy that had played an important role in shaping the evolution of the earlier postwar period. In order to legitimise their own strategic interventions, the Thatcher governments discursively narrated the crisis of the 1970s as a crisis of an overloaded state, caused by the overwhelming dominance of expansionist ideas throughout the postwar period. Thus, to the Thatcherites, the development of policy in the postwar period had occurred along a single evolutionary trajectory, involving a consensual movement towards Keynesianism, corporatism, active government and the conciliation of trade unions.

The major problem within the literature has been that, after the election of the first Thatcher government in 1979, the vast majority of political scientists and historians were willing to acquiesce to this view in their eagerness to assert the novelty and radicalism of Thatcherism. Admittedly many of these attempts, as with the efforts of Hall *et al.*, were provoked by the desire to demonise the Thatcher project by highlighting its assault upon the left. Yet, by doing so, most authors were being unreflexively absorbed into a particular interpretation of the early postwar period which accorded favourably with Thatcherite ideology and which, more importantly, was far from accurate. As a result, the established narrative of the postwar period played an important role in the development of Thatcherite hegemony; for, by characterising the postwar era as a period dominated by expansionist and collectivist ideas, the Thatcherites could point to these factors as a major cause of Britain's economic decline. This enabled the Conservatives legitimately to make the claim that there was 'no alternative' to their strategy of rescuing the market from the claws of an overloaded social-democratic state.

Throughout this book therefore, there has been an underlying critique of the active role that political scientists and historians have played in unwittingly legitimising Thatcherite hegemony. Clearly, there is much cause for alarm when the so-called organic intellectuals of the left subscribe to a similar historical narrative to that of right-wing politicians and liberal historians. However, we should not perhaps be too surprised that this has been the case, since a central element of Gramsci's own work concerns the important role that intellectuals play in reinforcing and strengthening common-sense assumptions. Throughout the literature on the postwar period the intellectual establishment has provided a ringing endorsement of the basic historical narrative of the New Right, abandoning previous assumptions about the adversarial nature of the political system in favour of the idea of a social-democratic consensus. Certainly, the aim of most authors has not been to endorse Thatcherism per se, but this is not the point; the central issue here, whether we are supporters or opponents of the Thatcher project, has been the lack of reflexivity involved in most studies, and the willingness passively to absorb government rhetoric without any accompanying penetrative critical assessment.

The established narrative as non-sense

In an attempt to move beyond the prevailing accounts of the period, this book has posited many reasons for rejecting the established narrative. First, it has asserted the inadequacy of the conventional storyline at an empirical level. As we have seen, the Attlee administration, though responsible for implementing many important changes, did not fundamentally alter the nature of the postwar British state to the extent that most authors have thus far implied. Apart from having laid down the structures of the welfare state (which as we have seen, represented a reform in line with both the evolution of progressive liberal ideas and the underlying commitment of the wartime Coalition), the Attlee government abandoned the majority of its erstwhile commitments to radical institutional reform, in favour of a retreat back into liberal retrenchment. Moreover, the idea of a so-called era of consensus dominated by continuity also fails to stand up to empirical examination. Rather, the period after 1947 was one which was dominated by continual conflict over government strategy, resulting in a whole series of policy reversals and strategic adaptations. Similarly, I have shown that the radicalism of the Thatcher project came into play a lot later and more gradually than most authors have thus far acknowledged.

Second, at a theoretical level, I have shown that the established narrative has many important flaws. Foremost amongst these has been the overall neglect of a consideration of the temporal dimension of political change. Overall, the established narrative has bequeathed us with a series of somewhat crude temporal sequences; specifically, the period can be summarised as being constituted by radical change followed by relative stasis, followed by radical change followed by relative stasis. At no point has there been any adequate attempt to take account of the constraints upon change and to acknowledge that, in the face of these constraints, strategies continually adapt and evolve. Thus, change is inherent in politics and, although the pace of change may alter dramatically, it is always present. As we have seen, this is particularly evident during the so-called consensus era, when in place of continuity and stasis, the period was dominated by a whole series of changes which, in many respects, gave the era a dynamic that was no less forceful than the Thatcher years. The second main theoretical flaw within the literature has been the tendency of most authors to employ uni-dimensional explanations of the period. This has been particularly prevalent within the literature on Thatcherism. Overall, most explanations have either concentrated upon political *or* economic *or* ideological factors. At the same time, these explanations alternate between either structural or agency inputs into the process of policy formulation. Throughout the liter-ature, there have been few attempts to link these disparate elements into a coherent explanatory framework that offers a multi-layered perspective.

Third, there has been an overall lack of attention paid within the litera-ture to the historical dimensions of change. Again, this is particularly true in the case of the literature on Thatcherism. Few attempts have been made to consider Thatcherism as having evolved *out of* a particular historical back-ground; rather, the aim of most authors has been to assert Thatcherism as representing merely *a reaction to* particular historical events. As a result, Thatcherism has most often been separated from its historical ancestry; few attempts have been made to assess the important lines of continuity that exist between the Thatcher period and the earlier postwar era.

Overall then, these problems have contributed to the fact that Thatcherism has most often been presented as a singular, static 'snapshot' in time, dislocated from its historical precedents, while primary explanatory emphasis has alternated between ethno/agency centred accounts of change or strict structural determinism. The legacy of these analyses is that we are left with an inanimate picture of the development of postwar British politics, in which our understanding of the evolution of state structures and governmental strategies has been compromised by a series of static representations that merely caricature change and obscure important continuities. What has been missing has been a proper analysis of the complexity of change through the dynamic and dialectical interplay between structure, agency and strategy.

Towards an alternative explanation: bringing evolution back in

In order to overcome these problems, this book has drawn upon and devel-oped an evolutionary account of political change. As we have seen, evolutionary theorising in social science has long been discredited due to its association with certain types of unfavourable theoretical baggage. Among these have been: an emphasis upon change as a unilinear path to 'progress'; a reliance upon functionalist explanation; a tendency to assert certain 'laws' of structural determination; and the failure to acknowledge the crucial role of human agency as a primary factor shaping historical development. Overall, these problems have meant that evolutionary theorising in social science has been exposed to a wide array of criticisms and, cumulatively, these have left it stripped of a great deal of its former credibility.

Nevertheless, as we have also seen, evolutionary theory itself has since evolved considerably in order to overcome these problems and re-emerge as an exciting new paradigm spanning a range of other disciplines, including economics, sociology, organizational theory and state theory. Within these other branches of social science research, the utility of an evolutionary theory as a sophisticated and multi-layered explanation of change is being widely recognised. This recognition has led to an attempt to strip evolutionary theories of their inherent functionalism and structural determination. The idea of progress has been dropped, while the lack of recognition of the role of human agency has been addressed. The result is that a new brand of neo-evolutionary theory has emerged that asserts the inherent contingency and randomness in the process of change, as well as the multiplicity of factors which can generate it.

Here, an attempt has been made to draw upon these revised conceptions of evolutionary change in order to provide a more adequate explanation of the postwar period that avoids the empirical and theoretical problems inherent within the literature. As such, I have identified evolutionary theory as having four main distinguishing features: a concern with both time and the processes that generate change; a focus upon the selection of variables; an emphasis upon adaptive process; and a concern to emphasise that change is at once both contingent and path dependent. The combination of these intrinsic elements within evolutionary theory provides the approach with many advantages for explaining political change. Overall, an evolutionary account of political and economic change pre-supposes a heightened sensitivity to the constantly changing relationship between strategic actors and the environment in which they are forced to operate. Change is conceived of here as being *both* contingent and path-dependent; as a conditioned response to environmental exigencies and crises filtered through the limited ideological heuristics of state actors.

In these respects, an evolutionary explanation entails a proper consideration of the dialectical interplay between structure, agency and strategy by focusing our attention upon the ways in which actors articulate strategies in order to negotiate the structural and strategic demands of the environment that they inhabit. It is this heightened sensitivity to the relational and contingent articulation of strategy that provides an evolutionary account with the explanatory depth required to elucidate periods of intensified political change such as the Thatcher years. Thus, an evolutionary explanation of Thatcherism, a priori, precludes the type of static, ahistorical, ethno-centred and reductionist accounts that have so far dominated the literature, by directing our focus onto the inherent dynamism of the Conservatives' strategy and the multi-layered historical processes and mechanisms which generated, facilitated and constrained it. This then also implies a proper consideration of the temporality of change that allows us to view Thatcherism as a series of contingent interventions which unfolded and evolved through time.

Establishing an alternative narrative: from conflict to consensus

Through the application of an evolutionary approach, therefore, this book has provided an alternative account of postwar British politics that, in effect, turns the established narrative on its head. By focusing upon the range of strategic adaptations in the earlier postwar period, we have seen that, instead of representing a long era of continuity dominated by consensus, the pre-Thatcher period reflected fundamental shifts and reversals of governmental strategy due to the inherent conflicts at the heart of the policy-making arena. This 'struggle for survival' between competing conceptions of government strategy resulted from a combination of environmental and agency factors.

First, policy in the postwar period had been shaped by the pre-war crisis of maladaptation to changing conditions in the productive base. The shift towards Fordist production techniques had placed significant pressures upon all advanced capitalist nations to re-regulate the conditions for future economic growth. This required the stimulation of mass demand through Keynesian macro-economic management, the creation of welfare structures, and the maintenance of full employment. However, Britain's peculiar position within the global economy – that of a former hegemony – invoked cross-cutting pressures for the selection of policies aimed at maintaining the country's status within the international environment. The decision to pursue such a foreign policy placed contradictory pressures upon all postwar governments which made the mutual reconciliation of domestic and foreign demands virtually impossible over the long term.

These contradictory pressures were mirrored within the domestic environment where the combination of factors such as the dominance of finance capital, the weakness of the state, and the fragmentation of industrial capital and trade unions, all served to enhance the inherent conflicts at the heart of policy-making. The overall result, as we have seen, was a fitful evolution, involving fundamental reversals and adaptations in government strategy as politicians struggled to balance the competing and contradictory demands placed upon them. All in all, this fitful evolution and policy oscillation between state expansion and liberal retreat can only be taken to reflect the fundamental lack of any firm or coherent postwar settlement. Far from being 'settled', the story of the early postwar era is one of continual conflict, and a battle between progressive and classical liberal ideas fought out within a strategically selective environment that favoured the latter over the former.

In this sense then, Thatcherism emerged out of a historical environment which was, in many ways, conducive to its inherent anti-statism and its overall emphasis upon traditional monetary concerns. As a response to international pressures to re-regulate the productive base, and domestic environmental pressures to resolve Britain's long-running postwar conflicts and fitful evolution, Thatcherism emerged as Britain's first real postwar settlement. Although faced initially with the final residues of earlier postwar conflicts, the Thatcher project was able successfully to dissipate these in order to create a relatively favourable environment for the evolution of its highly abstract strategic objective of rolling back the state.

Through a constant process of experimentation, strategic learning, ad hoc decision-making and policy adaptation within an environment relatively free from fundamental conflict at the heart of the policy-making apparatus, the Conservatives' strategy could evolve over time into a more concrete response to an abstract formula. The culmination of this evolution was the series of radical institutional reforms implemented in the public sector during the Conservatives' third and fourth terms in office. Yet, despite the Conservatives' success in implementing many of their strategic objectives, the overall success of the strategy in reversing Britain's economic decline was severely hampered by the narrow ideological heuristics which informed the Conservatives' strategic interventions. In particular, the dogmatic attachment to an anti-statist, neo-liberal ideology directed their attention away from the need to learn the appropriate means by which state mechanisms could be used to generate growth and successful accumulation. In place of this, the Conservatives proved merely content to engage in an almost constant and ongoing process of learning how to satisfy their twin fetishes for welfare retrenchment and depoliticisation of the very areas that could generate successful adaptation to the environmental crises brought about by the failure of Fordism.

Notes

1 Introduction: what's the story?

1 The only period which has so far failed to provoke any substantial debate is the Major administration. As we shall see in Chapter Two, far from stimulating debate, the premiership of John Major failed to spark any general interest at all.
2 For a review see D. Porter 1994.
3 By referring to 'the Thatcher years', I do not simply mean the period 1979–90. It is important to remember here that the 'Thatcherite' critique of postwar British government maintained a gradual ascendancy throughout the late 1960s and into the 1970s.
4 Tiratsoo is quoting Hennessey (1989: 50)
5 The attempts by political science to turn the spotlight upon itself have been limited. However, there have more recent tentative efforts to remedy this. See for example Leftwich (1984a), Hayward and Norton (1986), Zuckerman (1991), Lekhi (1995a).
6 As Lekhi points out, it is important to emphasise that the discipline faces increasing political impediments to achieving this type of broad remit. Thus, the author states: 'The need to survive (and even prosper) as an academic has acquired a short-termism, a need to direct research to the current desires of policy-makers or to the latest fads and fashions of the popular media. . . . Desperate to secure scarce resources, the tendency is increasingly for political studies to accede to crude instrumentalist judgements of what constitutes serious political inquiry' (Lekhi 1995b: 1–2)
7 This is perhaps best reflected in the fact that the concept of 'class' has generally been reduced by mainstream studies of British politics to a mere variable which helps to decide each party's share of the vote at elections.

2 Evolution, not revolution

1 The literature on Thatcherism has been reviewed by a number of authors. Marsh (1994, 1995a) has provided the most comprehensive survey to date. For less rigorous, but no less useful reviews see; Jessop *et al.* (1988: 22–51) Douglas (1989), Evans and Taylor (1996: 219–46). For summaries of the legacy of the Thatcher governments see Gamble (1990), Crewe (1993). More extensive surveys are provided by Riddell (1991), Cloke (1992), Marsh and Rhodes (1992), Ludlam and Smith (1996).
2 See Hall *et al.* (1978), Hall (1979), Jacques (1979).
3 To some extent, this point has been backed by Mrs Thatcher herself, who writes in her memoirs: 'we had also taken apprenticeships in advertising and learnt how to put a complex, and sophisticated case in direct, clear and simple

language. We had been arguing that case for the best part of four years, so our agenda would, with luck, strike people as familiar common sense rather than a wild radical project' (Thatcher 1993: 5).

4   The exceptions here are Hay (1996) and McAnulla (1997; 1999).

5   Although see Gamble (1988), Jessop *et al.* (1988), Taylor (1989), Overbeek (1990), Hay (1996).

6   For an informed analysis and critique of the literature on decline see Johnston (1997, 1999).

7   See in particular: Tomlinson 1981, 1984; Booth 1983; Thompson 1984; Bulpitt 1986; Cronin 1991.

8   See in particular: Ingham 1984; Fine and Harris 1985; Jessop 1992; Hutton 1996.

9   See for example Hall (1979, 1988), Gamble (1988), Jessop *et al.* (1988), Overbeek (1990), Taylor (1992), Hay (1996). As Marsh has highlighted however, although these analyses do succeed in providing more holistic approaches to Thatcherism, each fails in different ways to provide a proper multi-dimensional theoretical perspective which is elastic enough to pay sufficient weight to the range of political, economic and ideological inputs to the Conservatives' strategy. Thus, Gamble affords a primacy of explanation to the political dimensions to Thatcherism, Hall and Hay emphasise ideational factors while Jessop *et al.*, Overbeek and Taylor ultimately rely upon analyses which are, at times, strictly economistic. Having stated this, it is perhaps worth noting that Evans and Taylor (1996: 232) have criticised Marsh for failing to categorise Gamble's thesis as multi-dimensional. These authors claim that due weight is given by Gamble to the ideological and economic factors which impinged upon the Thatcherite strategy. To a large extent this criticism is justifiable; however, while Marsh recognises this, his response is that: 'one is ultimately left dissatisfied because again the articulation between economic, ideological and political factors is under-theorised; the theoretical nettle is not really grasped' (Marsh 1994). Nevertheless, it would be fair to say that Gamble does come closest to a multi-dimensional explanation.

10   Attempts to overcome the rigid dichotomy between structuralist and intentionalist accounts of change, and to re-assert the need for a heightened sensitivity to the dialectical interplay between structure, agency and strategy, have become more common in recent years. Unfortunately, however, these seem largely to have failed to impinge upon the concerns of political scientists. See for example Bhaskar 1979; Giddens 1984; Stzompka 1991, 1993; Archer 1995; Hay 1995; Jessop 1996.

11   As Wallerstein (1991: 264–5) explains: 'we have been bequeathed a terrible legacy by nineteenth-century social science. It is the assertion that social reality occurs in three different and separate arenas: the political, the economic and the socio-cultural. . . . This is nonsense in terms of how the world really works. . . . The holy trinity of politics/economics/society has no intellectual heuristic value today'.

3   Conflict, not consensus

1   A wealth of studies have emerged in the past decade devoted to summarising the political and economic trends of the latter half of the twentieth century. General studies include: Gourvish and O'Day (1991); Morgan (1992); Obelkevich and Catterall (1994); Childs (1995); Tiratsoo (1997). On the politics of the period see: Dutton (1991); Dorey (1995); Ridley and Rush (1995); Robins and Jones (1997); Marsh *et al.* (1999). Economic developments are reviewed by: Crafts and Woodward (1991); Cairncross (1992); Floud and McCloskey (1994). For analyses of social policy and welfare see: Lowe (1993);

Glennester (1995). On elections and parties see: Stevenson (1993); Butler (1995); Shaw (1996). On ideas and ideology see: Marquand and Seldon (1996).

2 It is important to emphasise that historians have been more inclined than political scientists towards challenging the accepted assumptions of the established narrative.

3 As Dutton (1991: 9) explains, until Addison's (1975) original publication, the Second World War had remained 'something of a backwater as far as British domestic political history was concerned'. Today however, both the war period and its aftermath have been served well by recent research, including: Morgan 1984; Barnett 1986; Jefferys 1991; Tiratsoo 1991a; Brooke 1992; Mercer, Rollings and Tomlinson 1992; Fyrth 1993; Hennessey 1992; Tiratsoo and Tomlinson 1993, Fielding, Thompson and Tiratsoo 1996.

4 Kavanagh and Morris do not directly cite this as a separate pillar of the consensus. However, the move towards active government is recognised by most authors, including Kavanagh (1987) himself, as a central feature of the policies pursued by all postwar governments up until the election of the first Thatcher government in 1979.

5 Again, some may object that this claim rests upon shaky foundations. It is true to say that Addison's work does not provide the first reference to the consensual nature of British politics in the postwar period. Indeed, the term can be traced to a scattered assortment of previous references. For example, Robert McKenzie (1955: 581) noted an 'agreement on fundamentals' between the two main parties. Likewise, Samuel Beer (1965: 357) acknowledged the 'massive continuity' between consecutive Labour and Conservative governments, while Angus Calder (1969) remarked that the wartime consensus had acted as a major factor in shaping the postwar welfare state. However, it is important to emphasise that as a distinct thesis, used to describe the nature of the political system as a whole, the idea of consensus did not start to cement until Addison's publication in 1975. Therefore, although we can detect previous points of reference, Addison's work is normally accredited as being the closest we come to a seminal piece in the literature (see Kavanagh and Morris 1994: 1; Seldon 1994: 501). However, we only need to examine any detailed bibliography on consensus politics to realise that the literature is a relatively new phenomenon.

6 The context of Russell's work could hardly be further removed from the supposed harmony and agreement associated with the consensus era. These remarks are taken from one of his attempts to revise the assumptions which are normally made about the causes of the English Civil War.

7 Interestingly enough, while the left and right seemed to consent to consensus, the view from the centre sought to dispute the notion of consensus by advocating the 'adversarial politics' thesis. It was this thesis which held most sway until the onset of Thatcherism. Indeed, it is this view that Pimlott (1988) subscribes to.

4 Reconstructing our perspective

1 In its most sinister guise, evolutionary thinking has been used by some 'social Darwinists' to promote malign ideological assumptions about racial and sexual hierarchies (see Hawkins, 1997). In particular, 'social Darwinism' as a strand of evolutionary theorising has been linked to the doctrine of fascism, while other proponents have used it to justify the practice of laissez-faire capitalism.

2 For economists see for example Nelson and Winter (1982); Clark and Calestous (1987); De Bresson (1987); Anderson, Arrow and Pines (1988); Dosi *et al.* (1988); Saviotti and Metcalfe (1991); Hodgson (1993a); Magnusson (1994); Vromen (1995). For a review see Hodgson (1993b); Nelson (1995). As

regards organization theorists see for example the various contributions to Singh (1990). For sociobiologists see, among others, Cavalli-Sforza and Feldman (1981); Lumsden and Wilson (1981); Lopreato (1984); Boyd and Richerson (1985); Durham (1991). For a review see: Nelson (1995: 59–60); Hawkins (1997: 292–313).

3   See for example Rueschemeyer (1986); Alexander (1988); Alexander and Colomy (1988); Sanderson (1990, 1995) regarding historical sociology. In political economy recent interest has been shown by some political economists in the study of long waves of economic growth and stagnation. Inspired mainly by the work of Kondratieff and Schumpeter, various authors (see for example: Mandel 1964, 1995; Gordon 1978, 1980; Freeman 1982; Van Duijn 1983; Kleinknecht 1987; Tylecote 1992) have attempted to demonstrate the existence of regular evolutionary patterns of capitalist development. Although most of this work can only be described as implicitly 'evolutionary', the aim of these authors has been to demonstrate the processes and stages through which capitalist economic relations and correlative institutions adapt and evolve in response to periodic crises within the world economy. Moreover, the renewed interest in long-wave theory has also provoked other theoretical responses such as the world-systems approach applied by Wallerstein and others (see for example: Wallerstein 1974, 1980, 1983, 1989; Frank 1980; Hopkins and Wallerstein 1982; Taylor 1989; Frank and Gillis 1996; Hopkins and Wallerstein *et al.* 1996) and the regulation approach derived from the French regulation school of political economy (see for example: Aglietta 1979; Lipietz 1987; Boyer 1990; Jessop 1990b). Again, although these authors only implicitly rely upon formal evolutionary concepts, their aim has been to demonstrate the adaptation of institutional structures and economic and political relations to the wider evolutionary trajectory of capitalist growth patterns.

4   As regards state theorists see, for example: Jessop (1990a); Ward (1993, 1997); Hay (1996, 1997). It is important to emphasise here that these approaches differ markedly in the extent to which they employ evolutionary concepts. For historical institutionalists see, for example: Skocpol (1992); Steinmo *et al.* (1992); Hall (1993); Pierson (1993, 1996). For a review of the historical institutionalist literature and its relationship to new institutionalism more broadly see Hall and Taylor (1996), Kato (1996). It should be emphasised that these authors are much more implicit in their use of formal evolutionary concepts and analogies. However, their work does represent one of the closest systematic attempts within an orthodox political science discourse to formulate a broad evolutionary schema given their emphasis upon change as a path-dependent evolutionary process which is (*under*)-determined by the historical formation of institutional structures.

5   The exceptions amid this recent trend of neo-evolutionary thought could perhaps be considered to be certain streams of sociobiology and long-run economics. Whereas the latter has often been criticised for its latent technological determinism, the former has come under sustained criticism and condemnation for its 'renascent Social Darwinism' (Hawkins 1997: 295). In this respect, sociobiology in particular still retains a largely discredited reputation in social science circles for its alleged biological determinism. See for example: Samuelson (1975); Thompson (1982).

6   At this point, it is important to provide some qualification to these remarks. For it would be inappropriate to charge Giddens too directly with having misrepresented evolutionary theory. At the time of writing most of the authors' criticisms were entirely apt in relation to the type of impaired conception of evolutionary change that had hitherto been applied in the social sciences. In this respect, it is the earlier advocates of evolutionary theorising who must ulti-

mately be blamed for having distorted the general principles of an evolutionary approach. Moreover, it is equally important to acknowledge the crucial role which critics such as Giddens have played in forcing neo-evolutionary theorists to adapt their theoretical premises in order to provide a more sophisticated conception of change.

7 Some conventional theories of policy change can be loosely characterised as 'evolutionary' in their basic premise that change occurs in an iterative fashion due to the constraints which the institutional environment, and the inheritance from past policy choices place upon actors' abilities to affect radical policy outcomes. Here, we could include the 'incrementalism' of Lindblom (1959) and others. Meanwhile, some authors have explicitly referred to the constraints which past 'inheritance' places upon the evolution of public policy (Rose and Davies 1994), while others (Cohen, March and Olson 1972; Kingdon 1984) argue that, although solutions to problems are often arbitrarily taken from the 'garbage can' of ideas, successful solutions can only come to fruition when ideas converge with an appropriate policy climate or environment.

8 Here, it is important to emphasise that discursive formations are widely recognised to be open to continual contestation. Thus: 'it is important to avoid an image of discursive change as a unilinear, top-down process: there is struggle over the structuring of texts and orders of discourse, and people may resist or appropriate changes coming from above, as well as merely go along with them' (Fairclough 1992: 9). In this respect then: 'discourse as a political practice is not only a site of power struggle, but also a stake in power struggle: discursive practice draws upon conventions which naturalise particular power relations and ideologies, and these conventions themselves, and the way in which they are articulated, are a focus of struggle' (ibid.: 67).

9 It is perhaps worth noting here that incrementalism, or gradualism, is not an intrinsic property of an evolutionary process. However, it is likely to appear as the dominant characteristic of the process, given that it is intrinsic to evolution that changes are inherently path-dependent. Given the complex array of factors which shape evolution, the 'limits' upon strategic action are likely most often to outweigh the potentialities.

5 Go . . . stop . . . go . . . stop!

1 For an evolutionary account of the creation of the welfare state, see Fraser (1984). As the author states: 'the Welfare State is subject to those same evolutionary forces which were its ancestors. The Welfare State was thus not a final heroic victory after centuries of struggle, but the welfare complex of a particular period adapting to the needs of the next generation' (ibid.: 243).

2 In a footnote to this passage, Gamble (1994: 240) adds: 'the paucity of labour's constitutional reforms showed the extent to which the Labour leadership had become reconciled to the existing state'.

3 Cronin (1991: 161) identifies five major crises which hampered Labour's ability to put into effect its longer-term aims: the mounting problem of the dollar drain; the fuel crisis during the winter of 1946–7; the convertibility crisis in the summer of 1947; the 30 per cent devaluation of Sterling in 1949; and rearmament in 1950. However, we may also add to this list the ending of American financial support through lend–lease immediately after the war and Britain's subsequent negotiations for an American loan to prevent virtual bankruptcy.

4 Certainly it is true to say that the pursuit of full employment had now become a governmental priority. However, the reality is that no real steps had been

taken towards ensuring that this goal would be maintained. As Alex Cairncross, an economic adviser to the Attlee government, explains: 'the maintenance of a high level of employment was only to a limited extent the government's doing. It was made easy because world markets remained in a state of boom. . . . What can be claimed for the Labour government is that the one thing that it had to plan, and did plan – the balance of payments – was effectively planned' (quoted in Cliff and Gluckstein 1996: 227–8).

5   This heightened economic decline was also being accompanied by a gradual retreat from empire. Cuts in public expenditure on the domestic front were being mirrored by a dramatic cut in Britain's overseas defence commitments.

6   In many ways, Heath's ideological conviction was no different either from the corporate-liberalism of his predecessors (Overbeek 1990: 155). According to Middlemas (1979: 423), 'Heath attempted to reimpose the genial statism of the fifties but had to concede to his opponents the so-called "Selsdon doctrine" in 1969, at immense cost to the support of his subsequent government from both sides of industry'. As a result, Overbeek (1990: 155; emphasis added) argues that, given Heath's general reluctance fully to subscribe to a policy of dogmatic *laissez-faire* liberalism, 'the Heath government embarked on a course characterised by *rhetorical radicalism*'.

6 Struggling for survival

1   The first element is sometimes referred to as a 'technological paradigm' or an 'industrialisation model' (Lipietz: 1992: 2). It refers to the dominant set of general principles governing the division of labour both within and between firms. Sectors which are most advanced in the pursuit of these principles will determine how other sectors evolve (ibid.). The second element refers to the dominant system of macro-economic management that is used to consolidate the labour process model. The regime of accumulation determines the primary conditions of production (such as labour productivity and the degree of mechanisation) as well as factors which affect the use of production (such as consumption and investment levels, government spending) (ibid.). The third element, the mode of regulation, refers to the regulatory mechanisms which ensure that individual groups conform to the 'collective principles of the regime of accumulation' (ibid.). These include institutionalised procedures governing such things as the rules of the market, the level of welfare provision and the distribution of wealth. Such regulatory mechanisms are normally enforced by the state; however, they can also be the product of private or semi-public institutions.

2   The term 'Fordism' dates as far back as the 1920s when theorists such as Antonio Gramsci applied it to describe the new production methods being used in the United States. These combined the 'scientific management' techniques adapted by Frederick Taylor with the mass production methods employed by Henry Ford. Taylor's ideas involved the rationalisation of production, whereby the mental and manual aspects of work were separated and the division of labour organized so that most people in the production process were left to carry out repetitive tasks (Lipietz 1992: 4). Although the introduction of these techniques at the beginning of the century met heavy opposition from craft workers and trade unions, a compromise was eventually reached which allowed unions to acquire a greater share of the productivity gains made from rationalisation. Henry Ford was one of the first employers to accept this compromise when he began mass production of his Model-T motor car.

3   For a discussion on the distinction between selection *of* and selection *for* certain variables see Chapter Five (also Sober 1984: 100; Vromen 1995: 98).

4   Lend–Lease, which had been established in 1942, had provided Britain with $27 billion of aid over the three years.

5   So determined were British policy-makers to secure Britain's financial status that an inordinate amount of the Marshall Aid fund was devoted to under-pinning this policy rather than, in line with the expressed aims of the Marshall Plan, modernising British industry (Overbeek 1990: 91). In comparative terms, Britain used only 8.8 per cent of its share of aid to invest in machinery and equipment compared to 11.9 per cent in France.

6   Here, Cronin is quoting G. Sutherland (1972) *Studies in the Growth of Nineteenth Century Government* (London: Routledge).

7 Struggling for definition

1   In actual fact, it would be just as plausible to argue, as some authors have, that 1975 represented the true end to the attempts at state expansion. As we saw in the previous chapter, Labour had already effectively abandoned its strategy some time before the intervention of the IMF.

2   Here, it is important to note, as Marsh (1992: 49; also Hay 1996: 120) has pointed out, that despite the lack of commitment to formalised procedures of securing wage restraint, the social contract was still, in effect, an incomes policy under a different name.

3   Indeed, between 1975 and 1978, real wages fell by an average of 13 per cent a year, a rate of reduction not experienced by British workers since 1931–2 (Gourevitch *et al.* 1984: 56; Middlemas 1979: 156; Hay 1996: 118).

4   According to Belsey (1986: 173; also Overbeek 1990: 197), ideal-typical *neo-liberalism* involved an emphasis upon individualism, freedom of choice, the market society, laissez-faire and limited government. *Neo-Conservatism* on the other hand emphasised strong government, social authoritarianism, a disci-plined society, hierarchy and subordination, and nationhood.

Bibliography

Addison, P. (1975) *The Road to 1945: British Politics and the Second World War* (London: Cape).

—— (1985) *Now The War Is Over* (London: BBC).

—— (1987) 'The Road From 1945', in P. Hennessey and A. Seldon (eds) *Ruling Performance* (Oxford: Blackwell).

—— (1993) 'Consensus Revisited', *Twentieth Century British History* vol. 4 no. 1.

Adonis, A. and Hames, T. (eds) (1994) *A Conservative Revolution? The Thatcher–Reagan Decade in Perspective* (Manchester: Manchester University Press).

Aglietta, M. (1979) *A Theory of Capitalist Regulation: The US Experience* (London: New Left Books).

Alexander, J. (1988) *Action and its Environments* (New York: Columbia University Press).

Alexander, J. and Colomy, P. (eds) (1988) *Differentiation Theory and Social Change: Historical and Comparative Approaches* (New York: Columbia University Press).

Anderson, P. (1987) 'Figures of Descent', *New Left Review* 161.

Anderson, P. W., Arrow, K. J., Pines, D. (eds) (1988) *The Economy as an Evolving Complex System* (Redwood City: Addison-Wesley).

Archer, M. (1995) *Realist Social Theory: The Morphogenetic Approach* (Cambridge: Cambridge University Press).

Arrighi, G. (1994) *The Long Twentieth Century* (London: Verso).

Ball, A. R. (1981) *British Political Parties* (London: Macmillan).

Barker, A. (1995) 'Major's Government in a Major Key: Conservative Ideological Aggressiveness Since Thatcher', *New Political Science* 33.

Barnett, C. (1986) *The Audit of War: The Illusion and Reality of Britain as a Great Nation* (London: Macmillan).

—— (1996) *The Lost Victory: British Dreams, British Realities 1945–1950* (London: Pan).

Bartlett, C. J. (1977) *A History of Post-war Britain, 1945–74* (Longman: London).

Beer, S. (1965) *Modern British Politics* (London: Faber).

Belsey, A. (1986) 'The New Right, Social Order and Civil Liberties', in R. Levitas (ed.) *The Ideology of the New Right* (Cambridge: Polity).

Benn, T. (1987) 'British Politics, 1945–87: Four Perspectives', in P. Hennessey and A. Seldon (eds) *Ruling Performance* (Oxford: Blackwell).

Berki, R. N. (1986) 'The Belated Impact of Marxism', in J. Hayward and P. Norton (eds) *The Political Science of British Politics* (Sussex: Wheatsheaf).

Bertramsen, R. (1988) 'Towards a Strategic Relational Approach to State Analysis', *Essex Papers in Politics and Government* 56.

Bhaskar, R. (1979) *The Possibility of Naturalism* (Hemel Hempstead: Harvester Wheatsheaf).

Blank, S. (1978) 'Britain: The Politics of Foreign Economic Policy, the Domestic Economy and the Problem of Pluralistic Stagnation', in P. Katzenstein (ed.) *Between Power and Plenty* (Madison: Wisconsin Press).

—— (1986) 'The Impact of Foreign Economic Policy', in D. Coates and J. Hillard (eds) *The Economic Decline of Modern Britain: The Debate Between Left and Right* (Hemel Hempstead: Harvester Wheatsheaf).

Booth, A. (1983) 'Simple Keynsianism and Whitehall 1936–44', *Economy and Society* 15.

Boyd, R. and Richerson, P. J. (1985) *Culture and the Evolutionary Process* (Chicago: Chicago University Press).

Boyer, R. (1990) *The Regulation School: A Critical Introduction* (New York: Columbia University Press).

Brett, T. (1985) *The World Economy Since the War* (London: Macmillan).

Brittan, S. (1977) *The Economic Consequences of Democracy* (London: Temple Smith).

Britton, A. J. C. (1991) *Macroeconomic Policy In Britain 1974–1987* (Cambridge: Cambridge University Press).

Brooke, S. (1992) *Labour's War: The Labour Party during the Second World War* (Oxford: Oxford University Press).

Bulpitt, J. (1986) 'The Discipline of the New Democracy: Mrs Thatcher's Domestic Statecraft', *Political Studies* vol. 34 no. 1.

Burch, M. and Wood, B. (1997) 'From Provider to Enabler: The Changing Role of the State', in L. Robins and B. Jones (eds) *Half a Century of British Politics* (Manchester: University Press).

Burnham, P. (1990) *The Political Economy of Postwar Reconstruction* (London: Macmillan).

Burns, T. R. and Dietz, T. (1992) 'Cultural Evolution: Social Rule Systems, Selection and Human Agency', *International Sociology* vol. 7 no. 3.

Burrow, J. W. (1966) Evolution and Society (Cambridge: Cambridge University Press).

Butler, A. (1993) 'The End of Post-war Consensus: Reflections on the Scholarly Uses of Political Rhetoric', *Political Quarterly* vol. 64 no. 4.

Butler, D. (1995) *British General Elections Since 1945* (Oxford: Blackwell).

Butler, D. and Kavanagh, D. (1980) *The British General Election of 1979* (London: Macmillan).

Cain, P. J. and Hopkins, A. G. (1993) *British Imperialism: Crisis and Deconstruction 1914–1990* (London: Longman).

Cairncross, A. (1991) 'Reconversion, 1945–51', in N. F. R. Crafts and N. W. C. Woodward (eds) *The British Economy Since 1945* (Oxford: Oxford University Press).

—— (1992) *The British Economy Since 1945: Economic Policy and Performance* (Oxford: Blackwell).

—— (1994) 'Economic Policy and Performance, 1945–1964', in R. Floud and D. McCloskey (eds) *The Economic History of Britain Since 1700*, vol. 3: 1939–1992 (Cambridge: Cambridge University Press).

Calder, A. (1969) *The People's War* (London: Cape).

Catterall, P. (1989) 'The State of the Literature on post-war British History', in A. Gorst, L. Johnman and W. S. Lucas (eds) *Post-war Britain, 1945–64: Themes and Perspectives* (London: Pinter).

Cavalli-Sforza, L. L. and Feldman, M. W. (1981) *Cultural Transmission and Evolution: A Quantitative Approach* (Princeton: Princeton University Press).

Ceadel, M. (1991) 'Labour as a Governing Party: Balancing Left and Right', in T. Gourvish and A. O'Day (eds) *Britain Since 1945* (London: Macmillan).

Childs, D. (1995) *Britain Since 1939: Progress and Decline* (London: Macmillan).

Clark, N. and Calestous, J. (1987) *Long Run Economics: An Evolutionary Approach to Economic Growth* (London: Pinter).

Cliff, T. and Gluckstein, D. (1996) *The Labour Party: A Marxist History* (London: Bookmarks).

Cloke, P. (ed.) (1992) *Policy and Change in Thatcher's Britain* (Oxford: Pergamon).

Coates, D. (1975) *The Labour Party and the Struggle for Socialism* (Cambridge: Cambridge University Press).

—— (1980) *Labour in Power?* (London: Longman).

—— (1986) 'The Character and Origins of Britain's Economic Decline', in D. Coates and J. Hillard (eds) *The Economic Decline of Modern Britain: The Debate Between Left and Right* (Hemel Hempstead: Harvester Wheatsheaf).

—— (1989) *The Crisis of Labour* (Oxford: Philip Allen).

Cohen, M., March, J. and Olsen, J. (1972) 'A Garbage Can Model of Organisational Choice', *Administrative Science Quarterly* 17.

Coopey, R. and Woodward, N. (1996) *Britain in the 1970s: The Troubled Economy* (London: UCL Press).

Cox, A. W. (1986) 'Political Science and the Economy: An Unconsummated Relationship', in J. Hayward and P. Norton (eds) *The Political Science of British Politics* (Sussex: Wheatsheaf).

Crafts, N. F. R. and Woodward, N. (1991) *The British Economy Since 1945* (Oxford: Clarendon).

Crewe, I. (1988) 'Has the Electorate Become Thatcherite?', in R. Skidelsky (ed.) *Thatcherism* (London: Chatto and Windus).

—— (1993) 'The Thatcher Legacy', in A. King, I. Crewe, D. Denner, K. Newton, P. Norton, D. Sanders and P. Slyd (eds) *Britain at the Polls 1992* (Chatham, N.J.: Chatham House).

Cronin, J. E. (1991) *The Politics of State Expansion: War, State and Society in Twentieth-Century Britain* (London: Routledge).

—— (1996) *The World the Cold War Made: Order, Chaos and the Return of History* (London: Routledge).

Crosland, C. A. R. (1956) *The Future of Socialism* (London: Jonathan Cape).

Crouch, C. (1979) *The Politics of Industrial Relations* (Manchester: Manchester University Press).

Dalton, H. (1962) *High Tide and After* (London: Muller).

De Bresson, C. (1987) 'The Evolutionary Paradigm and the Economics of Technical Change', *Journal of Economic Issues* vol. 21 no. 2.

Debray, R. (1973) 'Time and Politics', in *Prison Writings* (London: Allen Lane).

Dearlove, J. and Saunders, P. (1991) *Introduction to British Politics* (Cambridge: Polity).

Dolowitz, D. (1998) *Learning From America: Policy Transfer and the Development of the British Workfare State* (Brighton: Sussex Academic Press).

Dolowitz, D., Marsh, D., O'Neill, F. and Richards, D. (1996) 'Thatcherism and the Three R's: Radicalism, Realism and Rhetoric in the Third Term of the Thatcher Government', *Parliamentary Affairs*.

Dorey, P. (1993) 'One Step at a Time: The Conservative Government's Reform of Industrial Relations Since 1979', *Political Quarterly* vol. 64 no. 1.

—— (1995) *British Politics Since 1945* (Oxford: Blackwell).

Dorfman, G. (1979) *Government versus Trade Unionism in British Politics since 1968* (London: Macmillan).

—— (1983) *British Trade Unionism Against the TUC* (London: Macmillan).

Dosi, G., Freeman, C., Nelson, R. R., Silverberg, G. and Cowete, L. (eds) (1988) *Technical Change and Economic Theory* (London: Pinter).

Douglas, J. (1989) 'The Changing Tide: Some Recent Studies of Thatcherism', *British Journal of Political Science* 19.

Dowse, R. E. (1986) 'The Recourse to Political Sociology', in J. Hayward and P. Norton (eds) *The Political Science of British Politics* (Sussex: Wheatsheaf).

Dunleavy, P. (1989) 'Britain: The Paradox of Ungrounded Statism', in F. Castle (ed.) *The Comparative History of Public Policy* (London: Polity).

Dunleavy, P. and O'Leary, B. (1987) *Theories of the State* (London: Macmillan).

Durham, W. H. (1991) *Coevolution: Genes, Culture and Human Diversity* (Stanford: Stanford University Press).

Dutton, D. (1991) *British Politics Since 1945: The Rise and Fall of Consensus* (Oxford: Blackwell).

Eatwell, R. (1979) *The 1945–51 Labour Governments* (London: Batsford).

Economist (1954) 'Mr Butskell's Dilemma', 13 February.

Elster, J. (1983) *Explaining Technical Change* (Cambridge: Cambridge University Press).

—— (1989) *Nuts and Bolts for the Social Sciences* (Cambridge: Cambridge University Press).

Evans, B. and Taylor, A. (1996) *From Salisbury to Major: Continuity and Change in Conservative Politics* (Manchester: Manchester University Press).

Evans, P. B., Rueschemeyer, D. and Skocpol, T. (1985) 'On the Road Towards a More Adequate Understanding of the State', in P. B. Evans, D. Rueschemeyer and T. Skocpol (eds) *Bringing the State Back In* (Cambridge: Cambridge University Press).

Fairclough, N. (1989) *Language and Power* (Harlow: Longman).

—— (1992) *Discourse and Social Change* (Cambridge: Polity).

Fielding, S., Thompson, P. and Tiratsoo, N. (1996) *England Arise: The Labour Party and Popular Politics in 1940s Britain* (Manchester: Manchester University Press).

Fine, B. and Harris, L. (1985) *The Peculiarities of the British Economy* (London: Lawrence and Wishart).

Floud, R. and McCloskey, D. (1994) *The Economic History of Britain Since 1700, vol. 3: 1939–1992* (Cambridge: Cambridge University Press).

Frank, A. G. (1980) *Crisis: In the World Economy* (London: Heinemann).

Frank, A. G. and Gillis, K. G. (eds) (1996) *The World System* (London: Routledge).

Fraser, D. (1984) *The Evolution of the British Welfare State* (London: Macmillan).

Fraser, M. (1987) 'British Politics, 1945–87: Four Perspectives', in P. Hennessey and A. Seldon (eds) *Ruling Performance* (Oxford: Blackwell).

Freeman, C. (ed.) (1982) *Long Waves in the World Economy* (London: Butterworths).

Fyrth, J. (ed.) (1993) *Labour's High Noon: The Government and the Economy 1945–51* (London: Lawrence and Wishart).

Gamble, A. (1988) *The Free Economy and the Strong State: The Politics of Thatcherism* (London: Macmillan).

—— (1990) 'The Thatcher Decade in Perspective', in P. Dunleavy, A. Gamble and G. Peele (eds) *Developments in British Politics 3* (London: Macmillan).

—— (1994) *Britain in Decline: Economic Policy, Political Strategy and the British State* (London: Macmillan).

—— (1996) 'An Ideological Party', in S. Ludlam and M. J. Smith (eds) *Contemporary British Conservatism* (London: Macmillan).

Garnett, M. (1996) *Principles and Politics in Contemporary Britain* (London: Longman).

Giddens, A. (1984) *The Constitution of Society* (Cambridge: Polity).

Gilpin, R. (1987) *The Political Economy of International Relations* (Princeton: Princeton University Press).

Glennester, H. (1995) *British Social Policy Since 1945* (Oxford: Blackwell).

Gordon, D. M. (1978) 'Up and Down the Long Roller Coaster', in Union for Radical Political Economics (ed.) *US Capitalism in Crisis* (New York: URPE).

—— (1980) 'Stages of Accumulation and Long Economic Cycles', in T. K. Hopkins and I. Wallerstein (eds) *Processes of the World-System* (London: Sage).

Gould, S. J. (1981) *The Mismeasure of Man* (New York: Norton).

Gourevitch, P., Marint, A., Ross, G., Allen, C., Bornstein, S. and Markovits, A. (1984) *Unions and Economic Crisis: Britain, West Germany and Sweden* (London: Allen and Unwin).

Gourvish, T. and O'Day, A. (1991) *Britain Since 1945* (London: Macmillan).

Gramsci, A. (1971) *Selections From Prison Notebooks* (London: Lawrence and Wishart).

Grant, W. (1987) *Business and Politics in Britain* (London: Macmillan).

—— (1993) *Business and Politics in Britain* (London: Macmillan).

Grant, W. and Marsh, D. (1977) *The CBI* (London: Hodder and Stoughton).

Hain, P. (1986) *Political Strikes: The State and Trade Unionism in Britain* (London: Viking).

Hall, J. (1986) *Powers and Liberties* (London: Penguin).

Hall, P. (1986) *Governing the Economy: The Politics of State Intervention in Britain and France* (Cambridge: Polity).

—— (1989) 'Introduction', in P. Hall (ed.) *The Political Power of Economic Ideas* (Princeton: Princeton University Press).

—— (1993) 'Policy Paradigms, Social Learning and the State: The Case of Economic Policy-Making in Britain', *Comparative Politics* vol. 25 no. 3.

Hall, P. and Taylor, R. C. R. (1996) 'Political Science and the Three New Institutionalisms', *Political Studies* vol. 44 no. 4.

Hall, S. (1983) 'The Great Moving Right Show', *Marxism Today* January, reprinted in S. Hall and M. Jacques (eds) *The Politics of Thatcherism*, pp. 19–39 (London: Lawrence and Wishart).

—— (1985) 'Authoritarian Populism: A Reply', *New Left Review* 151.

—— (1988) *The Hard Road to Renewal: Thatcherism and the Crisis of the Left* (London: Lawrence and Wishart).

—— (1991) 'And Not a Shot Fired', *Marxism Today* December.

Hall, S. and Jacques, M. (eds) (1983) *The Politics of Thatcherism* (London: Lawrence and Wishart).

Hall, S., Critcher, C. and Jefferson, J. (1978) *Policing the Crisis: Mugging, the State and Law and Order* (London: Macmillan).

Harden, I. (1992) *The Contracting State* (Milton Keynes: Open University Press).

Harris, K. (1982) *Attlee* (London: Weidenfeld and Nicolson).

—— (1988) *Thatcher* (London: Fontana).

Harris, L. (1985) 'British Capital: Manufacturing, Finance and Multinational Corporations', in D. Coates, G. Johnston and R. Bush (eds) *A Socialist Anatomy of Britain* (Cambridge: Polity).

Hawkins, M. (1997) *Social Darwinism in European and American Thought, 1860–1945* (Cambridge: Cambridge University Press).

Hay, C. (1995) 'Structure and Agency', in D. Marsh and G. Stoker (eds) *Theory and Methods in Political Science* (London: Macmillan).

—— (1996) *Re-stating Social and Political Change* (Buckingham: Open University Press).

—— (1997) '"Political Time and the Temporality of Crisis": On Institutional Change as "Punctuated Evolution"', paper presented at the Department of Politics, York University, 10 March.

—— (1998) '"Punctuated Evolution"' and the Uneven Temporality of Institutional Change: The "Crisis" of Keynesianism and the rise of Neo-liberalism in Britain', paper presented to the Eleventh Conference of Europeanists, Omni Harbor Hotel, Baltimore, 26–8 February.

—— (1999) 'Crisis and British Political Development', in D. Marsh, J. Buller, C. Hay, J. Johnston, P. Kerr, S. McAnulla and M. Watson *Postwar British Politics in Perspective* (Cambridge: Polity).

Hay, C. and Jessop, B. (1997) 'The Governance of Local Economic Development and the Development of Local Economic Governance: A Strategic Relational Approach', unpublished article, mimeo.

Hayward, J. and Norton, P. (eds) (1986) *The Political Science of British Politics* (Sussex: Wheatsheaf).

Hennessey, P. (1989) 'The Attlee Governments, 1945–51', in P. Hennessey and A. Seldon (eds) *Ruling Performance* (Oxford: Blackwell).

—— (1992) *Never Again* (London: Cape).

Hirst, P. Q. (1976) *Social Evolution and Sociological Categories* (London: Allen and Unwin).

Hodgson, G. M. (1993) *Economics and Evolution: Bringing Life Back into Economics* (Cambridge: Polity).

—— (1993b) 'Theories of Economic Evolution: A Preliminary Taxonomy', *Manchester School of Economic and Social Studies* vol. LXI no. 2.

Holmes, M. (1985) *The Labour Government, 1974–79* (London: Macmillan).

—— (1985) *The First Thatcher Government 1979–83* (London: Macmillan).

Hopkins, T. K. and Wallerstein, I. (eds) (1982) *World-Systems Analysis* (London: Sage).

Hopkins, T. K., Wallerstein, I. *et al.* (1996) *The Age of Transition: Trajectory of the World-System 1945–2025* (London: Zed Books).

Howell, D. (1976) *British Social Democracy* (London: Crook Helm).

Hudson, R. (1989) 'Rewriting History and Reshaping Geography: The Nationalised Industries and the Political Economy of Thatcherism', in J. Mohan (ed.) *The Political Geography of Contemporary Britain* (London: Macmillan).

Hutton, W. (1996) *The State We're In* (London: Vintage).

Ikeda, S. (1996) 'World Production', in T. K. Hopkins, I. Wallerstein *et al.* (eds) *The Age of Transition: Trajectory of the World-System, 1945–2025* (London: Zed Books).

Ingham, G. (1984) *Capitalism Divided? The City and Industry in British Social Development* (London: Macmillan).

Jabri, V. (1996) *Discourses on Violence: Conflict Analysis Reconsidered* (Manchester: Manchester University Press).

Jacques, M. (1979) 'Breaking out of the Impasse', *Marxism Today* October.

Jay, P. (1994) 'The Economy 1990–94', in D. Kavanagh and A. Seldon (eds) *The Major Effect* (London: Macmillan).

Jefferys, K. (1991) *The Churchill Coalition and Wartime Politics 1940–45* (Manchester: Manchester University Press).

—— (1993) 'Perspectives on Postwar Britain', *Twentieth Century British History* vol. 4 no. 3.

——— (1997) *Retreat From New Jerusalem: British Politics, 1951–64* (London: Macmillan).

Jenkins, P. (1988) *Mrs Thatcher's Revolution* (London: Cape).

Jenkins, S. (1995) *Accountable To None: The Tory Nationalisation of Britain* (London: Hamish Hamilton).

Jessop, B. (1980) 'The Transformation of the State in postwar Britain', in R. Scase (ed.) *The State in Western Europe* (London: Crook Helm).

——— (1982) *The Capitalist State* (Oxford: Blackwell).

——— (1988) 'Thatcherism: The British Road to Post-Fordism?', *Essex Papers in Politics and Government* no. 68.

——— (1990a) *State Theory: Putting Capitalist States in their Place* (Cambridge: Polity).

——— (1990b) 'Regulation Theories in Retrospect and Prospect', *Economy and Society* vol. 19 no. 2.

——— (1992) 'From Social Democracy to Thatcherism: Twenty-Five Years of British Politics', in N. Abercrombie and A. Warde (eds) *Social Change in Contemprary Britain* (Cambridge: Polity).

——— (1994) 'The Transition to post-Fordism and the Schumpterian Workfare State', in R. Burrows and B. Loader (eds) *Towards a Post-Fordist Welfare State?* (London: Routledge).

——— (1996) 'Interpretive Sociology and the Dialectic of Structure and Agency', *Theory, Culture and Society* vol. 13 no. 1.

Jessop, B., Bonnett, K., Bromley, S. and Link, T. (1988) *Thatcherism: A Tale of Two Nations* (Cambridge: Polity).

John, P. (1998a) 'Ideas and Interests; Agendas and Implementation: Evolutionary Explanations of Policy Change in British Local Government Finance, 1986–93', paper presented to the ECPR Joint Sessions Workshop, 'The Evolution and Transformation of the Modern State: Processes of Change', 23–8 March.

——— (1998b) *Analysing Public Policy* (London: Cassell).

Johnson, P. S. (1985) *British Industry: An Economic Introduction* (Oxford: Blackwell).

Johnston, J. (1997) 'Economic Decline Revisited: Challenging Idealist Fallacies Within the Literature', in J. Stanyer and G. Stoker (eds) *Contemporary Political Studies 1997, vol. 2* (Exeter: PSA).

——— (1999) 'Questions of Change and Continuity in Attlee's Britain', in D. Marsh, J. Buller, C. Hay, J. Johnston, P. Kerr, S. McAnulla and M. Watson *Postwar British Politics in Perspective* (Cambridge: Polity).

——— (1999) 'Britain's Economic Decline: Cultural Versus Structural Explanations', in D. Marsh, J. Buller, C. Hay, J. Johnston, P. Kerr, S. McAnulla and M. Watson *Postwar British Politics in Perspective* (Cambridge: Polity).

Kato, J. (1996) 'Review Article: Institutions and Rationality in Politics: Three Varieties of Neo-Institutionalists', *British Journal of Political Science* 26.

Kavanagh, D. (1985) 'Whatever Happened to Consensual Politics?', *Political Studies*.

——— (1987) *Thatcherism and British Politics: The End of Consensus?* (Oxford: Oxford University Press).

——— (1990) *Thatcherism and British Politics* (Oxford: Oxford University Press).

——— (1992) 'The Postwar Consensus', *Twentieth Century British History* vol. 3 no. 2.

Kavanagh, D. and Morris, P. (1989) *Consensus Politics: From Attlee to Thatcher* (Oxford: Blackwell).

——— (1994) *Consensus Politics: From Attlee to Major* (Oxford: Blackwell).

Kavanagh, D. and Seldon, A. (eds) (1994) *The Major Effect* (London: Macmillan).

Keegan, W. (1984) *Mrs Thatcher's Economic Experiment* (Harmondsworth: Penguin).

Keegan, W. and Pennant-Rae, R. (1979) *Who Runs the Economy?* (London: Temple Smith).

Kemp, P. (1993) *Beyond Next Steps: A Civil Service for the 21st Century* (London: Social Market Foundation).

Kerr, P. (1995) 'The Island Mentality in the Study of British Politics', in R. Lekhi (ed.) *The State of the Academy: New Reflections on Political Studies* (London: Network).

—— (1999) 'The Postwar Consensus: A Woozle That Wasn't', in D. Marsh, J. Buller, C. Hay, J. Johnston, P. Kerr, S. McAnulla and M. Watson *Postwar British Politics in Perspective* (London: Polity).

Kerr, P., McAnulla, S. and Marsh, D. (1997) 'Charting Late-Thatcherism: British Politics Under Major', in S. Lancaster (ed.) *Developments in Politics* (Ormskirk: Causeway).

Kerr, P. and Marsh, D. (1996) 'False Dichotomies and Failed Assumptions: Revisiting and Revising the Consensus Debate', in I. Hampshire-Monk and J. Stanyer (eds) *Contemporary Political Studies* vol. 2 (Exeter: PSA).

—— (1999) 'The Evolution of Thatcherism: Towards a Multi-Dimensional Perspective', in D. Marsh, J. Buller, C. Hay, J. Johnston, P. Kerr, S. McAnulla and M. Watson *Postwar British Politics in Perspective* (London: Polity).

King, A. (1985) 'Margaret Thatcher: The Style of a Prime Minister', in A. King (ed.) *The British Prime Minister* (London: Macmillan).

King, D. S. (1987) *The New Right: Politics, Markets and Citizenship* (London: Macmillan).

Kingdom, J. (1991) *Government and Politics in Britain: An Introduction* (Cambridge: Polity).

—— (1984) *Agendas, Alternatives and Public Choices* (Boston: Little Brown).

Kleinknecht, A. (1987) *Innovation Patterns in Crisis and Prosperity: Schumpeter's Long Cycle Reconsidered* (London: Macmillan).

Krieger, J. (1986) *Reagan, Thatcher and the Politics of Decline* (Cambridge: Polity).

Laclau, E. and Mouffe, C. (1985) *Hegemony and Socialist Strategy* (London: Verso).

Layder, D. (1997) *Modern Social Theory: Key Debates and New Directions* (London: UCL Press).

Leftwich, A. (ed.) (1984a) *What Is Politics? The Activity and Its Study* (Oxford: Blackwell).

—— (1984b) 'On the Politics of Politics', in A. Leftwich (ed.) *What Is Politics?: The Activity and Its Study* (Oxford: Blackwell).

Lekhi, R. (ed.) (1995a) *The State of the Academy: New Reflections on Political Studies* (London: Network).

—— (1995b) 'Introduction: New Reflections in Political Studies', in R. Lekhi (ed.) *The State of the Academy: New Reflections on Political Studies* (London: Network).

Lereuz, J. (1975) *Economic Planning and Politics in Britain* (Oxford).

Letwin, S. (1992) *Anatomy of Thatcherism* (London: Fontana).

Leys, C. (1996) 'The Formation of British Capital', *New Left Review* 160.

Lindblom, C. E. (1959) 'The Science of Muddling Through', *Public Administration Review* 14.

Lipietz, A. (1987) *Mirages and Miracles: The Crises of Global Fordism* (London: Verso).

—— (1992) *Towards a New Economic Order: Postfordism, Ecology and Democracy* (Cambridge: Polity).

Lopreato, J. (1984) *Human Nature and Biocultural Evolution* (Boston: Allen and Unwin).

Lowe, R. (1990) 'The Second World War, Consensus and the Foundation of the Welfare State', *Twentieth Century British History* vol. 1 no. 2.

—— (1993) *The Welfare State Since 1945* (London: Macmillan).

Ludlam, S. (1996) 'The Spectre Haunting Conservatism: Europe and Backbench Rebellion', in S. Ludlam and M. J. Smith (eds) *Contemporary British Conservatism* (London: Macmillan).

Ludlam, S. and Smith, M. J. (eds) (1996) *Contemporary British Conservatism* (London: Macmillan).

Lumsden, C. J. and Wilson, E. O. (1981) *Genes, Mind and Culture* (Cambridge: Harvard University Press).

McAnulla, S. (1997) 'Fade to Grey? Symbolic Politics in the Post-Thatcher Era', in J. Stanyer and G. Stoker (eds) *Contemporary Political Studies, vol. 1* (PSA: Exeter).

—— (1999) 'The Post-Thatcher Era', in D. Marsh, J. Buller, C. Hay, J. Johnston, P. Kerr, S. McAnulla and M. Watson *Postwar British Politics in Perspective* (Cambridge: Polity).

McKenzie, R. (1955) *British Political Parties* (London: Heinemann).

Magnusson, L. (ed.) (1994) *Evolutionary and Neo-Schumpeterian Approaches to Economics* (London: Kluwer).

Mandel, E. (1964) 'The Economics of Neo-Capitalism', *Socialist Register*.

—— (1995) *Long Waves of Capitalist Development* (London: Verso).

Marlow, J. D. (1995) 'Questioning the Postwar Consensus Thesis: Towards an Alternative Account, A Different Understanding', Ph.D. Thesis, Dept of Sociology, University of Essex.

—— (1996) *Questioning the Postwar Consensus Thesis: Towards an Alternative Account* (Aldershot: Dartmouth Publishing).

—— (1997) 'Metaphor, Intertextuality and the Postwar Consensus', *Politics* vol. 17 no. 2.

Marquand, D. (1988a) *The Unprincipled Society* (London: Cape).

—— (1988b) 'The Paradoxes of Thatcherism', in R. Skidelsky (ed.) *Thatcherism* (London: Chatto and Windus).

—— (1989) 'The Decline of Postwar Consensus', in A. Gorst, L. Johnman and W. S. Lucas (eds) *Post-war Britain, 1945–64: Themes and Perspectives* (London: Pinter).

Marquand, D. and Seldon, A. (eds) (1996) *The Ideas That Shaped Postwar Britain* (London: Fontana).

Marsh, D. (1991) 'Privatisation Under Mrs Thatcher', *Public Administration* 69.

—— (1992) *The New Politics of British Trade Unionism: Union Power and the Thatcher Legacy* (London: Macmillan).

—— (1994) 'Explaining Thatcherism: Beyond Uni-Dimensional Explanation', paper presented at the Political Studies Association Annual Conference, Swansea, March.

—— (1995a) 'Explaining Thatcherite Policies: Beyond Uni-Dimensional Explanation', *Political Studies* vol. 43 no. 4.

—— (1995b) 'Thatcherism and the Post-war Consensus', paper presented at the Institute of Contemporary History Conference, London, July 1995.

Marsh, D. and Locksley, G. (1983) 'Labour: The Dominant Force in British Politics?', in D. Marsh (ed.) *Pressure Politics* (London: Junction).

Marsh, D. and Rhodes, R. (eds) (1992) *Implementing Thatcherite Policies: Audit of an Era* (Buckingham: Open University Press).

—— (1995) 'Evaluating Thatcherism: Over the Moon or as Sick as a Parrot?', *Politics* vol. 15 no. 1.

Marsh, D. and Stoker, G. (eds) (1995) *Theory and Methods in Political Science* (London: Macmillan).

Marsh, D. and Tant, T. (1989) 'There is No Alternative: Mrs Thatcher and the British Political Tradition', *Essex Papers in Politics and Government* no. 69.

Marsh, D., Buller, J., Hay, C., Johnston, J., Kerr, P., McAnulla, S. and Watson, M. (1999) *Postwar British Politics in Perspective* (Cambridge: Polity).

Marshall, A. (1907) *Principles of Economics* (fifth edition), (London: Macmillan).

—— (1948) *Principles of Economics* (eighth Edition) (London: Macmillan).

Martin, J. (1998) 'Interpreting Italy's Crisis: The Discursive Constraints of State Transformation', paper presented to the ECPR Joint Sessions Workshop, 'The Evolution and Transformation of the Modern State: Processes of Change', 23–8 March.

Martin, R. (1992) 'Has the British Economy Been Transformed? Critical Reflections on the Policies of the Thatcher Era', in P. Cloke (ed.) *Policy and Change in Thatcher's Britain* (London: Macmillan).

Mercer, H. (1991) 'The Labour Governments of 1945–51 and Private Industry', in N. Tiratsoo (ed.) *The Attlee Years* (London: Pinter).

Mercer, H., Rollings, R. and Tomlinson, J. (eds) (1992) *Labour Governments and Private Industry: The Experience of 1945–51* (Edinburgh: Edinburgh University Press).

Middlemas, K. (1979) *Politics in Industrial Society* (London: Andre Deutsch).

Minogue, K. and Biddiss, M. (eds) (1987) *Thatcherism: Personality and Politics* (London: Macmillan).

Morgan, K. (1984) *Labour in Power 1945–51* (Oxford: Oxford University Press).

—— (1992) *The People's Peace: British History 1945–90* (Oxford: Oxford University Press).

Murray, R. (1990) 'Fordism and Post-Fordism', in S. Hall and M. Jacques (eds) *New Times: The Changing Face of Politics in the 1990s* (London: Lawrence and Wishart).

Nairn, T. (1964) 'The British Political Elite', *New Left Review* 23.

—— (1977) 'The Twilight of the British State', *New Left Review* 101.

—— (1981) 'The Crisis of the British State', *New Left Review* 130.

—— (1986) 'The Nature of the British State', in D. Coates and D. Hillard (eds) *The Economic Decline of Modern Britain: The Debate Between Left and Right* (Hemel Hempstead: Harvester Wheatsheaf).

Nelson, R. R. (1995) 'Recent Evolutionary Theorising about Economic Change', *Journal of Economic Literature* 33.

Nelson, R. R. and Winter, S. G. (1982) *An Evolutionary Theory of Economic Change* (Cambridge: Harvard University Press).

Nisbet, A. (1969) *Social Change and History* (London: Oxford).

Norton, P. and Hayward, J. (1986) 'Retrospective Reflections', in J. Hayward and P. Norton (eds) *The Political Science of British Politics* (Sussex: Wheatsheaf).

Obelkevich, J. and Catterall, P. (1994) *Understanding Postwar British Society* (London: Routledge).

O'Connor, J. (1973) *The Fiscal Crisis of the State* (New York: St Martin's Press).

Offe, C. (1974) 'Structural Problems of the Capitalist State', in K. von Beyme (ed.) *German Political Studies* (London: Russell Sage).

Osbourne, D. and Gaebler, T. (1992) *Reinventing Government* (London: Plume).

O'Shea, A. (1984) 'Trusting the People: How Does Thatcherism Work?', in A. O'Shea *Formations of Nation and People* (London: Routledge).

Overbeek, H. (1990) *Global Capitalism and National Decline: The Thatcher Decade in Perspective* (London: Unwin Hyman).

Page, E. (1990) 'British Political Science and Comparative Politics', *Political Studies* 38.

Painter, J. (1995) *Politics, Geography and 'Political Geography'* (London: Arnold).

Parsons, T. (1966) *Societies: Evolutionary and Comparative Perspectives* (Englewood Cliffs: Prentice Hall).

—— (1971) *The System of Modern Societies* (Englewood Cliffs: Prentice Hall).

Peden, G. C. (1991) *British Economic and Social Policy: From Lloyd George to Margaret Thatcher* (London: Philip Allan).

Pelizzon, S. and Casparis, J. (1996) 'World Human Welfare', in T. K. Hopkins, I. Wallerstein *et al.* (eds) *The Age of Transition: Trajectory of the World-System, 1945–2025* (London: Zed Books).

Philips, L. (1996) 'Rhetoric and the Spread of the Discourse of Thatcherism', *Discourse and Society* vol. 7 no. 2.

Pierson, C. (1996) 'Social Policy Under Thatcher and Major', in S. Ludlam and M. J. Smith (eds) *Contemporary British Conservatism* (London: Mamillan).

Pierson, P. (1993) 'When Effect Becomes Cause: Policy Feedback and Political Change', *World Politics* 45.

—— (1996) 'The Path to European Integration: A Historical Institutionalist Analysis', *Comparative Political Studies* vol. 29 no. 2.

Pimlott, B. (1988) 'The Myth of Consensus', in L. M. Smith (ed.) *The Making of Britain: Echoes of Greatness* (London, Macmillan).

—— (1989) 'Is the Postwar Consensus A Myth?', *Contemporary Record* vol. 2 no. 6.

Potter, J. and Wetherell, M. (1987) *Discourse and Social Psychology: Beyond Attitudes and Behaviour* (London: Sage).

Porter, B. (1994) '"Though Not an Historian Myself . . .": Margaret Thatcher and the Historians', *Twentieth Century British History* vol. 5 no. 2.

Porter, D. (1994) 'The Attlee Years Re-assessed', *Contemporary European History* vol. 4 no. 1.

Poulantzas, N. (1978) *State, Power, Socialism* (London: Verso).

Punnett, R. M. (1987) *British Government and Politics* (Aldershot: Gower).

Radice, H. (1984) 'The National Economy: A Keynesian Myth?', *Capital and Class* 22.

Reifer T. and Sudler, J. (1996) 'The Interstate System', in T. K. Hopkins, I. Wallerstein *et al.* (eds) *The Age of Transition: Trajectory of the World-System, 1945–2025* (London: Zed Books).

Rhodes, R. A. W. (1994) 'The Hollowing Out of the State: The Changing Nature of the Public Service in Britain', *Public Quarterly* 65.

Richter, I. (1973) *Political Purpose in British Trade Unionism* (London: Allen and Unwin).

Riddell, P. (1983) *The Thatcher Government* (Oxford: Martin Robertson).

—— (1989) *The Thatcher Decade* (Oxford: Blackwell).

—— (1991) *The Thatcher Era and its Legacy* (Oxford: Blackwell).

Ritschel, D. (1995) 'The Making of Consensus: The Nuffield College Conferences During the Second World War', *Twentieth Century British History* vol. 6 no. 3.

Robins, L. and Jones, B. (eds) (1997) *Half a Century of British Politics* (Manchester: Manchester University Press).

Rollings, N. (1988) 'British Budgetory Policy, 1945–1954: A "Keynesian Revolution"?' *Economic History Review* 41.

—— (1994) 'Poor Mr Butskell: A Short Life, Wrecked by Schizophrenia?', *Twentieth Century British History* vol. 5 no. 2.

Rose, R. and Davies, P. L. (1994) *Inheritance in Public Policy: Change Without Choice in Britain* (New Haven: Yale University Press).

Rowthorn, B. (1986) 'The Passivity of the State', in D. Coates and J. Hillard (eds) *The Economic Decline of Modern Britain: The Debate Between Left and Right* (Hemel Hempstead: Harvester Wheatsheaf).

Rueschemeyer, D. (1986) *Power and the Division of Labour* (Stanford: Stanford University Press).

Russell, C. (1976) 'Parliamentary History in Perspective, 1604–1629', *History* 16.

Samuelson, P. (1975) 'Sociobiology: A New Social Darwinism', *Newsweek* 7 July.

Sanderson, S. K. (1990) *Social Evolutionism: A Critical History* (Oxford: Blackwell).

—— (1995) *Social Transformations* (Oxford: Blackwell).

Saviotti, P. and Metcalfe, J. S. (eds) (1991) *Evolutionary Theories of Economic and Technical Change* (Reading: Addison-Wesley).

Seldon, A. (1994) 'Consensus: A Debate Too Long?', *Parliamentary Affairs* 47.

Shaw, E. (1996) *The Labour Party Since 1945: Old Labour; New Labour* (Oxford: Blackwell).

Simon, H. A. (1959) 'Theories of Decision-Making in Economics and Behavioural Science', *American Economic Review* 49.

—— (1982) *Models of Bounded Rationality, vol. 2* (Cambridge, Mass.: MIT Press).

—— (1983) *Reason in Human Affairs* (Oxford: Blackwell).

Singh, J. V. (1990) *Organisational Evolution: New Directions* (London: Sage).

Skocpol, T. (1979) *States and Social Revolutions* (Cambridge: Harvard University Press).

—— (1992) *Protecting Soldiers and Mothers: The Political Origins of Social Policy in the United States* (Cambridge: Belknap Harvard).

Smith, K. (1989) *The British Economic Crisis: It's Past and Future* (London: Penguin).

Smith, M. (1996) 'Reforming the State', in S. Ludlam and M. Smith (eds) *Contemporary British Conservatism* (London: Macmillan).

Smith, M. and Ludlam, S. (1996) 'Introduction', in S. Ludlam and M. Smith (eds) *Contemporary British Conservatism* (London: Macmillan).

Sober, E. (1984) *The Nature of Selection: Evolutionary Theory in Philosophical Focus* (Cambridge, Mass.: MIT Press).

Spencer, H. (1887) *The Factors of Organic Evolution* (London: Williams and Norgate).

Steinmo, S., Thelen, K. and Longstreth, F. (eds) (1992) *Structuring Politics: Historical Institutionalism in Comparative Analysis* (Cambridge: Cambridge University Press).

Stevenson, J. (1993) *Third Party Politics Since 1945* (Oxford: Blackwell).

Strange, S. (1971) *Sterling and British Policy: A Political Study of an International Currency in Decline* (Oxford: Oxford University Press).

Stzompka, P. (1991) *Society in Action: The Theory of Social Becoming* (Cambridge: Polity).

—— (1993) *The Sociology of Social Change* (Oxford: Blackwell).

Sutherland, G. (1972) *Studies in the Growth of Nineteenth Century Government* (London: Routledge).

Tant, A. P. (1993) *British Government: The Triumph of Elitism* (Aldershot: Dartmouth).

Taylor, P. (1992) 'Changing Political Relations', in P. Cloke (ed.) *Policy and Change in Thatcher's Britain* (Oxford: Pergamon).

Taylor, P. J. (1989) *Political Geography: World-Economy, Nation-State and Locality* (London: Longman).

Taylor, R. (1993) *The Trade Union Question in British Politics* (Oxford: Blackwell).

Thatcher, M. (1993) *The Downing Street Years* (London: Harper Collins).

Thompson, G. (1984) 'Economic Intervention in the Postwar Economy', in G. McLennan, D. Held and S. Hall(eds) *State and Society in Contemporary Britain: A Critical Introduction* (Oxford: Blackwell).

Thompson, H. (1996) 'Economic Policy Under Thatcher and Major', in S. Ludlam and M. J. Smith (eds) *Contemporary British Conservatism* (London: Macmillan).

Thompson, J. (1982) 'The New Social Darwinism: The Politics of Sociobiology', *Politics* 17.

Tiratsoo, N. (ed.) (1991a) *The Attlee Years* (London: Pinter).

—— (1991b) 'Introduction', in N. Tiratsoo *The Attlee Years* (London: Pinter).

—— (ed.) (1997) *From Blitz to Blair: A New History of Britain Since 1939* (London: Phoenix).

Tiratsoo, N. and Tomlinson, J. (1993) *Industrial Efficiency and State Intervention: Labour 1939–51* (London: LSE/Routledge).

Tomlinson, J. (1981) 'Why Was There Never a "Keynesian Revolution" in Economic Policy?', *Economy and Society* 10.

—— (1984) 'A "Keynesian Revolution" in Economic Policy-Making?', *Economic History Review* 37.

—— (1987) *Employment Policy: The Crucial Years, 1939–1955* (Oxford: Clarendon).

—— (1994) 'British Economic Policy Since 1945', in R. Floud and D. McCloskey (eds) *The Economic History of Britain Since 1700, vol. 3: 1939–1992* (Cambridge: Cambridge University Press).

Turner, J. (1989) 'The Decline of Post-war Consensus: Commentary Three', in A. Gorst, L. Johnman and W. S. Lucas (eds) *Post-war Britain, 1945–64: Themes and Perspectives* (London: Pinter).

Tylecote, A. (1992) *The Long Wave in the World Economy: The Current Crisis in Historical Perspective* (New York: Routledge).

Van Duijn, J. J. (1983) *The Long Wave in Economic Life* (Sydney: Allen and Unwin).

Van Parijs, P. (1981) *Evolutionary Explanation in the Social Sciences: An Emerging Paradigm* (London: Tavistock).

Veblen, T. (1898) 'Why is Economics not an Evolutionary Science', *Quarterly Journal of Economics* 12.

Vromen, J. J. (1995) *Economic Evolution* (London: Routledge).

Wallerstein, I. (1974) *The Modern World-System I* (New York: Academic Press).

—— (1980) *The Modern World-System II* (New York: Academic Press).

—— (1983) *Historical Capitalism* (London: Verso).

—— (1989) *The Modern World-System III* (New York: Academic Press).

—— (1991) *Unthinking Social Science: The Limits of Nineteenth-Centuary Paradigms* (Cambridge: Polity).

—— (1996) 'The Global Picture, 1945–90', in T. K. Hopkins, I. Wallerstein *et al.* (eds) *The Age of Transition: Trajectory of the World System, 1945–2025* (London: Zed Books).

Ward, H. (1989) 'Evolution and Regulation: Economism Rediscovered' *Essex Papers in Politics and Government* no. 64.

—— (1993) 'State Exploitation, Capital Accumulation and the Evolution of the State's Role in Modes of Regulation', paper presented at the Annual Conference of the Political Studies Association, Leicester.

—— (1995) 'Evolutionary Explanation' (first draft copy: mimeo).

—— (1997) 'The Possibility of an Evolutionary Explanation of the State's Role in Modes of Regulation', in J. Stanyer and G. Stoker (eds) *Contemporary Political Studies, 1997, vol. 1* (Exeter: PSA).

—— (1998) '"Bandwagons Roll" . . . or Not: The Co-Evolution of Modes of Regulation and Patterns of Rule', paper presented at the Workshop on 'The Evolution and Transformation of the State: Processes of Change', 26th Joint Sessions of the European Consortium for Political Research, University of Warwick, 23–8 March.

Warde, A. (1982) *Consensus and Beyond* (Manchester: Manchester University Press).

Weiner, M. J. (1981) *English Culture and the Decline of the Industrial Spirit 1850–1980* (Cambridge: Cambridge University Press).

Wilson, E. O. (1978) *On Human Nature* (Cambridge: Harvard University Press).

Winter, S. G. (1990) 'Survival, Selection and Inheritance in Evolutionary Theories of Organisation', in J. V. Singh *Organisational Evolution: New Directions* (London: Sage).

Whitehead, A. N. (1925) *Science and the Modern World* (New York: Macmillan).

Wolfe, J. (1991) 'State, Power and Ideology in Britain: Mrs Thatcher's Privatisation Programme', *Political Studies* 39.

Wolinetz, S. B. *Parties and Party Systems in Liberal Democracies* (London, Routledge).

Wright, A. (1989) 'Endpiece', in L. Tivey and A. Wright, *Party Ideologies in Britain* (London: Routledge).

Young, H. and Sloman, A. (1986) *The Thatcher Phenomenon* (London: BBC).

Zuckerman, A. (1991) *Doing Political Science* (Boulder, Col.: Westview).

Index